Understanding Urban Tourism

Image, Culture and Experience

Martin Selby

I.B. TAURIS

LONDON · NEW YORK

Published in 2004 by I.B.Tauris & Co Ltd
6 Salem Road, London W2 4BU
175 Fifth Avenue, New York NY 10010
www.ibtauris.com

In the United States and Canada distributed by Palgrave Macmillan
a division of St. Martin's Press
175 Fifth Avenue, New York NY 10010

ISBN   hardback 1 86064 800 2
          paperback 1 86064 801 0

A full CIP record for this book is available from the British Library
A full CIP record for this book is available from the Library of Congress
Library of Congress catalog card: available

Typeset in Bodoni by Dexter Haven Associates Ltd, London
Printed and bound in Malaysia by SRM Production Services Sdn. Bhd.

Dedicated to my Dad
John Sylvester Selby

Contents

Tables, Figures and Illustrations

Figures

Tables

Illustrations

Preface

To me at least, urban tourism is a fascinating phenomenon. It is possible to sense its significance to everyday life from peoples' frequent conversations about visiting towns and cities. Whilst people seek the unique in places, urban tourism is increasingly part of the culture of contemporary life. Academic interest in urban tourism has also developed rapidly in recent years. In terms of tourism in general, new degree courses are springing up around the world, new journals are emerging, and the field is maturing. Understanding urban tourism as a student or researcher, however, is surprisingly challenging. This is partly due to the nature of urban tourism itself, with its complex and fragmented industry, and inherent dichotomies such as supply and demand, inside and outside, images and experiences. In many ways, urban tourism polarises academic disciplines, revealing the weaknesses, and producing divergent explanations.

Having researched and taught urban tourism in various British universities over recent years, I feel rather sorry for students of urban tourism. I have often reflected on the fact that I have worked with a fantastic but very diverse collection of colleagues. They have included management specialists, planners, marketers, food specialists, microbiologists, lawyers, accountants, geographers, psychologists, sociologists, and even a marine biologist. Tourism education and research is multi-disciplinary, and most university departments, not unlike in industry, consist of a team with different specialisms. This, in effect, means that the student of tourism needs to master a whole range of disciplines and skills, making tourism rather more challenging as an area of study than it is given credit for. Having taught urban tourism to students on both tourism and geography degrees, it is noticeable that the two tend to have different ways of looking at urban tourism. Whilst geography students are fairly familiar with social science issues and debates, they have rarely applied them to urban tourism. Whilst tourism students have a sound knowledge of tourism, they have rarely explored urban tourism from social science perspectives.

The urban tourism literature, however, contributes to these difficulties, as it does not fully reflect the multi-disciplinary nature of the field. Influential authors such as Law (1993, 2002), Page (1995), Page and Hall (2003), Ashworth and Voogd (1990), Pearce (2001) have provided a thorough understanding of management, marketing, planning, visitor management and service quality in urban tourism. Contributions from contemporary social science, however, have been minimal. Human geographers and sociologists, for example, have had a relatively minor influence on how we understand urban tourism. There are some impressive and sensitive studies, but they tend to be scattered amongst different areas of the literature, and fairly inaccessible to the urban tourism student or researcher. On the rare occasions that social science has been explicitly applied to urban tourism, it tends to be of a fairly retrospective and quantitative variety. This is despite a profound transformation of the social sciences in the last decade, known as the 'cultural turn'. This provides new ways of looking at phenomena such as urban tourism, and it also questions the validity of any knowledge produced by researchers.

This book, therefore, is intended to address this lack of a contemporary social science understanding of urban tourism, through an emphasis on image, culture and experience. The chapters generally present a review of studies adopting a particular perspective, a discussion of the concepts in more detail, an evaluation of the limitations of the perspective, and suggestions for possible solutions. Whilst different epistemologies are in evidence in each chapter, the emphasis in on themes and fields of the literature, and these may not have such neat boundaries. A synthesis of the perspectives is also presented, and this is intended to draw the diverse range of concepts and methods together.

The substantive contribution, therefore, is in bringing together the methods, concepts, and knowledge of a diverse range of social science studies, and making them accessible to students and researchers of urban tourism. Whilst it is not always possible to do justice to them in the space available, I have attempted to provide depth as well as variety. When authors are discussed in depth, it is because they have important contributions to make to future urban tourism research. It has also been necessary to be selective, and there are themes and perspectives that might have been included. The book should be useful for students of both tourism *per se*, and cognate social science disciplines. If the book makes the job of students, researchers, or even teachers of urban tourism a little easier, then the effort to produce it will have been worthwhile.

The constructive comments and support of the editors Gareth Shaw and Dimitri Ioannides is greatly appreciated. I am also grateful for the comments and guidance of Nigel Morgan, David Herbert, and Bill Bramwell. Over several years, David Botterill has been a great source of support and inspiration. The case studies would not have been possible without the enthusiasm and co-operation of Pam Wilsher and Chris Brown (Mersey Tourism), Gaynor Bagnall (Liverpool John Moores University), Monder Ram (De Montford University), Ffion Lloyd, Susanah Bulpin, Melissa Freeland, Dr Brian Hay, Cardiff Marketing, and Cardiff Bay Visitor Centre. Photographs have been generously provided by the Mersey Partnership, Las Vegas Tourism and Conference Bureau, Tourism New South Wales, Jan Rath (University of Amsterdam), Dan Heibert (University of Vancouver), and Phil Cubbin (Liverpool John Moores University).

The research and writing process has also been hugely influential in personal terms. This personal development includes a tendency to use phrases peculiar to phenomenology and cultural studies, several tons of paper encroaching upon my living space, friends who research beaches for a living, and considerably less hair. My ethnographic research of places of consumption has been extremely enjoyable, and would not have been possible without the company of the friends I have met along the way. I would like to express my gratitude to them, and particularly to Andrea. Most importantly, I would like to dedicate the book to my Dad who we lost suddenly last year. Always interested, always supportive, and always asking 'have you finished that book yet?'.

Chapter 1

Introduction

The following topics are covered in this chapter:

- An introduction to urban tourism as a field of study and research.
- The aims and objectives of the book.
- An introduction to the different perspectives on urban tourism presented throughout the book.

Studying Urban Tourism

This book is intended to add to the existing literature on urban tourism by presenting perspectives which draw upon social science. Although increasing numbers of practitioners, researchers and students are seeking to understand the phenomenon of tourism in towns and cities, the potential of contemporary social science has yet to be fully realised. In particular, the concepts and methods of social and cultural research have rarely been applied to urban tourism. This is despite the well-documented cultural turn within the social sciences. With some notable exceptions, the field of urban tourism has been rather insulated from the tectonic shifts in our understanding of the social and cultural world. This is not to say that the more applied and pragmatic approaches common to tourism studies have nothing to offer in terms of understanding urban tourism. Rather, there is an urgent need to complement established urban tourism research with concepts and methods currently enhancing our understanding of society.

The phenomenon of urban tourism has important and divisive implications for the pursuit of both social science and management. Whilst in practice the phenomenon of urban tourism unites people, place and consumption, their synthesis in the academic arena of conceptualisation and research is extremely problematic. Some years ago, Ashworth (1989:33) argued that a double neglect of urban tourism had occurred: tourism researchers had neglected the context in which urban tourism takes place, while urban studies researchers had neglected tourism. Around the same time, Hughes (1991:266) comments on the 'pre-social state' of tourism studies. Whilst one might expect that developments within both the social sciences and tourism studies

1

have enabled considerable progress to be made, unfortunately there has been relatively little. In the tourism literature, it is common for urban tourism to be given an atheoretical and descriptive treatment. As Page (1995:5) argues, urban tourism '...is poorly understood in theoretical and conceptual terms...'. He also points out the 'tendency for urban tourism research to be based on descriptive and empirical case studies which do not contribute to a greater theoretical or methodological understanding of urban tourism' (Page 1999:163).

The urban tourism field exemplifies how an understanding of the social and cultural nature of tourism lags behind the redefinition and reconceptualisation seen in other disciplinary sub-fields (Squire 1994:19). According to Rojek and Urry (1997:2), a 'response to the problematic nature of tourism is to abstract most of the important issues of social and cultural practice and only consider tourism as a set of economic activities'. They point out that most tourism textbooks conceptualise tourism as a set of economic activities, and tourists merely as bundles of preferences. It is relatively rare in tourism studies for individual voices and interpretations to be heard, as they are usually mediated by the tourism researcher who privileges the collective over the particular (Squire 1994:84). As Franklin and Crang (2001:5) argue, tourism studies has often been concerned with tracking and recording the growth of tourism through case studies which internalise industry-led perspectives. They also point out that much of this effort has been made by 'people whose disciplinary origins do not include the tools necessary to analyse and theorise complex social and cultural processes' (Franklin and Crang 2001:5). Theoretical development thus becomes dependent on a small core of theorists who provide standardised explanations.

Urban tourism, however, is also problematic for established social science disciplines. The challenging dichotomies of supply and demand, structure and agency, representations and landscapes, inside and outside the destination, make for a very difficult field of study. Problems are compounded by the notorious difficulties of conducting research within such a complex, fragmented and heterogeneous industry. Where geographers have devoted attention to urban tourism, for example, work has tended to be concerned with monitoring and describing patterns of land use and tourist flows. Multiplier effects, visitor flows and destination life-cycles have also dominated geographical studies of urban tourism. As Hughes (1997) points out, these patterns and flows are often discussed as if they are dependent on more fundamental causes. According to Squire (1994:81), it is only recently that researchers have begun to integrate 'economic and growth-related concerns with other, more qualitative and interpretive dimensions of touristic experience'. Cultural studies, concerned with cultural texts, representation and consumption, has transformed intellectual enquiry in numerous fields. Not only does urban tourism play a major role in forming the identity of people and places through representation, but the tourist destination is a social and cultural construction, the meaning of which is contested by various groups. As Squire (1994) argues, however, there have been few points of contact between cultural analysts and tourism specialists. She points out that in cultural geography, for example, edited collections rarely engage with tourism, and even in studies focusing on travel writing, tourism scholarship is rarely cited. It would seem, therefore, that the phenomenon of urban tourism also poses problems to cultural researchers, better equipped than most to capture such a slippery phenomenon. Whilst the analysis of landscapes and representations *per se* has been convincing, an understanding of how ordinary people consume and experience the cultural texts of urban tourism has emerged sporadically and rather reluctantly.

Social scientists are beginning to recognise that leisure and tourism are actually central to social life, and are primary determinants of space in their own right. Urban tourism thus plays a major role in the development of the 'ludic space' which dominates contemporary environments. The semiology of urban tourism is also of significance to society in general, as representations of places become the common currency of both place-marketing organisations and the mass media. Urban tourism works through dreams and myths, and these play a vital role in differentiating space into places. As urban tourism is symptomatic of an increasingly mobile society, rather than being marginal, it is actually centre-stage in explanations of contemporary society. There have, however, been relatively few social scientists willing to grapple with the messy phenomenon of urban tourism. It is necessary, therefore, to take a slightly more lateral journey, positioning oneself towards different genres of writing and research in order to gain alternative insights. As Franklin and Crang (2001:6) argue, 'the theoretical net needs to be cast much wider so that tourist studies is constantly renewed by developments in social and cultural theory and theory from other disciplines'.

As one attempts to delimit the concerns of a student or researcher of urban tourism, it becomes apparent that there is no single unifying discipline on which to draw. This book, therefore, develops different theoretical perspectives on urban tourism, drawing upon both the tourism and marketing literature, and different social science perspectives. The book also develops a theoretical model which synthesises the different perspectives and incorporates concepts relating to the neglected yet crucial experience and culture of urban tourism. It is not intended to provide a standardised and universal understanding of urban tourism, as it is necessarily selective. This selectivity also extends to disciplines, and sociology and human geography figure most prominently. The book deliberately focuses on perspectives neglected within the urban tourism literature, such as postmodernity, culture and experience. However, it is not the theory *per se* which is of interest to students and researchers of urban tourism. Instead, the book explores the unique insights into urban tourism provided by different and relatively neglected theoretical perspectives.

It is intended that the theoretical evaluation of urban tourism is a contribution salient to a diverse range of tourism students, researchers and practitioners. Whilst some readers may be interested in following the lines of argument to the model presented in chapter seven, others may be much more selective. It is intended that the book is useful in its entirety to researchers and students seeking an in-depth understanding of urban tourism, the culture of tourism and the tourist experience. It is perhaps more likely, however, that readers will use particular sections of the book, focusing on specific perspectives according to their own interests. To facilitate the latter use in particular, a different perspective is addressed in each chapter, and the reader is presented with both the contributions and limitations of each. A summary of these, and other key points, is presented in the form of bullet-points at the end of each chapter. Although much of the content of the book is of a theoretical nature, examples, case studies, figures and photographs are used within each chapter to illustrate the different ways of looking at the phenomenon of urban tourism.

The book aims, therefore, to explore the images, culture and experience of urban tourism, evaluating the implications of such themes for conceptualisation and research. In exploring how urban tourism is conceptualised and researched according to different theoretical perspectives, there is an attempt to identify the advantages and disadvantages of each. The discussions emphasise the significance of urban tourism within debates concerning the contemporary city, postmodernity and the pursuit of social science. Incorporating contributions from a range of literature, a conceptual model and a research agenda for urban tourism are presented.

Urban Tourism Perspectives

Chapter two considers the theory and practice of urban tourism, in an attempt to locate useful avenues of conceptualisation and research. Whilst the practice of urban tourism management and place marketing has increased greatly in scale and sophistication in recent years, challenges remain. These relate both to evidence of incoherence and inconsistencies between different organisations and spatial scales, and a lack of true differentiation of individual localities within urban tourism markets. To an extent, both of these problems appear to stem from a difficulty in co-ordinating activities relating to both the demand and supply sides of urban tourism.

Interest in urban tourism within the tourism literature has also developed in recent years. Authors such as Page, for example, seek to consider a 'framework for the analysis of the tourist's experience of urban tourism' (1997:112–13). A promising development, it would seem, is the application of the service-quality model (Parasuraman et al. 1985) to urban tourism. As authors such as Gilbert and Joshi (1992) argue, managing the gap between the expectations and experiences of urban tourists is vital. Unfortunately, the urban tourism literature also has some quite serious limitations. Particularly problematic, according to Page, is 'a failure to relate cases to wider issues' (1997:112). Pearce (1987:209) has long identified '... a need to move away from isolated, ideographic case study ...' in urban tourism research. Both Page (1995) and Ashworth (1989) have identified a neglect of urban tourism amongst researchers. Page (1995:8) attributes the problems to a vicious circle, whereby the lack of quality research on urban tourism results in a lack of interest within the public sector – and the lack of interest limits both funding and data sources. Echoing observations by authors such as Vetter (1985), Page (1995:5) argues that urban tourism '... is poorly understood in theoretical and conceptual terms since few researchers adopt an integrated approach'.

More specifically, it would seem that the literature on the experience of urban tourists is particularly weak. Shaw and Williams (1994:2087) point to a 'somewhat limited literature on visitor activity in urban areas'. Page considers it particularly important 'to constantly evaluate to establish if the actual experience met the tourist's expectations' (1995:24). Despite such a consensus concerning the deficiencies of urban tourism research, however, little progress appears to have been made in addressing them. Only a narrow range of theoretical perspectives has been drawn upon by urban tourism researchers. Several urban tourism researchers advocate behaviouralist approaches to research the experience of urban tourists (Page 1995, 1997; Pearce and Fagence 1996; Walmsey and Jenkins 1992). Behaviouralist research, however, has been extensively criticised for its atheoretical nature and its inability to incorporate social relations or culture (see Phillips 1993; Werlen 1993; Knox 1992; Ley 1981a; Cullen 1976).

Chapter three explores the role of urban tourism in postmodernity. The chapter discusses the materialist position on urban tourism, contrasting it with an alternative which draws upon authors such as Lyotard (1984), Lefebvre (1970) and Soja (1989). It is apparent that there is a dichotomy between conceptualisations of the city concerned with human agency, experience and culture, and materialist approaches attributing urban tourism merely to a symptom of 'late capitalism' (Jameson 1984). Harvey (1989a) is used to exemplify the materialist position, arguing that place marketing and urban tourism development is merely a reaction to the latest phase of capitalism, and in any case, will result in a 'zero-sum game' as every city gains a waterfront development. Ironically titled, *The Urban Experience* (Harvey 1989b) actually demonstrates the universalising tendencies of materialist conceptualisations of urban culture. Harvey reveals that he prefers to climb to the highest point in a city and look down at 'the city as a whole' (Harvey 1989b:1). The scathing critique of urban tourism, heritage and place marketing within the materialist literature is examined. This includes an alleged appropriation of local history and culture as a means of accumulating capital, the packaging and selling of a 'bogus history' (Hewison 1987) and the ultimate failure of most towns and cities to differentiate themselves in urban tourism markets (Harvey 1989a). The heritage industry is 'expected more and more to replace the real industry upon which this country depends' (Hewison 1987:11).

The limitations of the materialist position are alluded to in one of Hewison's few references to heritage consumers, the pensioners of an English heritage site called Wigan Pier 'who seem to throng the centre' (ibid.:21). As authors such as Bagnall (1998) demonstrate, however, if anyone can judge the authenticity of the Wigan Pier experience, it is those consumers sufficiently advanced in years to have memories of the exhibits. It would seem that, however convincing the materialist perspective is at the macro-scale, it offers a conceptualisation of urban tourism and place marketing which is devoid of people. In stark contrast to the materialist view, authors such as Lyotard (1984) draw attention to 'local knowledge', emphasising local context and 'ground rules' rather than universal and macro-level studies. Lyotard uses the term 'language games' to discuss the complexity and speed of images produced in contemporary society, destroying universal or fixed meanings. Lefebvre (1967, 1986) also challenges the materialist perspective, conceptualising the city as 'actually lived and socially created spatiality' (Soja 1989:18), and a place of encounter and experience. Lefebvre (1986) was interested in the rhythm of the body within the city, while also emphasising the influence of social groups on experience. Such authors, therefore, challenge the materialist perspective by emphasising the culture and experience of the city.

As chapter four argues, particularly pertinent to urban tourism development and place marketing have been promising developments in the field of place image. As the literature on postmodernity indicates, images have become crucial to postmodern society in general. Chapter four demonstrates how images are both the raw material and the product of place marketing, reviewing some of the important developments within this field of the tourism and place-marketing literature. In particular, there has been an interesting and valuable genre of research aiming to compare and contrast different types of images of destinations (e.g. Ashworth and Voogd 1990). Research has indicated the overwhelming significance of place images in tourist decision-making. Furthermore, it would seem that unofficial or 'organic' images are often considered to be more credible by tourists than the official 'projected' variety of marketing organisations. Particularly useful in terms of informing urban tourism and place-marketing policy have been studies aiming to compare and contrast the 'naive images' of potential visitors with the first-hand experience of actual visitors. This type of research appears to offer the potential of highlighting policy implications in terms of place-product development, place promotion and destination positioning.

It is also argued in chapter four, however, that the place image literature has some limitations, apparent in both theory and research. In terms of research, an overemphasis on statistical techniques at the expense of epistemological underpinning is identified. There is often very little consideration of the constructs used in surveys, and whether or not they are salient to consumers. If the epistemology of place image studies is considered, again it is behaviouralism which is dominant. Influential place image authors drawing heavily on behaviouralism, and particularly the work of Lynch (1960), include Ankomah and Crompton (1992), and Pearce and Fagence (1996). Although the behaviouralist approach has been unquestioningly adopted by numerous place image researchers, for several decades writers have been drawing attention to a number of inherent limitations. These include a lack of theoretical underpinning (Knox 1992), difficulties in incorporating emotions and feelings (Richards 1974), problems concerning universal claims about subjective processes (Phillips 1993), parallels with 'Skinnerian' psychology (Ley 1981a) and confusion between 'behaviour' and 'action' (Werlen 1993). In the context of contemporary urban tourism, it is also clear that behaviouralism has no place for the contested meanings and realities of places currently being addressed within cultural studies. While there are valuable contributions within the place image literature, it is argued that the experience, social relations and culture of urban tourism are neglected.

The focus of chapter five is the culture of urban tourism, as an engagement with cultural geography is argued to offer great potential in overcoming some of the limitations of urban tourism research and theory. In particular, we are offered a conceptualisation of representations and landscapes as contested and negotiated, in stark contrast to some of the more deterministic tourism studies. Cultural studies offer a powerful approach to conceptualising and researching the 'cultural texts' of urban tourism.

While cultural geography's emphasis on representation would seem to have great potential in terms of understanding urban tourism, it is argued in chapter five that there are limitations. The chapter explores the tendency within cultural geography to focus on cultural texts themselves – reading them on behalf of place consumers – rather than seeking an understanding of how they are read by place consumers. Gregson (1995) argues that in the context of the shopping mall, despite the endless metaphors created by cultural researchers, the shoppers themselves are rarely even mentioned. Jackson and Taylor (1996) demonstrate that even in studies of advertising, there is little regard for the various ways in which texts are read by different groups of consumers. Despite the importance of understanding the ways in which the texts of urban tourism are interpreted, the researcher still 'retains the position of power, telling readers what tourism means' (Squire 1994:8).

It is argued in chapter five that the apparent preoccupation with cultural texts themselves at the expense of the consumers is addressed by Johnson's 'Circuit of Culture' model (1986:284). Johnson conceptualises different 'moments' in which the form of a cultural text changes as it moves from production to consumption. Significantly, in contrast to cultural studies which are concerned with merely the text itself, the socially conditioned consumption of the text is emphasised. Recent studies which focus on the performativity of tourism (e.g. Edensor 2000a) also devote more attention to the ways in which the city is consumed. Place consumption is analysed in terms of the embodied experience of being in the tourist destination, rather than merely the 'tourist gaze'.

By chapter six, an adequate conceptualisation of experience is still somewhat lacking. This chapter, therefore, turns towards a more humanistic approach to understanding urban tourism. It begins by reviewing the limited literature on the experience of urban tourism, including past attempts to 'people' geographical research. The limitations of humanistic and experiential studies are discussed, emphasising particularly the problems associated with individualistic studies. The subsequent discussion attempts to illustrate the benefits of imbuing urban tourism studies with an appreciation of human experience, while avoiding an individualistic approach divorced from the practice of urban tourism.

The discussion draws initially on existential approaches inspired by writers such as Merleau-Ponty (1962). Although existentialism has sometimes inspired individualistic studies, it is argued that explanations of the embodied nature of experience are invaluable to urban tourism research. Attention turns to a somewhat neglected yet inspirational author, the phenomenologist Alfred Schutz. Schutz captures the varied but intersubjective nature of experience, and provides a link between place images and cultural texts (1972). Central to a Schutzian perspective is the 'stock of knowledge', representing a collection of first-hand and mediated experiences (Schutz and Luckmann 1974). Schutz also develops a sophisticated theory of action (1970), providing alternative insights into urban tourist decision-making.

Chapter seven re-examines the different perspectives, identifying concepts and principles of particular relevance to researching urban tourism. The chapter provides a summary of the contributions of each theoretical area, before presenting a conceptual model of urban tourism. Following the discussions within the preceding chapters, it is considered particularly important to conceptualise the culture and experience of urban tourism. The model traces both a consumptive and non-consumptive route taken by place consumers, depending on whether or not they experience the destination first hand. While representations and images of the urban destination are crucial to the non-consumptive circuit, the consumptive circuit includes first-hand experiences of the urban landscape. Although the model might be considered 'experiential' in nature, the concepts are drawn from the different perspectives explored in the book. The humanistic perspective, place image research and cultural studies make explicit contributions. The urban tourism literature and the 'postmodernity debate' also have an implicit influence.

Attention subsequently turns to urban tourism research, and the chapter provides an urban tourism research agenda. The aim is not to prescribe specific methodologies but to encourage the development of theoretically informed urban tourism research which addresses the perspectives currently neglected. Although specific method-ologies can only ever be determined by the aims and objectives of the particular study, the research agenda attempts to integrate the different genres of research into the context of urban tourism. Complemented by the case studies throughout the book, it is intended to act as a guide to a diverse range of tourism researchers, from undergraduates writing dissertations to experienced researchers.

Chapter eight provides a conclusion to the book, summarising the main arguments and perspectives. The chapter evaluates the theoretical discussion throughout the chapters, the implications for urban tourism research and the implications for the practice of urban tourism. It is considered whether such ideas have a contribution to make to commercial research conducted by tourism practitioners, in addition to academic research and studies. The chapter ends by considering the praxis of urban tourism research, suggesting possible reasons for the relative neglect of such a chal-lenging and fascinating contemporary phenomenon.

Chapter summary:

- Urban tourism is an exciting, challenging and multi-disciplinary field of study.
- Different social science perspectives can help us to understand urban tourism, but it is also important to recognise the limitations of each perspective.
- This book aims to evaluate different theoretical perspectives and suggest how they can be synthesised in order to provide a more complete understanding of urban tourism.
- This book is not concerned with theory *per se*, but with the application of different types of knowledge and understanding to urban tourism research and management.

Chapter 2
Urban Tourism

The following topics are covered in this chapter:

- An introduction to the characteristics of urban tourism and place marketing.
- An evaluation of the practical problems of developing urban tourism in a destination.
- The strengths of urban tourism research, and insights provided by urban tourism researchers.
- The limitations and weaknesses of research into urban tourism.
- Possible solutions to the limitations of urban tourism research.

Introduction

In this chapter, the philosophy and practice of urban tourism will be considered, along with the role of tourism within place-marketing and economic development strategies. In historic cities, urban tourism is an established phenomenon, and contemporary policy is often concerned with minimising the negative impact of tourism. More striking and widespread, however, is the proactive use of urban tourism in economic development and place-marketing strategies. This chapter focuses on the management, planning and marketing of urban tourism. Place marketing deserves particular attention, as it plays an important role in both the theory and the practice of urban tourism. Place marketing has become both a philosophy of urban governance and management and a major industry in itself. A major aim is to differentiate a particular city from its competitors, attracting a share of spatially mobile capital. It has increasingly been recognised that an attractive place to visit tends to be an attractive place to live and work. Tourism has therefore become an important component of economic development.

It would appear, however, that urban tourism has sometimes been developed in a rather evangelical, short-term and uncritical manner. Alternative views have sometimes been ignored, and dismissed with a rather defensive rhetoric. It would also seem that as well as possibly representing a costly 'zero-sum game' (Harvey 1989a), many strategies are ill-conceived and incoherent (see Haider 1989). It will be recognised in both this chapter and chapter three that, although tourism offers great potential in terms of economic development, there is certainly no consensus on its merits.

While one would expect tourism researchers to provide a holistic understanding of urban tourism, the literature has some significant theoretical and methodological weaknesses. Recent urban tourism work has addressed place marketing, management, planning and service quality. Urban tourism researchers, however, rarely draw upon theoretical debates within the social sciences, and problems are exacerbated by a lack of engagement with urban tourism within social science disciplines. Methodological weaknesses often stem from an overemphasis on quantitative results, irrespective of the validity of research. With some notable exceptions, urban tourism research informed by contemporary social science seems to be very rare. It is argued at the end of this chapter that, although marketing necessarily focuses on the consumer, a neglect of the experience and culture of urban tourism detracts from a full understanding of urban tourism.

Contemporary Urban Tourism
What is Urban Tourism?

According to Pearce (2001), the increased academic interest in urban tourism is related to the growth of tourism in cities. While the challenges of coping with ever-growing demand in historic cities has been influential, in many cities there has been a proactive strategy of attracting tourists. In terms of the former, Ashworth and Tunbridge (1990) have drawn attention to both the benefits and the problems of tourism in historic cities, and how planning and management might foster a mutually beneficial relationship. However, the latter – the proactive marketing of cities – is probably of wider significance to both practitioners and urban tourism researchers. Law's (1993) text, for example, is devoted more to the entrepreneurial approach to urban tourism, focusing on tourism development in large cities. Law seeks to 'describe, interpret, and evaluate tourism in large cities'. Rather than focus on historic cities and resorts, the book aims to 'determine why some cities have been successful in developing the industry, and why others have not, and what lessons can be learnt' (Law 1993:xi). By contrast, Page (1995:xvii) considers the use of tourism in urban-regeneration strategies to be well documented, and prefers to concentrate on 'recent innovations in the management of urban tourism problems', including visitor management in small historic cities. Page's (1995) text generally takes a management and marketing approach to urban tourism, developing an 'interdisciplinary systems approach'. He places 'tourist experience' at the centre of his systems framework, and ultimately draws upon the service quality literature as a means of managing the urban tourist experience. The influence of the service quality literature is also clear in Murphy's (1997) *Quality Management in Urban Tourism*, and particularly in Postina and Jenkins (1997) and Haywood and Muller (1988).

From a US perspective, Judd and Fainstein (1999) provide a fairly detailed discussion of themes as varied as casinos and gambling, major sporting events, 'Disneyisation', and urban regeneration. Among the more focused of the conference proceedings related to urban tourism, Tyler et al. (1998) addresses policy and planing, managing visitors and resources, tourists and space, and city events and the tourism product. The techniques of place marketing and urban tourism have been developed by marketing texts such as Kotler et al. (1993) and Ashworth and Voogd (1990). The latter, however, combines marketing and planning approaches, and adopts a more critical perspective on the transformation of towns and cities into place products. Perhaps the title *Selling the City* is a deliberate misnomer, as the emphasis is on the challenges of managing both the demand and supply sides of urban tourism.

As Law (1992:599) noted several years ago, urban tourism is relatively neglected, as 'most textbooks on tourism make hardly any reference to it'. Law (1993:vi) refers to a 'general absence of material on the subject', and Shaw and Williams (1994:207) state that there is a 'somewhat limited literature on visitor activity in urban areas'. While the limitations of urban tourism research are discussed later in the chapter, it is worth noting that the field is characterised by its fragmented and rather inaccessible nature. Although Shaw and Williams (1994) note that urban tourism has received more attention in recent years, research has been conducted on a bewildering range of spatial scales and *ad hoc* themes. A minority of researchers focus on the scale of individual attractions or urban tourism sites. Researchers such as Prentice et al. (1998) and Bagnall (2003), for example, provide theoretically informed accounts of the consumption of heritage sites.

The scale of tourism districts within cities, emphasising the clustering of facilities and attractions, has been more attractive to researchers. As Pearce (2001:933–35) points out, various types of tourism district have been studied, including historic districts, redevelopment zones, sacred spaces, entertainment destinations and functional tourism districts. The historic tourist district has been comprehensively addressed by Ashworth and Tunbridge (1990), with researchers such as Laws and Le Pelley (2000) providing detailed case studies. Mellor (1991) exemplifies research on redeveloped areas, providing a theoretically informed evaluation of Liverpool's regenerated waterfront. Ram et al. (2000) and Briggs (2000) evaluate ethnic tourism enclaves, albeit from rather different perspectives. Pearce (2001:933–44) also cites Dahles' analysis of the historic inner city of Amsterdam, and Chang's accounts of ethnic districts in Singapore. According to Pearce (2001), researchers have also been concerned with sacred spaces, such as in Jerusalem and Lourdes.

There is a large body of research into entertainment spaces such as shopping malls and theme parks (e.g. Shields 1989), although this rarely addresses urban tourism *per se*. Pearce (2001) also notes how the concept of the 'functional tourism district' and 'tourism business district' has also caught the attention of urban tourism researchers. Judd (1993) emphasises the agglomerative nature of the components of urban tourism, and subsequently Judd and Fainstein (1999:39) develop the concept of the 'urban tourist bubble'. The latter concept concerns the trend towards areas of cities exclusively designed for tourists. Not only do they consist of a typical and conspicuous tourist landscape, but they are also isolated from the city's environmental and social problems, such as dereliction, crime and poverty.

The majority of urban tourism research has been undertaken on the scale of the town or city itself. Many such studies are both empirical and descriptive in nature, although the focus and level of theoretical underpinning does vary. Law (1996), for example, provides comprehensive case studies of major cities, while Paddison (1993) provides a more critical examination of place marketing in the city of Glasgow. Authors such as Bramwell (1998; Bramwell and Rawding 1994, 1996) provide informative case studies of British cities such as Sheffield. Early and influential examples of comparative case studies of urban tourism include Buckley and Witt (1985, 1989), who concentrate on tourism in difficult deindustrialised areas. Van den Berg et al. (1995) present eight case studies of European cities, and Mazanec (1997) provides empirical European case studies. Pearce (2001:936) argues that urban tourism researchers also need to explore the phenomenon at regional, national and international levels. There is potential in analysing the functional roles and linkages within tourism systems. Pearce (2001:936–37) cites research into gateways, hubs, distribution channels and intermediaries, and transport. There is perhaps a much more urgent need, however, for theoretically informed work into the relationship between urban tourism, place and globalisation. Boniface and Fowler (1993) provide a sensitive evaluation of the role of heritage in this context. Pearce (2001) quite rightly points to the valuable work by Chang et al. (1996), which illustrates how urban tourism embodies both the forces of globalisation and the social construction of place at the local scale. Considering the interest in these themes within the social science literature (e.g. Soja 1989; Urry 1987; Featherstone 1991; Lash and Urry 1994, 1997), however, there is a paucity of studies which even mention urban tourism.

While this brief review of influential contributions to urban tourism scholarship does not define the field of study, it at least provides a flavour of what is currently considered within the realms of 'urban tourism'. Although urban tourism can be defined simply as tourism in towns and cities, it is apparent that the field is more complex. Ashworth (1989), in asking whether urban tourism exists, identifies three approaches to urban tourism research. Urban tourism might be understood through the supply-side, particularly the facilities for tourists in the city. The focus might be on the demand-side, including motivations, perceptions and behaviour. Alternatively, researchers might address urban tourism policy, including that of both the public and private sectors. Pearce (2001) provides an integrative framework, intended to organise the object of enquiry. This consists of a matrix which includes both key themes and the scale of analysis. According to Pearce (2001:929), therefore, urban tourism may be studied in terms of demand, supply, development, marketing, planning, organisation, operations and impact assessment. The spatial scale of enquiry may be the individual site, district or city, or regional, national or international. Although the scope of such 'key themes' will be discussed towards the end of the chapter, the framework at least enables researchers to establish both what is known and where the gaps in knowledge lie, encouraging a 'more systematic and integrative approach' (ibid.:941).

As Law (1993:4) points out, the term 'tourism' is often used as if it is unproblematic. In the US, tourism refers to leisure travel, whilst in Europe it tends to denote travel of any purpose. Whilst perhaps two-thirds of travel is primarily for leisure purposes, many business travellers also consume the urban destination in their leisure time, often accompanied by partners. According to the World Tourism Organisation (cited in Law 1993:4), a tourist is someone who spends at least 24 hours away from home. Yet, for urban tourism purposes, this definition is very restrictive, as day visitors (excursionists) are often significant. Although in the UK, day-trippers have been defined as people spending at least three hours away from home and making a round journey of 20 miles, this excludes residents consuming facilities shared with urban tourists and groups such as students. For the purposes of this book, urban tourism refers to both day-trippers and staying tourists. Likewise, urban tourism includes those visiting for both leisure and business. Additionally, this understanding of urban tourism also incorporates residents, whether temporary or permanent, who consume the city along with 'tourists'. In parts of this book, therefore, the term 'place consumer' is considered more appropriate. Guided by these points, this book engages with tourism in towns and cities, involving leisure and business visitors, excursionists and residents as consumers.

Selling the City

Deindustrialisation in Western Europe since the 1970s has been well documented. So too has the dramatic growth of the tertiary sector, and the emergence of the 'post-industrial city' (Bell 1973). As authors such as Fothergill et al. (1988) have argued, the deindustrialisation of major cities was due to both intense competition in global economies and the fact that cities became increasingly unattractive to new forms of industry. The flexibility, accessibility and quality of life offered by greenfield sites placed the city in a seemingly inescapable cycle of decline. It was increasingly recognised, however, that the city did have some unique and attractive resources, if not for traditional manufacturing industry, at least for consumption. The expanding tertiary sectors, therefore, were increasingly seen by urban authorities as offering a silver lining in terms of economic development and urban regeneration.

Not surprisingly, throughout the 1980s, urban policy-makers and local government increasingly adopted the style of 'entrepreneurial government' and place marketing. There has been an effort to provide the sites, environment, incentives and images to attract not only high-tech manufacturing and quaternary industry, but also a range of producer and personal-service industries. In addition to providing the physical infrastructure for new forms of manufacturing and service industries, the most ambitious and comprehensive programmes of regeneration also sought to develop the tourism and leisure sectors. Tourism, heritage and the cultural industries were increasingly linked to both economic development strategies in terms of employment and income generation, and place-marketing strategies concerned with image reconstruction.

The increase in the spatial mobility of capital, and the devastating effects of deindustrialisation on many cities, has led to the development of a new industry – place marketing. The practice of place marketing involves the activities of both public- and private-sector agencies, aimed at 'selling' the image of a particular locality in order to make it attractive to commercial organisations, tourists and inhabitants. The emphasis is on encouraging footloose industries to locate and tourists to visit. The economic logic of place marketing, therefore, is concerned with economic development, job creation – and often urban regeneration. Localities compete with each other for a share of mobile capital in a range of 'place-market segments'.

Place Marketing

The last decade and a half has seen a transformation of place marketing, from an essentially amateur activity to a vast and professionalised form of urban governance. Holcomb (1990) shows that in the US place marketing is a multibillion dollar industry in its own right, employing marketing and public-relations consultants to 'sell' towns, cities and states. Guskind (1987:4) estimates that in the US in 1986, $3–6 billion was spent 'selling' cities and states. The Tourist and Convention Agency in the city of Las Vegas has a budget of $81 million (Law 1993). Bailey's analysis of the urban development programmes of 23 US cities concluded that marketing 'is now the principal driving force in urban economic development' (1989:3). There is little sign of urban marketing activity decreasing, as cities in particular are likely to be sold even more aggressively in future years (Ashworth and Voogd 1990).

Authors such as Ashworth and Voogd (1988:68) emphasise that, although place marketing is sometimes considered to be synonymous with 'place promotion', it is necessary to use all of the 'geographical marketing mix'. The development of the place product to meet the needs of target market segments is particularly important. According to Kotler et al. (1993:18), place marketing is concerned with designing an appropriate mix of features and services, devising attractive incentives for current and potential consumers, delivering products and services in an efficient and accessible way, and promoting the attributes and image of the locality. Place marketers should take a strategic approach, positioning the locality according to its strengths and weaknesses relative to competitors. Ashworth and Voogd (1988:68) suggest that strategies may be defensive, concerned with maintaining existing services; quality-orientated, concerned with enhancing facilities; expansionist, concerned with promoting attractive heritage resources; or aimed at diversification, whereby new markets are targeted.

As economic development and often regeneration is an important aim, marketers see their role as that 'through which economy is integrated into society to serve human needs' (Drucker and Parlin cited in Bailey 1989:1). Deindustrialisation has been an important catalyst for applying the marketing philosophy to localities. A cycle of unemployment, dereliction and social problems has contributed to and been created by the unattractiveness of many places to industry. A falling tax base and the rise of *laissez-faire* economic strategies also fostered a strong marketing ethos. As Harvey asked, 'how could regions blessed largely with a demand-side heritage adapt to a supply-side world?' (Harvey 1989a:8).

The answer, at least according to government ministries and business leaders, was to change the emphasis of the planning profession. Instead of merely controlling development and providing basic infrastructure, a proactive approach was increasingly adopted. From the unsophisticated promotion of the main attributes of localities grew a more targeted and comprehensive place-marketing approach. According to Harvey (1989a), this represented a transition from the 'managerial' approach to local government characteristic of the 1960s to an 'entrepreneurial' approach from the 1970s onwards. In Britain, the 1989 Local Government and Housing Act forced local authorities to develop their economic development programmes, including community consultation on its content. The marketing concept was increasingly being applied to non-profit organisations and places. Kotler, for example, was one of the first marketing writers to address the ideological divide between the traditional and contemporary concerns of local authorities (Kotler 1969, 1972). From an emphasis on the public good and social benefit, attention turned to 'social marketing' (Kotler 2002). The competitive ethos of the marketplace was imported, and the concept of the 'place market' became widespread.

Place marketing is therefore a process, 'whereby urban activities are as closely as possible related to the demands of targeted customers so as to maximise the efficient social and economic functioning of the area' (Ashworth and Voogd 1988:68).

Place Image

Fundamental to place marketing is the construction and projection of an attractive image of the locality. In many cases there will be an attempt to replace a vague or unfavourable image with one that is conducive to attracting tourists and investment. Stereotypes – simplified generalisations about people and places – are crucial to urban marketing, particularly as many post-industrial cities suffer from the negative variety. The attraction of investment and tourists has often been hampered by negative stereotypes, and a range of promotional tools are employed to alter, strengthen and project a favourable image. Mills and Young (1986) have estimated that well over 70 per cent of UK local authorities engage in some form of promotional activity. Since Burgess' survey in 1977, it would seem that there has been a considerable increase in the use of tourist guides, and industrial and commercial information (Barke and Harrop 1994). Qualitative changes are also apparent, with 'glossy' and professional-looking publications replacing the 'dour' varieties of the 1970s. The proportion of local authorities distributing tourist information appears to have more than doubled since 1977. Examples of this in British towns such as Bradford, Wigan and Halifax (Buckley and Witt 1985, 1989) would seem to indicate that tourism is increasingly being incorporated into the strategies of economic development departments (Law 1991; Jeffrey 1990).

Enhancing the image of the city is often integral to urban tourism development. Although stereotypical images of dirt and dereliction can represent a severe obstacle to tourism in post-industrial cities, tourism has an important image-enhancement role. As one practitioner puts it, 'visitors will be drawn, word will spread, and perceptions will change' (Collinge 1989:7). This has been the aim in cities such as Glasgow, where first an image-building campaign, then an arts and culture-based image reconstruction programme was used (Paddison 1993). Despite the success of the tourism sector in the city of Liverpool, negative images of the city persist in the domestic markets of both tourism and inward investment. The anti-Liverpool discourse of the London-based media is exemplified by a journalist several years ago who was determined to obtain a photograph of a pile of rubbish in front of the Liver Building. He eventually made imaginative use of a busy scrapyard on the opposite banks of the River Mersey. The contemporary place marketing of Liverpool increasingly targets key decision-makers and opinion-formers, through the use of familiarisation tours, advertising, and hosting events such Guild of Travel Writers' annual general meeting (1998). Mersey Tourism uses advertising to communicate 11 key positive facts about the locality which contradict negative images. These include the fact that 'Merseyside is the one of the safest city regions in the UK' (Mersey Partnership 2001). The advert, which refers to the Home Office Statistical Bulletin (January 2001), includes the text 'with crime rates comparable to the likes of Cambridge and Sussex, it gives you peace of mind to enjoy a real quality of life both night and day' (see figure 2.1).

Merseyside is one of the **safest** city regions in the **UK.**

2.1: Liverpool: safe city.

Most content analyses of promotional literature, including Holcombe and Beauregard (1980), Ryan (1990) and Watson (1991), reveal surprisingly uniform themes. The adoption of logos is common, with symbols representing industrial heritage, quality of life and renaissance/re-birth (Barke and Harrop 1994). Slogans are often used, with references to quality of life, locational advantages (being either central or a gateway) and business opportunities. Even Wallasey (Merseyside) is promoted as 'EuroWirral' and Middlesbrough (northeast England) as 'Gateway to Captain Cook Country'. In northwest England, industrial heritage is also influential, inspiring puns such as 'Cotton onto Burnley'. The Black Country in the West Midlands looks to 'an industrious future from an industrial past', whilst Bristol is 'rich in industrial history' (Barke and Harrop 1994).

According to Bramwell and Rawding in their study of five British cities, it is common for cities to be represented as lively, exciting, dynamic and cosmopolitan (Bramwell and Rawding 1996:208). The study also reveals some interesting differences between the promotion of UK cities. The approach in Manchester, for example, is encapsulated in the slogan 'The Life and Soul of Britain', emphasising vitality, energy, and youth culture. By contrast, marketing in Stoke-on-Trent emphasises shopping and the pottery industry, employing the slogan 'The City that Fires the Imagination' (Bramwell and Rawding 1996:208). A priority for The Mersey Partnership, responsible for marketing Liverpool, has been to develop a distinctive and positive brand image, emphasising a high quality of life for both residents and visitors.

The Urban Tourism Product
Planning and Development

Place-marketing strategies which emphasise the quality of life of a locality tend to sit the most comfortably with the development of tourism. In the US, the emphasis on consumption and services in economic development is characterised by the development of Pittsburgh's huge waterside amusement park and Cleveland waterfront's collection of jazz clubs and restaurants. Likewise, the docks of Boston, New York and Baltimore have been transformed into festival markets (Law 1993). Getz (1991) describes how the downtown areas of Baltimore have been transformed by urban

2.2: Liverpool's waterfront. Courtesy of the Mersey Partnership.

development initiatives, fairs and the activities of the Baltimore Office of Promotion and Tourism. The image of a high-quality lifestyle, extensive facilities and a lively ambience are crucial to attract target market segments. Even places worst affected by deindustrialisation, such as Hartlepool in northeast England, where unemployment reached 22.3 per cent in the 1980s (DOE 1984), have invested heavily in waterfront developments. Most of Britain's redeveloped waterfront areas, such as the Albert Dock in Liverpool, or the Docklands in London, attempt to combine place promotion with extensive place-product development, exemplifying the marketing approach.

Tourism has increasingly been used as an important component of economic development strategies. Urban tourism can have immense income and employment-generating potential in itself, and it is widely considered to complement the attraction of inward investment. Direct benefits relate to job creation in facilities such as hotels, restaurants and attractions. Secondary rounds of expenditure occur, creating subsidiary and support industries, and the local economy also benefits from the induced affect on household incomes (see Fletcher and Archer 1991). On Merseyside, for example, it is estimated that even in the difficult 1980s, 14,000 jobs were supported by tourism (DRV 1986). By 2001, tourism expenditure on Merseyside was estimated at £602 million per year, supporting 22,000 jobs (Mersey Tourism 2001). Sheenan and Ritchie (1997:105) show that in North America, maximising the economic impact of

2.3: Sydney Opera House. Courtesy of Tourism New South Wales.

tourism is the priority of tourism bureaux. Even individual projects have significant employment-generating potential, such as the New Theatre in Cardiff which is estimated to sustain 200 jobs (Law 1993). Facilities, attractions and environmental improvements can also be of great benefit to a local population. In theory, they can also increase civic pride, enterprise and confidence.

As part of urban-tourism strategies, buildings are used as symbols of success for a city. Places can become renowned for certain landmarks, such as Sydney Opera House, the Statue of Liberty or the Eiffel Tower. As architecture helps to project a distinct image to potential tourists and investors, cities with waterfronts and listed buildings are at an advantage. The physical regeneration of derelict areas is an important benefit of developing tourism. As Law (1993) illustrates, the area on the fringe of the centre of industrial cities was usually the site of transport facilities, industry and warehouses. Although now derelict, this space does have potential in terms of tourism and cultural activities. The decline of transport facilities has been influential in St Louis (Union Station), Manchester (G-MEX Centre), Toronto (CN Tower and Skydive), and the docks and waterfronts in cities as varied as Boston, Baltimore, Barcelona, Liverpool and Cardiff.

As Walsh (1989) shows, planning departments have not been exempt from the adoption of techniques from marketing science. For the purpose of developing urban tourism strategies, Jansen-Verbeke (1988) classifies tourism resources into primary and secondary. Primary elements are those which actually attract visitors, such as historic buildings, urban landscapes, museums and art galleries, concerts, spectator sports, conferences, exhibitions and special events. Secondary elements include shopping, catering, accommodation, transport and tourism agencies. Cities such as Frankfurt in Germany also thrive as gateways to the surrounding area, in this case to the Rhine Gorge, Heidelberg and Gothenburg. As Ashworth and Tunbridge (1990) show, for tourist-historic cities the problem is not so much in attracting tourists. The challenge for the authorities of these cities, such as Groningen in the Netherlands is more concerned with balancing tourism, conservation, preservation and the needs of local residents. Urban tourism tends to be physically concentrated in historic districts, yet these districts are perceived very differently by architects, historians, urban planners and tourism specialists. Pearce (2001:933) cites Dahles' study of the historic inner city of Amsterdam, which contrasts the discourse produced to promote the district to the international tourism market with a more local discourse.

The Agents of Urban Tourism

Although the incorporation of tourism into economic development strategies is widespread, published documents are quite rare, perhaps reflecting a continuing ambiguity concerning the role of tourism. Law (1993) reports that a number of UK cities have produced comprehensive tourism plans, including Belfast (PIEDA 1987), Birmingham (Birmingham City Council 1987), Bristol (Bristol City Council Planning

Department 1990), Merseyside (MTB 1987), and Cardiff (Tibbalds, Colbourne, Karski 1988; Pannell et al. 1984; see also L & R Leisure Plc 1995). Some of the best case examples of urban tourism development suggest that tourism should be a component of general economic development. In the UK, Bradford's economic development department, for example, overcame initial derision in the mass media, successfully developing national attractions, cultural events and festivals.

Although European and Australasian tourist agencies tend to operate on a smaller scale than in the US, Pearce (1992) suggests that most large cities have some form of tourism marketing organisation. The Munich City Tourist Office, for example, had a budget of some DM23.3 million in 1989, with 40 per cent allocated by the city council. In Auckland, New Zealand, Tourism Auckland has a limited budget of NZ$40,000 to promote the city as the country's gateway. Research in the US and Canada shows that a common funding arrangement involves the use of a hotel tax, accounting for 71.7 per cent of budget revenues (Sheenan and Ritchie 1997:114). With government grants contributing an average of 6.2 per cent, local city taxes 2.6 per cent and other taxes 1 per cent, it would seem that tourism bureaux are financially dependent on public funds (ibid.). As membership fees contribute an average of only 6.9 per cent of revenue, there is a clear need to increase the contribution of private-sector funding.

Arts and Culture

Arts and cultural facilities commonly form an important component of urban tourism strategies, particularly when a group of attractions are geographically clustered. Although one of the earliest examples was the Smithsonian Institute in Washington DC, cities around the world have adopted a similar approach. There is a grouping of museums in South Kensington in London, and Frankfurt created a total of 11 new museums throughout the 1980s, grouping 7 on the southern bank of the Main (Law 1993). Redeveloped docklands commonly feature groups of attractions and museums. Liverpool's waterfront, for example is home to the Merseyside Maritime Museum, the Tate Gallery, the Beatles Story, the Museum of Liverpool Life, HM Customs and Excise National Museum and Mersey Ferries. Most large British cities significantly increased museum attendance throughout the 1980s and 1990s, and it was increasingly appreciated that despite the relatively small proportion of the population attending such attractions, a cluster of facilities can benefit the economy and help to project a positive image.

There has been an increasing amount of interest in what has been termed 'cultural tourism' (e.g. Richards, 1996; Robinson et al. 1996). Not only is 'culture' considered to be an increasingly important motivation for tourism, but the relationship between culture and tourism is assumed to be mutually beneficial. As Hughes (2000) argues, however, there is by no means a consensus on the definition of cultural tourism. As Hughes (2000:113) points out, the terms 'arts tourism', 'cultural tourism' and 'heritage tourism' tend to have been 'used interchangeably to refer to tourism which includes visits to historic buildings and sites, museums and art galleries, visits to contemporary paintings and sculptures or to attend the performing arts'. What is certain is the importance of cultural tourism to the urban tourism product. According to Hughes, in the UK the relationship has long been encouraged by the Arts Council of Great Britain, the British Tourist Authority, and the English Tourist Council. Hughes (2000:112) cites the Society of London Theatres as admitting as early as 1982 that 'if it were not for the overseas visitors to London it is doubtful whether West End theatres could remain open during the summer'.

Briggs (2000) demonstrates how south Asian food has increasingly become a catalyst for urban tourism (see case study 2.1). In East London, for example, ethnic tourism initiatives have been led by an agency called Spitalfields Town Management. Although Spitalfields already attracted visitors, the emphasis of the strategy was on improving quality in order to capitalise on its neighbour, the City of London's financial district. Another major initiative in Spitalfields was the development of the Beisakhi Mela – the Bangladeshi New Year festival – attracting up to 45,000 visitors. The commodification of ethnic cuisine has been developed further in Leicester, a city in the Midlands of England. Asian cuisines have been incorporated into a short-break package, developed by Leicester Promotions Ltd. Funded by both the local authority and private-sector organisations, the agency has developed a weekend break called 'A Taste of Asia'. Ethnic enclaves in US cites have also been evaluated, with Conforti (1996) demonstrating the mixed fortunes of 'Little Italies' in New York, Baltimore, Boston and Philadelphia. Singapore has also exploited its ethnic diversity, using the slogan 'Instant Asia' to promote its Chinese, Indian and Malaysian districts (Chang 1997).

Economic development has embraced the arts to the extent that the term 'arts industry' is now in common usage (Bianchini and Parkinson 1993; Griffiths 1993). Although US research shows that typically, only 12 per cent of the population attends the theatre in a year, and 13 per cent a classical concert (Law 1993:89), the arts continue to have a high profile in place marketing. According to Shanahan (1980), their presence suggests a level of civility and culture, and a progressive and resourceful city. Whitt (1988) shows how they have been considered the centrepiece of US economic development strategies. Numerous European cities have adopted arts strategies, and in the US, arts districts have been created in cities such as Boston, Dallas and Pittsburgh.

The arts often play an important part in events and festivals which attract large numbers of visitors, the largest of which have been termed 'mega-events' (Syme et al. 1989; Getz 1991). While large-scale events may serve a wide range of corporate objectives, they are increasingly used as part of urban tourism and place-marketing strategies; while festivals may offer opportunities for expressions of local knowledge, communal identity and shared values, they are also a tool of urban tourism practi-tioners. Getz (1991) describes a 'hallmark event' as an event that increases the profile of a destination or provides the tourism theme for the destination. He considers that there is a mutually beneficial relationship between hallmark events and the host community. The income-generating and image-building potential of events such as Munich's Oktoberfest, the Tall Ships Race, and the Commonwealth and Olympic

Games, have been recognised for some time. Even unsuccessful bids to host events can be beneficial, with research showing that the familiarity with Manchester amongst 500 businesses increased by 10 per cent during its Olympic bid (Healey and Baker cited in Law 1993). By 1991, the number of arts-based festivals in the UK had increased to 557 (Rolfe 1992). The Edinburgh Festival attracts 600,000 visitors over three weeks, and generates £40 million (Law 1993:99).

Urban Tourism in Theory and Practice
The Complexity of Urban Tourism

Boniface and Fowler (1993) emphasise the potential of urban tourism and heritage in providing an outlet for expressing local difference and place identity in the context of globalisation. In this optimistic view, urban tourism can mediate between the external global forces of capital, and the perspectives of local residents, local governments, and entrepreneurs. Attention has been drawn to the tangible elements of urban tourism by authors such as Jansen (1989), Jacobs (1993) and Jansen-Verbeke (1990). Indirectly, such contributions have been significant in suggesting the way in which values and social practices become embodied through urban recreation and tourism. A dialectical process seems to operate, between the physical production of the urban landscape, and the cultural production of symbolic value. As Selwyn (1996) shows, urban tourism is also about the creation of myths, images and fantasies, particularly about the Other. Whether one considers Nepal (Hutt 1996), Brighton (Meethen 1996) or Cyprus (Dann 1988, 1996a), the development of tourism requires the production of mythical places and hosts, and these myths are underpinned by politico-economic and cultural dependencies. Selwyn also demonstrates that there is no simple and universal process in the production and consumption of tourist myths.

Herbert (1995) identifies a triad of interrelated phenomena, consisting of leisure, tourism and heritage. Despite the seemingly unproblematic dictionary definition of heritage as 'that which has been or may be inherited' (OED 1993), Herbert (1995) reminds us that this is not the case. Whereas conservation and preservation were once the priority, the need to improve access and market tourism and heritage sites to paying consumers is the predominant contemporary motivation. As the competition between tourist destinations and individual attractions increases, so does the emphasis on increasing visitor numbers and ensuring customer satisfaction. Herbert suggests that very few tourism organisations can avoid adopting the marketing philosophy, citing CADW (Welsh Historic Monuments), which feels it necessary to assure that 'the completion of projects...should boost attendances in 1993–94' (*Western Mail*, 16 December 1993 cited in Herbert 1995:9).

In applying marketing to urban tourist sites and destinations, it is worth noting that: 'marketing is a process of planning and movement of a product from the supplier to those who use it...and the marketing process is incomplete unless all its functions are performed' (Kotler 1992:7). As in any marketing system, in urban tourism consumers and products are brought together by the market of exchange. Although place marketing performs all of these functions – adopting a 'place-marketing mix' – there are significant differences in the nature of elements, particularly in the case of the product and promotion. As Gold and Ward (1990), Ashworth and Voogd (1990) and Lovelock and Weinberg (1984) show, the place product is intangible, especially when sold as an entity rather than a defined set of facilities or services. The urban tourism product, for instance, is both a container or stage for activity-based products, and a product in itself. Activity-based products typically consist of cultural facilities, attractions, events and festivals.

The city, however, also has a concentration of facilities which, although not solely for tourist use, contribute to the 'leisure setting' (Jansen-Verbeke 1987). Marketing approaches differ, therefore, depending on the degree of definition possible, but it is significant that the product consumed may not correspond to that which is promoted. In spatial terms, the boundaries of the place product rarely correspond with juris-dictional boundaries, but include socio-cultural characteristics of local populations, such as local customs, folklore and local traditions.

Spatial hierarchies also exist, with different spatial scales often targeted by different place-marketing organisations (Ashworth and Voogd 1990). Because the place product is multi-sold, the same facilities and geographical area is sold to many different groups of consumers. Although marketers take steps to avoid conflict, the process often leads to tensions and ambiguities. The co-ordination of the activities of different organisations is important, and there may be an emphasis on partnerships in order to avoid duplication of activities and a 'shadow effect' (Bramwell and Rawding 1994). It is necessary for the activities of marketing consortia, tourist boards and economic development departments to be consistent with those of development corpo-rations, developers and planning departments. As Pearce (1998) shows, in the context of Paris, although tourism plans exist at a variety of spatial scales, from individual districts to the metropolitan area, these are not part of a co-ordinated strategy. Discrepancies between the projected image of the locality and the place product are obviously to be avoided. Market segmentation is also challenging in urban tourism, as demand for the place product cannot simply be equated with participation. The same products and facilities are simultaneously being used by very different groups of consumers with different needs and desires.

As authors such Harvey (1989a) argue, place marketing can result in a 'zero-sum' game, whereby places are both developed and promoted in very similar ways. According to Harvey, there is a danger that every city will redevelop and promote its waterfront and festival market, perhaps conforming to the model advocated by the same place-marketing practitioners employed by several different cities. This may have the effect of making cities more alike, rather than celebrating their uniqueness. Judd and Fainstein (1999:39) discuss the development of 'tourist bubbles', containing the 'mayor's trophy collection' including 'an atrium hotel, festival mall, convention centre, restored historic neighbourhood, domed stadium, aquarium, new office towers, and redeveloped waterfront'. The tourist bubble resembles a theme park in that it provides

entertainment and excitement, yet within 'reassuringly clean and attractive surroundings' (ibid.:39). This sanitised version of urban tourism not only threatens to
erode the uniqueness of urban destinations, but it may also devalue the urban tourism
experience in a process similar to that operating in overdeveloped coastal resorts.

Problems with Place Promotion

Promotion is also a fundamental component of urban tourism strategies, representing
the official, specific, goal-directed means of influencing the behaviour of target groups
(Ashworth and Voogd 1990). The transmission of images of localities depends on a
range of channels, effectively forming a 'place-promotional mix'. The media chosen in
promotional activity significantly influences the credibility of the message. Research
is important in monitoring the transmission and reception of place images (see,
for example, Goodall 1988). A range of promotional strategies and communication
channels have been examined, including local-authority tourism promotion (Burgess
1982), press advertising (Pocock and Hudson 1978), slogan advertising (Mortalieau
1988), official letters from public authorities (Van der Veen and Voogd 1987), film
(Burgess and Gold 1995), television (Gould 1985), news reporting (Brooker-Gross
1985) and popular music (Jarvis 1985).

Despite the diversity of these studies, a common conclusion is that official
projected images are rarely the most significant influence on place consumer decision-
making. To be accepted into the individual's image of the locality, the information
must be credible, and this depends on the individual's evaluation of the medium of
transmission. Researchers seem to be agreed on the importance of the credibility of
media for the success of place promotion (see Crompton 1979; Giletson and Crompton
1983). More fundamentally, it would seem that place consumers, particularly tourists,
are influenced by a much wider spectrum of information sources than consumers of
other products. Cities, for example, may be subject to mass-media reporting of
environmental or social problems, and these unofficial images dominate the locality's
identity. It would also seem that these unofficial images are significant in purchasing
behaviour, with strong attitudes towards places developed without exposure to com-
mercially projected sources of information.

It would seem that a major influence on the success of a place-marketing strategy
is its level of coherence and precision. Place marketing is successful where the place
product can easily be defined, the target consumer groups are identifiable and accessible and the organisation can project a clear and uncontested image. Organisational
structure is often critical for the success of place marketing. The philosophy of
marketing needs to permeate the entire organisation, a development that some public-
sector organisations have adapted to better than others. Crucial to marketing is the
identification of a unique selling proposition, yet there is a remarkable uniformity and
blandness in the packaging of many localities. Evans et al. (1995) argue that very few
destinations are marketed with a strategic approach to positioning. Town planners have

had to become comfortable with the market, combining traditional planning techniques with vision and intuition (Hall 1987:130). As Fretter (1993) argues, this implies a new relationship between local authorities and their 'customers', and a demand-orientated and 'flexible' approach to development plans (see also Harloe et al. 1990). In short, the transition from Fordism to flexible accumulation has forced the planning profession to develop a flexible, market-orientated and proactive approach.

Urban Tourism Strategies

As localities have embraced marketing and increasingly competed with other places to attract tourists and inward investment, there have also been significant changes in patterns of consumption and employment. As Meethen (1996) points out, there has been a shift away from mass consumption and mass marketing, and towards flexible consumption and niche marketing. Places have actively sought to become places of consumption, none more so than in the urban tourism market. This active process of developing, packaging, branding and promoting places has profound implications. The urban environment itself becomes a commodity to be bought and sold, a commodity to be consumed.

Despite the huge sums of public and private money spent marketing localities on a range of spatial scales, the effectiveness of many strategies is questionable. In addition to the huge amounts spent by public organisations, place-dependent businesses such as utilities, financial institutions, local newspapers and, of course, tourism enterprises, use place marketing. Such organisations have significant infrastructure investment, local financial investment or a reliance on local markets. Despite research estimating that in the US alone, $3–6 billion was spent in 1986 to sell cities and states (Guskind 1987:4), Haider argues that 'many, if not most places do not have a well thought out marketing plan or strategy' (1992:10–11).

The high aggregate levels of expenditure and the apparent professionalism of place marketing does not imply that a coherent or accepted range of methods and principles exist. Problems are often related to the co-ordination of tourism and regen-eration policies. The plethora of organisations – including local authority departments, central governments and its ministries, autonomous agencies and public–private partnerships – do not necessarily work consistently. Coherence in policy requires a great deal of co-operation and co-ordination between diverse, and often politically polarised, organisations. There can be something of a dichotomy between organisations concerned with the place product, such as development corporations and planning departments, and organisations involved in place promotion, such as tourist boards and marketing consortia. Bramwell and Rawding (1994:431–32) argue that the private sector has become increasingly involved in tourism marketing as part of the partnership-based model. Whilst private-sector expertise (and increasingly revenue) is important, tourism promotion may increasingly reflect short-term profit motives rather than the longer-term interests of the community as a whole.

There has generally been a long-standing failure of planners, residents and business leaders to view tourism as a serious form of economic activity. The perception of tourism as a seasonal and marginal activity bringing in extra revenue is closely interrelated with a lack of academic research. Page (1995) describes the creation of a vicious circle, whereby the absence of public- and private-sector research makes access to research data difficult, whilst the funding necessary for primary research becomes less forthcoming. The catalyst for research and the creation of coherent urban tourism strategies has often been the pressure of high volumes of visitors on popular destinations. Visitor management must become part of coherent place-marketing strategies if tourism in cities such as Canterbury, York and Venice is to be sustainable (Page 1995).

As Paddison (1993) argues, the inflexibility of cities is a problem, with their regeneration requiring long lead times. As the outcome of large-scale investments in social capital and infrastructure, their renewal is an attenuated process requiring huge investments of money and expertise. It would seem, however, that measures of financial performance are problematic, often lacking context. Sheenan and Ritchie (1997:115) find that tourism bureaux often use absolute measures, instead of ratios which enable comparisons to be made between the performance of different organisations.

The scale of tourism necessary to create significant benefits in terms of economic development raises doubts. The impact will be very limited unless part of a comprehensive economic development strategy. The English Tourist Board's view of tourism as 'the catalyst for regeneration' (ETB 1980) requires millions of visitors per year, and much public investment. Overambitious projections of employment figures have often been quoted, resulting in disappointment concerning the number of direct tourism jobs created. The areas regenerated are usually small, due to the necessity of creating tourism 'honey pots' (Law 1993). As Harvey (1989a) argues, there is also a danger that all cities will be redeveloped in the same way, ruining any competitive edge they may have. Evans et al. (1995) urge destinations to pay more attention to strategic management, advocating the application of Porter's model (Porter 1980). While there may be a strong argument for destinations to concentrate on cost leadership, differentiation or a focus strategy, it would appear that positioning is neglected by many destination marketing organisations.

Political accountability is one of the most contentious issues. In theory, social marketing recognises notions of equity and accountability (Kotler 2002). In practice, urban tourism and marketing raises serious questions about how a city is to be represented. As Paddison (1993) demonstrates, Glasgow is a city where marketing and tourism have been used to radically restructure the image and the economic base. There is much polemical debate, however, about the direction taken regarding the new economy, and the image of the city. The urban development corporations also attracted much controversy due to their imposition on areas, their far-reaching powers, and their lack of accountability. As Burgess (1990) shows, the London Docklands Development Corporation spent over £2 million on national advertising between 1981 and 1984, with the aim of encoding a new gentrified identity for the docklands. Not only were thousands of residents physically displaced by the dockland redevelopment, but communities were also subjected to a complex reimaging which manipulated an East End already encoded in television programmes (Burgess 1990:144).

Effective management is, of course, essential – particularly in ensuring that resources are sustainable. Historic areas, for instance face dangers from overuse, traffic congestion and pollution (see Ashworth and Tunbridge 1990). Management is made more difficult by the ill-defined boundaries of tourist areas. Whilst marketing may be conducted at city level, its impacts often extend well beyond city boundaries. The economic complementarities once existing between industrial cities in close proximity is reversed, as competition becomes fierce between them. The organisation of local government has also resulted in competition between local authorities, in effect, wasting resources which would be better spent on regional co-ordinating bodies (Dicken and Tickall 1991).

CASE STUDY 2.1: THE CURRY DEBATE HOTS UP: OPPORTUNITIES AND THREATS FOR ETHNIC TOURISM

The potential of 'ethnic tourist attractions' is now widely recognised by local governments and tourist boards, encouraging the development of areas such as Brick Lane in London, Little Italy in Boston and the Balti Quarter in Birmingham. This case study illustrates both the potential of ethnic tourism – specifically Asian cuisine – and also the complexities and contradictions inherent in 'ethnic tourism enclaves'.

Briggs (2000) demonstrates how south Asian food has increasingly become a catalyst for urban regeneration. In Spitalfields, East London, it was recognised that intense competition between restaurants resulted in price-wars, with spiralling prices, cost-cutting and a loss of quality. The importance of attracting visitors motivated by quality rather than price was recognised. As Briggs (2000) explains, a series of work-shops were organised in order to consult the restaurant owners, along with trips to other competitors outside the Brick Lane area. Free training courses focusing on quality, health and hygiene were offered, followed by a promotional activities including a leaflet, website, improved visual merchandising and public-relations initiatives.

According to Briggs (2000), Leicester, a city in the Midlands of England, is actually one of the most cosmopolitan cities in Europe, with communities from India, East and West Africa, the Caribbean and east Asia. Leicester is also the focus of a short-break package, developed by Leicester Promotions Ltd. The package, 'Taste of Asia' includes accommodation, two three-course meals, a tour of Belgrave and 'Golden Mile' areas of the city, and an introductory course at the Asian Cookery School. The package – for which demand is steadily increasing – is promoted by a public-relations campaign, a promotional leaflet, two brochures and inclusion within several short-break operators' brochures.

According to Portes (1981:290–91): 'Enclaves consist of immigrant groups who concentrate in a specific location and organise a variety of enterprises servicing their own ethnic market and/or the general population.' The deliberate promotion of the 'cultural' features of minority communities to potential visitors is an increasingly common strategy of local policy-makers. Ethnic enclaves are argued to increase community cohesiveness, promoting reliance on co-ethnic suppliers, markets, labour and finance (Wilson and Portes 1980). Contesting views of the ethnic enclave, however, question the ethnic solidarity of these areas, and emphasise intense competition rather than collaboration (see Barrett et al. 1996:793). The picture is also complicated by the often *ad hoc* regulation of ethnic enclaves through the planning system, by the use of family labour and by unequal gender relations in many ethnic enterprises.

Despite the apparent success of ethnic tourism, researchers such as Ram et al. (2000) demonstrate the complexities of operationalising strategies based on the tourist potential of south Asian culture and cuisine. Focusing on the Balti Quarter of Birmingham, England, Ram et al. (ibid.) explore how local policy-makers attempt to capitalise on the entrepreneurial potential of clusters of south Asian businesses. Ram et al. (2000) focus on the balti restaurants located in the Sparkhill and Sparkbrook areas of inner-city Birmingham. These areas are also characterised by high levels of unemployment, a poor physical environment and a high proportion of empty properties. In-depth interviews were conducted with 35 restaurateurs from the Balti Quarter area. A total of 34 were Pakistani (with one Indian entrepreneur), and almost all the businesses were small and family run. A previous survey of 577 customers of the restaurants indicated that 60 per cent were white. The interview explored issues including the backgrounds of restaurateurs, their motivations, working practices and views of the local area. Interviews with key local council employees were also conducted. Two focus groups were also held, for both retailers and council officers.

The results revealed that over 50 per cent of owners had previous experience of self-employment (ibid.:46). Half of these respondents had previous experience of the restaurant trade. The decision to locate in the Balti Quarter was found to be related to the perception that the location provided a lucrative business opportunity, combined with the ease of access to the sector. There was also a perception amongst restaurant owners, however, that the balti concept was now widely used in Birmingham, with the number of restaurants doubling in the last five years. This provided an added incentive for businesses to locate next to each other, maximising their market share through the 'hotelling effect' (Hotelling 1929).

One of the most striking and problematic issues revealed by the research was the intense competition between restaurants. On one level, the competition was for the same trade in the immediate area. Respondents used phrases such as 'dog eat dog' to describe the proliferation of restaurants in the Ladypool Road area (Ram et al. 2000). The was also competition from non-balti restaurants offering similar products such as fish and chips. Outside the area competition came from the increasing number of balti restaurants in other parts of the city, detracting from the overall appeal of the Balti Quarter. As one owner put it, 'the typical white customer came for taxi, alcohol, food. But now customers were saving on the taxi fare' (ibid.:48). It seemed that even outlying villages now had balti restaurants, and the Balti Quarter no longer hosted 'coach loads...from small villages'. Finally, it was recognised that there were changing social patterns of eating out, typified by the popularity of McDonalds or Pizzaland amongst the younger generation.

The research suggested that the intense competition was related to several contentious issues surrounding the Balti Quarter. Some respondents were very critical of the local authority for granting too many licences and not regulating the number of restaurants. One owner went as far as to say that it was a policy of 'let's kill the Pakis off'. Other respondents and key informants at the local authority revealed a more complex situation, in which the local authority could not refuse planning applications on the basis of competition, only if it would cause 'inconvenience to other traders and residents'.

Another issue of some concern was the emphasis on reducing costs and competing on price. The widespread use of family labour was not particularly surprising, with family members representing nearly half of all employees. This was seen as an advantage, as family members 'take interest, enjoy what they are doing...the customers feel more comfortable' (ibid.:50). A slightly less positive comment was that 'you can shout at them'. The use of part-time labour was also pronounced, particularly as Friday and Saturday nights account for over half of total trade, with over 11,000 visitors spending an estimated £84,000 (ibid.:50). One response to this pattern of demand is to offer 'buffet' evenings, for as little as £5. The research revealed that owners overwhelmingly considered advertising and price to be the factors which attracted customers. It is of some concern that none considered quality of service or products to have a substantial effect. The tools of competition are therefore price-cutting and the use of promotional material. This has obvious consequences for both the quality of the products on offer and the market segments attracted. Not surprisingly, there was no evidence of formal training plans or budgets, although informal training by existing employees is the norm.

In conclusion, it can be seen that although ethnic diversity is increasingly used as a component of urban regeneration through tourism, the picture is a complex one. It is important to recognise the contextual factors, such as competition, the state of the labour market and working practices which complicate the phenomenon. In the context of place marketing, it is significant that such issues are neglected with the discourse of the cultural industry, which aims to attract visitors, rather than project a realistic representation. There is therefore a risk that inequalities and harsh working practices will be obscured, in order to project a positive image of a unified and consensual ethnic tourism area.

Urban Tourism Research

Acknowledging the Weaknesses

Recent urban tourism research has improved our understanding of marketing (e.g. Ashworth and Voogd 1990), management (e.g. van den Berg et al. 1995), planning (e.g. Pearce 1998), impacts (e.g. Parlett et al. 1995) and quality (Murphy 1997). However, with a limited number of exceptions (e.g. Prentice et al. 1998), there appears to be a very poor understanding of the composition of urban tourism and heritage consumers, an overemphasis on the socio-economic characteristics of visitors and a neglect of other important characteristics. Ashworth (1989) notes that, despite providing some useful data to tourist boards and planning departments, site-specific studies rarely consider the processes underlying urban tourism. It would seem that little has changed since Pearce suggested that there is 'a need to move away from the isolated, ideographic case study to more systematic and comparative research and replicate studies from place to place and time to time so that the general might be distinguished from the specific' (Pearce 1987:209).

Ashworth argues that despite its economic and social significance, urban tourism has been severely neglected as an area of academic research. According to Ashworth, 'a double neglect has occurred. Those interested in the study of tourism have tended to neglect the urban context in which much of it is set, while those interested in urban studies ... have been equally neglectful of the importance of the tourist function of cities' (Ashworth 1989:33). This neglect is surprising, as urban tourism is significant both in economic terms and in terms of the wider cultural implications for cities. Ashworth (1989) considers the problem in some detail, suggesting possible explanations. It would seem that considerable attention has been devoted to urban regeneration by researchers in disciplines such as geography, planning and sociology. This may have had the effect of marginalising tourism to a mere component of urban regeneration. It would also seem that tourism is rarely represented as a significant phenomenon by planners and local government officials. Page (1995:8) believes that urban tourism suffers from a vicious circle, whereby the lack of quality research results in a lack of interest within the public sector to understand urban tourists. The lack of interest makes further research difficult, as both funding and data sources are limited.

Whilst authors such as Shaw and Williams (1994) argue that recent years have seen an increase in urban tourism research, a lack of sophistication in studies is still apparent. Shaw and Williams (1994:207), for example, concede that there is a 'somewhat limited literature on visitor activity in urban areas'. According to Page (1995), the failure of researchers to analyse urban tourism was noted as early as the 1960s, when US researchers were reluctant to disaggregate the tourist and recreational functions of cities. Vetter (1985) and Page and Sinclair (1989) have come to similar conclusions.

It would seem that the limited understanding of urban tourism is partly the result of a lack of academic sophistication in tourism and marketing studies (Butler and Pearce 1993). Page (1995:5) believes that urban tourism research has tended to remain fragmented and methodologically unsophisticated. This has resulted in studies in which the emphasis is on the results, rather than theory and methodology. Page (1999:163) identifies a tendency for urban tourism research to be based on descriptive and empirical case studies which 'do not contribute to the greater theoretical or methodological understanding of urban tourism'. Commentators also blame the failure to relate findings to wider issues. Authors such as Butler and Pearce (1993) have identified a lack of methodological sophistication in tourism research in general. As Ashworth argues: 'Urban Tourism requires the development of a coherent body of theories, concepts, techniques and methods of analysis' (Ashworth, 1992:5). Page (1995:1) also believes that urban tourism '... is poorly understood in theoretical and conceptual terms since few researchers adopt an integrated approach'. Pearce (2001) obviously shares this view, as he seeks to develop an 'integrative framework' for urban tourism research. Pearce (2001:928) quotes Blank in pointing out that '... most urban tourism studies investigate only parts of the traveller pattern'. Partial studies lead to widespread misunderstanding of urban tourism. Pearce's framework consists of a matrix which identifies both key themes in urban tourism and different spatial scales for research, as described earlier. The key themes consist of demand, supply, development, marketing, planning, organisation, operations and impact assessment. As Pearce suggests, the framework is useful for integrating both different themes at the same spatial scale, and a theme across different spatial scales. It also helps to identify both the strengths and the gaps within urban tourism research.

As research focusing on the experience of urban tourists is particularly weak, Ashworth (1989:43) argues for a user-orientated approach, addressing issues such as who urban tourists are, what they do in the city, why they visit the city and what perceptions they have. Ashworth and Tunbridge (1990) distinguish between intentional users of urban tourism resources, motivated by the characteristics of a particular city, and incidental users, for whom the visit is of secondary importance. For some authors (e.g. Graefe and Vaske 1987), an interest in managing quality in tourism leads to a focus on motivations, activities within the destination and the extent to which expectations are met by experiences. Page (1995) argues that the output of urban tourism – the tourist experience – has received only very limited attention in the literature. Detailed data on the urban tourist, the activities undertaken in the city, and their impact on the urban environment, is rare. To Page (1995:9) 'conceptualising why tourists seek cities as places to visit is one starting point in trying to understand this phenomenon'.

Quality Management in Urban Tourism

Shaw and Williams (1994) have addressed these issues to an extent, emphasising the heterogeneity of urban destinations, and the way in which they are 'multi-sold' to place consumers with different needs and desires. It is significant that in advocating a 'systems approach' to urban tourism, Page (1995:17) places 'the tourist experience' at the centre of the model. It is argued that 'urban tourism should be conceptualised as a service encounter and experience' (Page 1995:18), due to the high level of customer involvement, the simultaneous supply component, inconsistent demand and an intangible product.

Urban tourist experience is explored in some detail in chapter six. It would seem that some of the most useful concepts within the urban tourism literature, however, draw upon service-quality models (e.g. Parasuraman et al. 1985). Gaps may exist between urban tourists' expectations of the product and their perception of its actual performance, resulting in dissatisfaction with a destination (Bramwell 1998:36). The potential for gaps between expected and perceived levels of service in tourism has inspired authors such as Postina and Jenkins (1997), Page (1997), Gilbert and Joshi (1992) and Haywood and Muller (1988). Indeed, Clewer et al. (1992) argue that urban tourists have particularly high expectations of service.

Although service-quality models traditionally identify five different gaps between expectations and perceptions, it would seem that the fifth gap is fundamental to the experience of urban tourists. This is the gap between consumers' perceptions of the service they received and their initial expectations of the service. It is argued that both this gap and the others, relating to the design and operationisation of service-quality specifications (table 2.1), can be identified through market research (Gilbert and Joshi 1992). Haywood and Muller (1988) develop a methodology for evaluating the quality of the urban tourist experience. The data on visitors' expectations prior to a visit, and their perceptions upon visiting, utilises a wide range of variables.

While service-quality models would appear to offer considerable potential in researching urban tourist experience, they are not without problems. The measurement of expectations and perceptions, and their translation into service specifications, is often problematic. It would seem that the complexities of leisure and tourism have rarely allowed the successful application of service-quality models (see Williams 1998). The application of service-quality models to tourist sites is often problematic due to the fact that consumers vary so significantly in their use of a site or destination. While some visitors consume the whole site, others are very selective and may actually seek aspects in a manner difficult to predict by the researcher. Although Haywood and Muller (1988) provide a list of factors to consider in evaluating the experience of urban tourists, and Postina and Jenkins (1997) construct a detailed framework for monitoring quality in urban tourism, there is little attempt to elicit attributes which are salient to the consumers themselves. The heterogeneous nature of urban tourist destinations means that researchers can not assume that consumers' understanding of 'quality' is self-evident. It may be extremely destination- and context-specific.

Table 2.1 Service quality in urban tourism

	Gap in Urban Tourism Service	Quality Benefits of Market Research
Gap 1	Gap between the expected service and the management's perception of the urban tourist experience.	Encouraging providers to elicit detailed information from customers on what they require.
Gap 2	Gap between the management's perception of the tourist needs and the translation of those needs into service-quality specifications.	Providing realistic specifications for the services to be provided which are guided by clear quality standards.
Gap 3	Gap between the quality specifications and the actual delivery of the service.	Enabling employees to deliver the service according to the specifications; these need to be closely monitored and staff training and development is essential.
Gap 4	Gap between the service delivery stage and the organisation's communication with the consumer.	Reflecting the promises made by service providers in their marketing and promotional messages in the actual quallty offered.
Gap 5	Gap between the consumer's perceptions of the service they received and experienced, and their initial expectations of the service.	Reducing the major gap between the perceived service and delivered service, through progressive improvements in the image which is marketed to visitors, and the private sector's ability to deliver the expected service efficiently.

Source: after Gilbert and Joshi (1992).

Dadgostar and Isotalo (1995) use a multiattribute model to examine the benefits sought by near-home tourists. Despite a welcome emphasis on both destination image and positioning, it would again appear that the actual consumers have a limited influence on the attributes included in the study. The selection of variables in many studies, therefore, remains rather arbitrary, limiting the validity of the approach. While studies need to include the images and experiences of consumers, it is common for researchers and managers to impose their own constructs. If research methodologies are unable to capture the salient expectations and perceptions of consumers, the exercise becomes less convincing.

CASE STUDY 2.2: DESTINATION BENCHMARKING – THE CITY OF LIVERPOOL

There are signs that it is becoming more common for destination-marketing organisations to conduct research concerned with perceptions of a destination. The destination-benchmarking exercise conducted in British towns and cities, – among them Liverpool – provides one such example. Benchmarking has been described as 'the continuing process of measuring product, services and practices against toughest competition or those recognised as leaders' (Mersey

Partnership 2000). In the context of urban tourism, therefore, it can enable the identification of areas in which the destination excels, in relation to comparable and competing destinations. Areas which are relatively weak in relation to competitors can also be identified, and corrective action planned using the data. Destination benchmarking is therefore significant in terms of product development, place promotion and the identification of best practice.

The research was commissioned by the Mersey Partnership, and conducted by the North West Tourist Board. The research was in the form of a standard survey, allowing comparisons with other participating towns and cities. The survey was designed to update information from previous research on the profile, behaviour, and opinions of tourists. The survey also included the regional tourist board's standard destination-benchmarking questions, designed both to indicate levels of satisfaction with the city of Liverpool *per se*, and to compare with other destinations participating in the 2000 programme.

It was intended that the Liverpool data would be compared to the average for 'large UK towns and cities' and 'all destinations' participating in the benchmarking exercise. It was also intended that comparisons would be made with the findings of a similar study conducted in 1998. A total of 402 face-to-face interviews were conducted over 30 interview days between June and October 2000. The interview days were spread as representatively as possible across times of day, days of the week and months of the year. The interviews were conducted at three sampling points in the city, chosen for their high proportion of visitor footfall.

In terms of the visitor profile, it was found that the largest proportion of visitors came from Chester (11.3 per cent, followed by Greater Manchester, with 8.3 per cent). Slightly less than one in five visitors were from overseas; 59 per cent of respondents were women, over 10 per cent were part of an organised group and over one-third of visitors were staying overnight. The proportion of visitors staying overnight was found to be significantly higher than for UK towns and cities in general. It was found that over three-quarters of visitors were on a leisure holiday or short break, again a relatively high proportion compared to other UK towns and cities.

The substantive findings, however, relate to the experience of visitors to Liverpool. Overall, the city produced high scores in terms of the satisfaction of visitors. The choice of night life and entertainment scored particularly highly, both absolutely and in relation to the average for large UK towns and cities. Also scoring highly – both absolutely and relatively – were 'likelihood to recommend', 'overall enjoyment' and 'overall impression'. Feeling safe was also one of Liverpool's strengths, with the proportion of visitors feeling safe well above the average for both large UK towns and cities, and that of all of the participating destinations. The high satisfaction concerning safety is interesting as, despite Liverpool's relatively low crime rate (Home Office 2001), this is rarely reflected in Liverpool's image.

The data also allowed these general perceptions to be examined in more detail. Surprisingly, it emerged that in terms of feeling of safety, visitors actually felt much safer from crime than they did from traffic. More specifically, 'feeling of welcome' and 'general atmosphere' scored highly, and represented a significant improvement since 1998. Tourism information centres were perceived highly, representing an improvement since 1998. Attractions scored above average for 'quality of service' and 'value for money', and accommodation for 'value for money', 'quality of service' and 'range'. Places to eat and drink scored very highly for 'range', representing a significant improvement on 1998. The range of shops had also significantly improved since 1998.

Despite the positive findings, the study also suggested several aspects of the destination which could be improved. The only aspect where Liverpool's score was lower than the average for 'all destinations' was cleanliness of streets. Liverpool's score, however, was higher than both the average of large UK towns and cities and the 1998 study. The upkeep of parks and open spaces scored above average, both for all destinations, and for large UK towns and cities. Cleanliness of streets, therefore, appears to be one of the few areas of the Liverpool place product in need of improvement.

The benchmarking exercise represents a powerful method of understanding the levels of satisfaction of urban tourists, relative to competing destinations. Although the research is still fairly quantitative in approach, the focus on the visitor experience is a welcome addition to traditional visitor surveys concerned with quantifying visitor numbers and expenditure. The Liverpool study provides powerful data relating to the strengths of the Liverpool product. Whilst there is no room for complacency, it would seem that the study has the potential to inform promotional activities, particularly in terms of improving both the image and awareness of the destination. It is interesting, for example, that Mersey Tourism has already emphasised the relative safety of Merseyside in the 'makeitmerseyside' advertising campaign. It is also encouraging that the few areas for improvement identified can be addressed by relatively inexpensive and simple measures. The findings of the study can only add to the confidence of Liverpool's tourism sector.

Urban Tourist Behaviour

There are relatively few studies of tourist behaviour within urban tourist destinations, due partly to the complexity of the urban environment. An innovative approach is the use of geographical information systems to map tourist flows around the destination. Middleton (for example) combines the use of a geographical information system, surveys, and in-depth interviews to map tourist behaviour in the city of Manchester. Hartmann (1988) uses a combination of interviews and participant and non-participant observation to understand tourist behaviour in the city of Munich. Page (1999:170) states that 'how individual tourists interact and acquire information about the urban environment remains a relatively poorly researched area on tourism studies'. This leads, therefore, to a consideration of 'behavioural issues' and 'tourist perception and cognition of the urban environment' (Page 1997:120–23). Page comments on the lack of tourism studies amongst social psychologists. According to Page (1999:170), human geographers have had an interest in space perception, the way people store spatial information and 'their choice of different activities and locations within the environment'.

Page (1999:170–71; 1995:224) provides a model of 'the process through which individuals perceive the urban environment' (figure 2.1). This includes an explanation of how the information an individual receives is subject to perception, relating to the information received by the senses, and cognition, the assembling of information in relation to the existing knowledge, values and attitudes of the individual. Drawing upon Powell (1978), he also lists 10 key features of an image. Perhaps the greatest influence on Page's conceptualisation of urban tourist experience, however, is the work of Lynch (1960). In developing a technique for people to draw their 'mental map' of a locality, Lynch emphasised the 'common elements in these mental maps' (Hollis and Burgess 1977:155), and the way individuals collect information about the city. In *The Image of the City* (1960), Lynch is interested in the nodes, paths, landmarks and districts structuring an individual's perceptions of the city. Mental-map researchers drawing upon Lynch have been concerned with the process by which individuals '…collect, organise, store, recall and manipulate information about the spatial environment' (Downs 1977:6). This represents a change in emphasis from 'objective assessment of geographical areas to an understanding of how perception influences human behaviour' (Wallace 1992:169).

The popularity and accessibility of mental-map research was increased by Gould and White's text *Mental Maps* (1974). Gould and White present what might be better termed 'preference maps' of American and British school-leavers, indicating their spatial preferences in terms of residential areas. A similar process is used to evaluate the cognitive maps of continents produced by groups of various nationalities. The fundamental assumption of these studies is that perception is a more significant influence on behaviour than objective reality. There is, therefore, an attempt to evaluate the

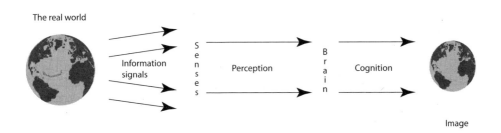

Figure 2.1: The process through which Individuals perceive the urban environment. Source: after Page (1995:224).

distinction between cartographically correct maps and maps representing an individual's perceptions of place.

The attraction of Lynch's work (1960) to urban tourism researchers is increased by his specific interest in the urban environment. Lynch's work is also attractive to authors such as Jameson (1988), because he suggests that the difficulties of mapping urban environments result in a feeling of alienation. Jameson (1988) uses the example of Boston, suggesting that its large and simple spatial form allows it to be mapped easily. This results in people's mental maps having 'a generally successful and continuous relation to the rest of the city' (Jameson 1988:353). Jameson applies this process of mapping the urban environment to the social and political environment – the mental map of society that people have in their minds. Jameson therefore argues that in the context of postmodernity, mental maps are useful in understanding the complex global totality which people perceive (Jameson 1988).

Although mental-map research was notable for attempting to introduce a human element into the urban planning of the 1950s, the approach has also been convincingly criticised. Page (1995) reports that advocates of Lynchian approaches acknowledge the issues involved in deriving generalisations from such research. It will be argued in chapter four, however, that the dangers of an overreliance on behavioural approaches may be underestimated. Human geographers have been particularly concerned with the deterministic assumptions underlying such studies. There is little attempt to account for the background or experience of respondents in such studies, the sources of their images or the production of space in its economic, social, or political context. Lynch himself admitted to finding theory 'dull' and 'difficult' (Knox 1992:231), and the literature on the city he called 'stupefying in its dullness' (Banerjee 1990:351). Not surprisingly, authors such as Knox (1992:231) argue that in Lynch's work 'there is little that qualifies as theory of any kind', due particularly to a 'heavy reliance on truisms and simplistic rhetoric'. The individual is assumed to be 'common man' and images are conceptualised as distortions of an objective reality. Cultural studies (e.g. Wood 1992) illustrate how cartographic maps – Lynch's objective reality – are also value-laden and always work towards the ends of those who commission them. As all map-makers are human, all maps can therefore be considered mental maps.

The Way Forward

Some of the limitations of urban tourism research have been addressed by contributions on urban tourist behaviour, satisfaction and quality management. However, it is difficult not to concur with the assessment of leading writers concerning the state of urban tourism research. There is little doubt that there is a lack of theoretical underpinning, a fragmented literature and a particular neglect of the experiences, behaviour and images of urban tourists. The solutions to these problems, however, are not self-explanatory. It is certainly useful to seek to address the gaps, as the contributions discussed above have hopefully demonstrated. It may be useful to attempt to map and integrate urban tourism studies on different themes and spatial scales.

It is curious, however, that many urban tourism writers call for the development of a coherent and integrated body of theories, methods and methods of analysis. This is almost advocating an urban tourism discipline, with a distinctive body of both theory and methods. Pearce (2001) identifies eight themes which supposedly delimit the concerns of urban tourism researchers. These themes, however, bear little resemblance to the concerns of contemporary social science. It is striking that although several leading urban tourism researchers declare themselves to be human geographers, it is the spatial modelling tradition to which they refer. Page (1995:10) at least acknowledges the limitations of the 'logical positivist tradition', but it is still this retrospective version of human geography which dominates much of the urban tourism literature. It is argued here that it is not the variety of urban tourism research which is the problem, but more the lack of theoretical underpinning within studies. Rather than reinventing the wheel, it may be more fruitful to encourage researchers to draw upon different epistemologies in order to engage with urban tourism.

It is striking that many of the gaps in urban tourism research identified are actually characterised by their buoyancy within the social science literature. The literature on the relationship between the local and the global, for example, has frequently been addressed as part of the debate on postmodernity. Places of consumption and the ways in which they are read is a significant branch of the cultural studies literature. There is also a growing body of literature concerned with the experience and embodiment of consumption, with considerable potential for understanding urban tourists. Another neglected area, the images and perceptions of urban tourists, is addressed by three decades of place image research within the tourism literature. While there is no doubt that social scientists have been extremely reticent towards urban tourism, it is possible that the urban tourism net needs to be cast further, rather than attempting a closer delimitation of the field.

The concept of the 'place consumer' is useful – representing an individual who experiences a tourist destination, and also representations of it. It is clear that comparing the expectations and perceptions of urban tourists is useful, and represents one of the most significant contributions of urban tourism researchers. Although the urban tourism and place-marketing literature conceptualises people as consumers, it is less capable of recognising that urban tourists have an attachment and an emotional sense of place which is different from other products. Urban tourism is closely bound up in the characteristics of globalisation and postmodernity, while also crucial to the interpretive significance of place, and the 'actually lived and socially created spatiality' (Soja 1989:18). It follows that urban tourism researchers should also have an interest in the landscapes and representations consumed by place consumers. There appears, therefore, to be an urgent need to explore alternative epistemologies and methodologies in order to evaluate the city from different perspectives.

Conclusion

The emergence of urban tourism, and the underlying economic, social and political forces, are well documented. Themes such as deindustrialisation and urban regeneration are well researched. There is also a growing body of literature focusing on place marketing and the development of urban tourism. Authors such as Kotler et al. (1993) and Ashworth and Voogd (1990) have made a valuable contribution to the theory of place marketing and urban tourism development. Within the urban tourism literature, there are numerous case studies, and some innovative applications of marketing and management approaches. Conversely, many urban tourism studies illustrate the problems associated with marketing place products. Researchers provide an insight into both the challenges faced by urban tourism practitioners, and the limitations of many urban tourism strategies.

It would seem, however, that the urban tourism literature is characterised by some recurring theoretical weaknesses. It has been argued that tourism researchers often fail to acknowledge important theoretical debates within the social sciences. It should also be recognised that this problem is exacerbated by a corresponding lack of engagement with urban tourism within social science disciplines. There can be little doubt that within the urban tourism literature, critical and discursive contributions are rare. The lack of theoretical debate in the field results in atheoretical studies of urban tourism. It would seem that prevailing perspectives are much more likely to draw upon established epistemologies such as positivism than the contested viewpoints with the social sciences, whether they be materialist, culturalist or humanist. Experiential approaches are explored in some detail in chapter six. Chapters three to five also engage with themes introduced in this chapter, exploring postmodernity, place image and the culture of urban tourism.

Chapter summary:

- The emergence of urban tourism is well documented, and rooted in economic, social and political change.
- Despite the immense scale of urban tourism and place marketing, there are practical problems in applying marketing to places.
- Urban tourism researchers provide insights into the marketing, management and planning of tourism in towns and cities.
- The application of service-quality models to urban tourism has particular potential.
- Urban tourism research also has serious limitations, with an overemphasis on descriptive and quantitative case studies.
- Despite calls by academics to explore the images, perceptions, behaviour and experience of urban tourists, these are neglected aspects of the urban tourism literature.

Further Reading

Ashworth, G.J. and H. Voogd (1990) *Selling the City: Marketing Approaches in Public Sector Urban Planning*, Belhaven, London.

Bramwell, B. (1998) 'User Satisfaction and Product Development in Urban Tourism', *Tourism Management* 18 (1), 35–47.

Bramwell, B. and L. Rawding (1994) 'Tourism Marketing Organisations in Industrial Cities', *Tourism Management* 15, 425–34.

— (1996) 'Tourism Marketing Images of Industrial Cities', *Annals of Tourism Research* 23, 201–21.

Chang, T.C., S. Milne, D. Fallon and C. Pohlmann (1996) 'Urban Heritage Tourism: the Global Nexus', *Annals of Tourism Research* 23, 1–19.

Gold, J.R. and S. Ward (1991) *Place Promotion: The Use of Publicity and Marketing to Sell Towns and Regions*, John Wiley and Sons, Chichester.

Kotler, P., D.M. Haider and I. Rein (1993) *Marketing Places: Attracting Investment, Industry, and Tourism to Cities, States, and Nations*, Macmillan, New York.

Law, C.M. (1993) *Urban Tourism, Attracting Visitors to Large Cities*, Mansell Publishing Ltd, London.

— (2002) *Urban Tourism: The Visitor Economy and the Growth of Large Cities*, Continuum, London.

Paddison, R. (1993) 'City Marketing, Image Reconstruction, and Urban Regeneration', *Urban Studies* 20 (2), 339–50.

Page, S. (1995) *Urban Tourism*, Routledge, London.

Page, S.J. and C.M. Hall (2003) *Managing Urban Tourism*, Prentice Hall, London.

Pearce, D.G. (2001) 'An Integrative Framework for Urban Tourism Research', *Annals of Tourism Research* 28 (1), 926–46.

Chapter 3

Urban Tourism and Postmodernity

The following topics are covered in this chapter:

- An introduction to the general characteristics of the postmodern city.
- Materialist perspectives on the postmodern city.
- A materialist critique of urban tourism and the heritage industry.
- Limitations of the materialist approach.
- An introduction to alternative perspectives which recognise the importance of human experience and culture in the city.

Introduction

There has been a general consensus among writers on the city that from the late 1970s onwards there has been an overwhelming need for cities to differentiate themselves in order to compete for spatially mobile capital. This has led to a dramatic surge in the contemporary significance of images and representations of the city from outside, and the packaging of the city itself. The city is often conceptualised as 'soft' (Raban 1974), in the sense of having a culture and identity which is open to manipulation and change by those seeking an identity for themselves and for the city. Whilst for authors such as Harvey (1989a) this largely represents a reaction to the alienating characteristics of late capitalism, this softness has also been represented as indicative of a more fundamental potentiality of human agency in the contemporary city (e.g. Lefebvre 1970). Whilst there has undoubtedly been a general increase in interest in the 'postmodern condition', and particularly consumption of the city, the city also reveals the very different epistemologies and agendas between academics and practitioners, materialists and culturalists. Much of the debate concerning postmodernity has centred on the city, and in many ways the city has polarised the different ways of conceptualising and researching contemporary society. In the context of studies focusing on urban tourism and place marketing, this represents rather an impasse.

Authors such as Harvey (1989a) have placed the city within the context of a 'condition of postmodernity', arguing that contemporary urban culture reflects the conditions of capitalism in the late twentieth century, particularly globalisation and the over-accumulation of capital. Authors drawing on these 'materialist' arguments have developed a powerful, scathing and dismissive discourse relating to the use of tourism and heritage in economic development (see especially Hewison 1987). This relates particularly to the appropriation and commodification of local arts, history and culture in order to attract tourists. The materialist meta-theory has some limitations, however, including the very passive conceptualisation of place consumers.

Authors such as Lyotard (1984) and Lefebvre (1970) have generally accredited urban culture with more autonomy, with Lefebvre coining terms such as 'consumer culture'. This chapter will draw upon this discussion, suggesting how a 'postmodern approach' has important implications for conceptualising and researching the city. The phenomenon of urban tourism will be used to illustrate the dramatic way in which both the consumption and marketing of the city polarises not only practitioners and academics, but also different epistemologies.

Urban Tourism and the Postmodern City

The term 'post-industrial city', perhaps most closely associated with the work of Daniel Bell (1973), encapsulates many of the long-running issues surrounding cities in the developed world. These include questions relating to whether or not we are now in a period that has succeeded industrial capitalism, whether the city has a meaning-ful ontological status if separated from global economics, and to what extent the local is significant in such processes. If one broadens the focus to consider the 'postmodern city', however, one begins to catch sight of the divergent pathways to explanation. A popular analogy, and one used to introduce Harvey's *Condition of Postmodernity*, is to conceptualise the contemporary city as 'soft', 'like a theatre, a series of stages upon which individuals could weave their own distinctive magic while performing a multiplicity of roles ... with colourful entities which have no relation to each other, no directing, rational or economic scheme' (Harvey 1989a:3). The city represented here is one without any coherence, rationality or recognisable shape. It is also one where images and signs flash before us in a seemingly chaotic and fleeting manner (Cloke et al. 1991). The period characterised as 'postmodern' appears to introduce 'much more open and fluid social identities as compared with ... the modern period' (Urry 1995:21). In the contemporary city, traditional class boundaries become blurred as the boundaries between art and high culture, and everyday life and popular culture, are dissolved. Culture becomes increasingly dominated by visual and aesthetic media, and the consumption of this culture has increased in pace. The postmodern city is argued to be characterised by a rich collage of signs and symbols from a wide range of genres and styles. A diverse range of buildings, places and cultural products have been described as postmodern. They all tend to exhibit a discontinuous and fragmentary nature, containing a collage of references to different styles and genres, often deliberately challenging the characteristics of modernism.

As authors such as Harvey (1989a), Dear (1986) and Huyssen (1984) have argued, modernism is perhaps best exemplified by the functionality and obsessive efficiency of architects such as Le Corbusier. The manufacturing-led economic boom of the 1950s and 1960s encouraged the mass construction of 'machines for living'. This endeavour was guided by a heroic, optimistic and rather deterministic ethos, which aimed to improve human nature and social organisation through town planning and science (Cloke et al. 1991). Not only did such a built environment, with its large-scale and featureless concrete structures, largely fail to improve human existence, but the worst examples actually alienated, marginalised and dehumanised urban communities. It is particularly this objective, rational and dehumanising aspect of modernism that postmodernism, including postmodern architecture, has sought to challenge. Architecturally, there has been an attempt to challenge the 'sheer blandness of modernist architecture', replacing it with 'variety, colourfulness, attention to detail, and the deliberate mixing of ... styles' (Huyssen 1984:14–15).

The built environment of the postmodern city is characterised, therefore, by a deliberate attempt to refer to the emotions, experiences and sense of place of inhabitants. While authors such as Harvey (1989a) and Jameson (1984) emphasise the superficiality and depthlessness of such architecture, it has been welcomed by humanist geographers such as Ley (1989) and Gregory (1989). A wide variety of urban landscapes have been used as postmodern objects of analysis, including redeveloped waterfronts and docklands (Short 1989), hotels (Jameson 1984), fringe festivals (Willems-Braun 1994) and shopping malls (Shields 1989; Hopkins 1990; Jackson and Johnson 1991). As Zukin demonstrates, the city has become a place of consumption, where spectacle and images create 'a dreamscape of visual consumption' (1992:21). Whilst postmodern urban populations are necessarily more flexible and mobile than the modern variety, contemporary landscapes attempt to recreate and simulate a sense of place. Whether this is achieved through theme parks, festivals, world fairs, waterfronts, museums, civic art or heritage centres, contemporary urban landscapes involve the paradoxical creation of a sense of place and history, to be consumed immediately.

As Urry (1995) argues, whilst there is a humanistic impulse in the creation of the postmodern environment and culture, the speeding up of time and space can dissolve one's identity. Television is used to exemplify the changes to the temporal and spatial organisation of social relations, providing 'a market identity as a consumer in the society of the spectacle' (Kellner 1992:145). It is argued that the image replaces narrative, and that the individual loses all depth and substance. In this scenario, the inauthenticity and simulated place of the contemporary urban environment seduces decentred consumers. Television exemplifies the need for instantaneous gratification, 'as a collage of disconnected stories, with no coherent geographical patterning, intrudes and shapes social life' (Urry 1995:23). The use of remote control 'channel hopping' and video recorders is argued to make television more of a private activity, removing the sense of a shared experience. Even the style of contemporary programmes reflects this fragmentation and speeding up of an ever-expanding popular culture.

The postmodern urban environment has received considerable attention in the social science literature, and will continue to be a theme here. This brief outline of some of the objects of postmodernism, rather than being substantive in itself, is intended to serve as an introduction to the epistemological and methodological implications of their explanation. It is with respect to the supposed processes in operation, and subsequent philosophical considerations, that the debate rages. It is worth noting at the outset that the economic restructuring of Western Europe and North America has been a subject of both analysis and inspiration to many commentators of the postmodern.

Empirical work over the last two decades shows the scale of restructuring, and associated changes to cities, to be quite immense. Between 1960 and 1981, for example, London lost nearly half of its manufacturing jobs (700,000), and the English conurbations lost more than one-third (1.3 million) (DOE 1984). Very significant in the process of restructuring has been the urban–rural contrast in manufacturing employment change, with stability or growth occurring in relatively remote towns and rural areas. Although there has been something of a dichotomy in explanation between the diseconomies and disadvantages of cities themselves (e.g. Scott 1982), and global restructuring intrinsic to the latest phase of capitalist production (Dunford 1977), it would seem that the interaction of the global and the local has been important. Global competition and mechanisation has confronted firms with pressures to reduce costs and size of workforce, whilst constraints on the supply of suitable sites in cities results in disproportionate growth in small towns and rural areas.

Such changes have resulted in the need for localities to differentiate themselves in order to attract a share of this spatially mobile capital. In the case of cities in particular, authorities ranging from local governments to marketing consortia have been striving to present localities as attractive to potential investors, employers, inhabitants and tourists (see Kearns and Philo 1993). Harvey succinctly sums up the implications of an increase in the spatial mobility of capital, noting that 'the less important the spatial barriers, the greater the sensitivity of capital to the variations of place within space, and the greater the incentive for places to be differentiated in ways attractive to capital' (Harvey 1989a:295–96). Whilst the empirical evidence for massive restructuring since the beginning of the 1960s is indisputable, conceptualising the changing culture and economies of cities is fundamental to the postmodern debate. It is also a useful starting point for considering prevailing materialist conceptualisations of the contemporary city.

Materialist Perspectives
Urban Tourism as the Cultural Logic of Capitalism

Harvey (1989a) develops a comprehensive argument linking postmodern culture and built environment to a transformation of space and time. Whether it is the way art parodies any attempt at interpretation, offering only irony, schizophrenia and indeterminacy, or the way that architecture appropriates the past in neovernacular designs, the roots are in the changing experience of space and time under flexible accumulation (Cloke et al. 1991). It is argued that the shift from Fordism to 'flexible accumulation' has caused changes to Western culture. Central to this thesis is the process of 'time-space compression', whereby contemporary capitalism has in effect caused the world to 'shrink'. Whereas Fordism relied on mass production and mass consumption, flexible accumulation 'is marked by a direct confrontation with the rigidities of Fordism. It rests on flexibility with respect to labour processes, new markets, products, and patterns of consumption…greatly intensified rates of commercial, technological and organisational innovation' (Harvey 1989a:147). Flexible accumulation (the predominant form of capitalism for the last three decades) implies a rapid increase in the pace of communication and transfers of money and people. Dramatic improvements in technology such as telecommunications, information technology and transport have had the effect of compressing time and space in the developed world. Significantly, it is the overaccumulation of capital which has prompted capitalism to develop in this way, and these developments should be viewed merely as the latest phase in the development of capitalism. Harvey therefore, in common with materialists such as Jameson (1984), views postmodernism as merely another chapter of capitalism, dictated by the logic of capitalism. Accordingly, 'shifts of this sort are by no means new, and…the most recent version of it is certainly within the grasp of materialist enquiry, even capable of theorisation by way of the meta-narratives of capitalist development that Marx proposed' (Harvey 1989a:146). Harvey, therefore, not only seeks to locate the economic changes associated with globalisation within the logic of capitalism, but he also employs the meta-narratives of Marx to explain postmodern culture. Culture, therefore, is not accredited any autonomy of its own, instead it is located within a superstructure which is largely determined by the economic developments associated with globalisation. Harvey advances the argument that different historical periods of capitalism create different conditions with respect to space. Within each of these periods, capitalism organises space in a manner most amenable to the maximisation of profit. Periods of crisis in the accumulation of capital, therefore, lead to reorganisations of space and time. Harvey's theory of time-space compression, drawing on Marx's ideas about the annihilation of space by time, describes this latest condition, in which 'space appears to shrink to a "global village" of telecommunications and a "spaceship earth" of economic and ecological inter-dependancies…an overwhelming sense of compression of our spatial and temporal worlds' (Harvey 1989a:240).

This process, driven by the development of capitalism, also has consequences for postmodern urban culture. The pace of life becomes greatly increased, with products purchased and consumed globally. Culture also becomes increasingly global, as instead of high culture and working-class culture, a global popular culture becomes dominant. Popular culture, however, is characterised by ephemerality and super-ficiality, with a range of media driving the rapid production and consumption of messages, signs and images. Significantly, Harvey maintains that the characteristics or 'condition' of postmodernity is wholly caused by the economic logic of flexible accumulation. Furthermore, Harvey questions the extent to which the cultural characteristics of flexible accumulation are different from the economic logic, referring to the 'equally speculative development of cultural, political, legal, and ideological values' (ibid.:336). Urban tourism, therefore, fits into the logic of flexible accumulation, as the 'odd thing about postmodern cultural production is how much sheer profit-seeking is determinant' (ibid.:336). To Harvey, even the imagery and spectacle of urban tourism, from docklands and shopping malls to world fairs and festivals, serves to mystify and glamorise the exploitation and oppression under capitalism in the search for profit.

The 'cultural capital' of postmodernism, particularly the role of 'spectacle' created by urban tourism, has received an increasing amount of attention in the literature (e.g. Lash and Urry 1994; Ley and Olds 1988; Kearns and Philo 1993), and is a subject to which we will return. Although Harvey has perhaps been most closely associated with the materialist approach to postmodernism, authors such as Jameson (1984:52) have been making the point for some time. Jameson also locates the characteristics of postmodern culture firmly within 'the cultural logic of late capitalism'. Jameson argues that due to the fundamental importance of power and control under flexible accumulation, the categories of Marxism have the same validity for multinational and media societies. Although traditional social classes may have been superseded, Jameson believes that there is a Marxian alternative to the theories of 'consumer' and 'post-industrial' societies (e.g. Bell 1973): 'postmodern (or multinational) space is not merely a cultural ideology, but has genuine historical (and socio-economic) reality as a third great original expansion of capitalism around the globe' (Jameson 1984:88–89). Jameson, therefore, argues that the shift away from

3.1: Vancouver: Glamorising capitalism through spectacle? Courtesy of Dan Heibert, University of Vancouver.

industrial technologies towards informational technologies is a powerful, original and global phase in the expansion of capitalism. Jameson also turns towards the 'aesthetic cognitive mapping' of localities to see the cultural logic of postmodernism and the associated power and control. He specifically refers to the work of Lynch (1960) on urban images. The 'post-industrial society', therefore, is argued to be indicative of the period in which all branches of the economy become industrialised, including the cultural industries. Urban tourism, therefore, is very much within the logic of capitalism.

The Growth of Heritage

Urban tourism consists not only of a collection of tourist facilities, but the consumption of signs, symbols and spectacle, creating aestheticised spaces of entertainment and pleasure (Cooke 1990; Featherstone 1991; Kearns and Philo 1993; Lash and Urry 1994). The manipulation of place images and the projection of a high quality of life represents a re-evaluation of urban space at the local level, in response to global processes. The deliberate creation of an attractive place product and place image, together with material processes creating the urban landscape, results in a range of spatial narratives (Zukin 1992). The existence of spatial narratives – ways of reading the landscape of the locality according to different sets of values – and the contested nature of these (Bourdieu 1984), is crucial to the debate concerning use of tourism, place marketing and heritage in economic development.

In his critique of the 'heritage industry', Hewison (1987) condemns the mythical and inauthentic English idyll represented by tourism and heritage organisations. Like other critics of tourism and heritage, he is concerned with what he sees as nostalgia, false memory, the fetishism of images and artefacts and the packaging of culture (see also Horne 1984; Lowenthal 1989; Samuel 1989; Ascherton 1995). He is particularly critical of the romanticised sense of community and the glamorisation of Britain's industrial past, 'creating a shallow veil that intervenes between our present lives and our history' (Hewison 1987:135). To such authors, the 'postmodern malaise' has caused history to lose its privileged position in Western society. 'Postmodernism is modernism with the optimism taken out' (Hewison 1987:132), and accordingly, it is the job of materialists to unmask the hidden ideologies of tourism and place marketing, unveiling the 'real'.

It is argued, therefore, that the commodification of local history and culture diverts attention from the present, as nostalgia is seen as a response to an unhealthy present. Hewison raises some useful points about the reliance on visual presentation and artefacts (Urry 1995), although he also seeks to judge whether or not repre-sentations of history are authentic. He cites comments concerning the growth of heritage made by the director of the Science Museum in London: 'You can't project that sort of growth much further before the whole country becomes one big open air museum, and you just join it as soon as you get off at Heathrow' (Hewison 1987:24). Wigan Pier plays an important role in the marketing of Wigan, exemplified by the publication 'I've never been to Wigan but I know what it's like' (Economic Development Wigan cited in Urry 1995). A major strand of Hewison's critique of Wigan Pier, and a preoccupation amongst other authors, is the role of heritage in the commodification of culture. Authors such as Boorstin have long argued that mass tourism transforms 'real' experiences into 'pseudo events' (Boorstin 1964). Tourism has been represented as an important force of commodification, with 'culture as process' being replaced by 'culture as product' (Richards 1996). It is this transformation of culture into a product which Hewison is so critical of, particularly if this allows the commodified history to meet political and economic ends.

The Appropriation of Culture

Authors such as Kearns and Philo (1993) emphasise the mobilisation of cultural resources in order to extract surplus capital within the city. Consistent with the arguments of Hewison (1987), urban culture is conceptualised as a means of social dominance used by the contemporary urban bourgeoisie. The contradictions inherent in 'New Right' rhetoric on individualism are emphasised, arguing that rather than allowing individuality, conformity is actually encouraged (Kearns and Philo 1993:20). Not only is place consumption tailored to the desirable and high-income individual, but superficial elements are used to produce similar 'attractive' images for numerous localities. Such authors direct attention to the surprisingly universal vocabulary used in place promotion. To authors such as Sorkin (1992), the postmodern city is characterised by the creation and marketing of 'cultural-historic packages', whether they be rituals, customs or monuments. The activities all have an economic logic, in terms of attracting the capital of tourists and inward investors; yet also a social control function in terms of specifying the activities and characteristics of the city which are desirable and attractive.

Following Harvey (1989a), authors such as Sorkin (1992) dwell on the irreverence and disrespect of place marketers for the realities of local culture and history. By arranging them in ways which attract capital, place marketers are conceptualised as appropriating and denigrating local culture. Kearns and Philo (1993) draw upon Umberto Eco's description of a museum (Eco 1986:8) to discuss the packaging and selling of history. It is emphasised that the packaging of history and culture is about extracting a surplus, but that cultural resources are also used for purposes of social control. As Sorkin (1992) argues, the postmodern city is designed to be marketed, with the packaging of cultural and historical elements, the simulation of rituals and events, the creation of monuments, and the playfulness inherent in postmodern architecture.

Drawing on examples such as the London Docklands, it is argued that the postmodern architecture of urban redevelopment performs the dual role of attracting capital, and reducing antagonism amongst the local population. The latter function is performed through the creation of a warm and friendly urban environment which manipulates and recreates attractive features of established town centres, including town squares, markets and courtyards. According to authors such as Harvey (1989a) and Sorkin (1992), this represents a manipulative disrespect for the real histories and cultures of such localities.

Urban tourism, therefore, attracts considerable criticism for its decontextual-isation of culture and history, and its use for economic and social ends. This is argued to represent an insensitive approach to the city, rather than postmodernism's supposed sensitivity. In reassembling cultural references in postmodern environments, they are believed to lose any link with their original context. In waterfront developments, for example, references to poor working conditions and low wages are conveniently omitted, whilst a collection of more attractive signs, symbols and architecture is celebrated. As Kearns and Philo (1993) argue, by claiming that the postmodern city is sensitive to the culture and history of groups of people, whilst decontextualising elements for economic ends, place marketers parallel the hypocrisy of the 'New Right' claims of promoting individuality.

Silencing the Other

Both Kearns and Philo (1993) and Harvey (1989a) emphasise the way urban tourism practitioners manipulate historical and cultural legacies in order to attract capital, in the process emptying them of their original meaning. Kearns and Philo, however, express an interest in cities' 'other peoples' (1993:25), and particularly the conflict that may arise between their experience of the city and the official version of place marketers. Kearns and Philo distinguish between history, consisting of a critical evaluation of claims about the past, and memory, consisting of a certain preferred account of the past. In this sense, memory involves the use of a certain version of past events to legitimise action in the present, often in an arrogant, exclusionary and chauvinistic way. It is suggested, therefore that the bourgeois form of memory is officially sanctioned by place marketers, including the use of heritage attractions, events and festivals. As Kearns and Philo put it:

> Integral to this transformation is the use of those many props from heritage centres to historical anniversaries which can be employed (more or less consciously) to create the impression of a truthful history with unavoidable lessons for the present, and the whole process is hence deeply embedded in the bourgeois project of selling places [Kearns and Philo 1993:26].

Such authors are concerned with revealing the distortions of 'bourgeois memory frozen into truth' (ibid.:26). While acknowledging the dangers of conceptualising more or less accurate versions of history, Kearns and Philo maintain that '...some accounts simply do have greater veracity than do others...' (ibid.:27). These versions are 'much nearer to the ground' and closer to 'the processes, struggles, and meanings that have shaped the existences of people' (ibid.:27).

Davis (1990:23) also writes of a 'city myth' in relation to the city of Los Angeles, emphasising the role of images in the transformation of the city. Again it is 'old fashioned material interest...' (Davis 1990:71) which drives place marketing and urban tourism. Authors such as Davis (1990) and Holcombe (1994) show how cities undergo a continuous 'revisioning'. In the case of Los Angeles, like many cities, this is based on the arts. As Davis points out, Los Angeles is sold just 'like automobiles, cigarettes and mouth wash' (Davis 1990:17), and this is a feature of place marketing everywhere. Images and myths are packaged as part of the commodification of a postmodern urban lifestyle. Authors such as Eco (1986) describe the result of this process as 'hyperreal', as the distinction between 'image' and 'reality' dissolves. The promotion of urban images is often a means of creating a new urban economics. The creation of new images, however is often contested by individuals, groups and institutions with a different image of the city.

Authors commonly point out the universal nature of place marketing, with every city seeking to be an arts Mecca, having a waterfront and a fascinating heritage. Indeed, a number of place-marketing practitioners have been quoted as admitting that they promoted exactly the same images working for other cites (see Burgess 1982:6). This is consistent with Harvey's view of place marketing as a 'zero-sum game' (Harvey 1989b). Perhaps more insidious in relation to the universality of strategies, is the universal absence of references to poverty, race, social problems and unemployment. As Holcomb (1993) shows, the ethnic composition of neighbourhoods in Cleveland is conveniently omitted by place marketers.

Place-marketing organisations are dubbed 'place-based ruling class alliances' by authors such as Sadler (1993:348). Sadler cites Cox (1989:81) in arguing that labour is extremely vulnerable to growth coalition ideologies, representing 'potent tools in the hand of capital'. Harvey, too, believes that 'the ideology of locality, place and community becomes central to the political rhetoric of urban governance...' (Harvey 1989a:14). Sadler (1993) highlights a tendency to quash dissent and alternative views by insisting that there is no alternative to place marketing and urban tourism. According to Sadler, this often includes accusations by place marketers that criticism by academics jeopardises jobs. Sadler maintains that despite the poor performance of the national and regional economies during the 1980s, the rhetoric of success continued in a vain attempt to improve business confidence.

This rhetoric of there being 'no alternative' to place marketing and urban tourism, together with the implication that criticism cannot be constructive, is common. The implication is that a dismissal of alternative views is inherent in place marketing. More insidious still, it is maintained, is a silencing of local views and a neglect and denial of 'other voices'. According to materialists, therefore, such activities are inherent to place marketing, oiling the machinery used by a bourgeois elite to commodify and package elements of local culture and history. This, of course, involves two inter-related processes: attracting and accumulating capital, and forcing the local population into compliance.

Limitations of the Materialist Perspective

It has become clear that the complex phenomenon of urban tourism raises some important questions. Authors increasingly discover a tension between the global and the local, revealed by urban tourism and heritage (see Chang et al. 1996). Although the materialist arguments engage with some important issues about the acceptability of images and cultural-historic packages to inhabitants, some dangerous assumptions are made.

Urban tourists are not merely passive, but are involved in both the creation and consumption of contemporary forms of culture. As Urry (1995) shows, Wigan Pier, one of Hewison's first targets, is visited and appreciated by both local and working-class people. It is ironic that the pensioners of Wigan Pier, on the receiving end of Hewison's (1987) tirade, are particularly adept in the practice of reminiscence, which is central to heritage consumption. As Kershaw (1993) argues, reminiscence is not the same as nostalgia, and offers considerable insights into history. In contrast to Hewison's derisory accounts of the pensioners of heritage sites, Kershaw uses the term 'reminiscence peak' to refer to the capacity of the elderly to draw upon longer-term memory in the practice of reminiscing. Many of those people have a family history which they can relate to presentations. In common with Kershaw (ibid.), Bagnall (2003) emphasises the performativity of heritage tourism. She shows how visitors to Wigan Pier actively engage in a form of reminiscence. The heritage centre presents historical themes through the performances of actors, yet visitors are also actively performing, drawing upon their memories, life histories and personal family narratives. Qualitative research (see case study 3.1) with both heritage-centre staff and visitors shows how this practice of reminiscence is central to the heritage consumption experience, with emotion playing a much greater role than cognition (Bagnall 2003).

According to Rojek and Urry (1997), there are various possible readings of the same heritage site. They identify 'a somewhat condescending, one-dimensional reading of such sites' (Rojek and Urry 1997:13) by Hewison (1987). The argument of authors such as Hewison (1987) rests upon a simple contrast between real history and false heritage. This assumes both that there is a true and authentic history, and that this real history is accessible in historical texts. Researchers such as McCrone et al. (1995), however, show how Scottish heritage is significant in developing cultural and political nationalism, and the formation of a Scottish identity. There is no evidence that heritage sites and urban tourist destinations are read in a uniform way by consumers; in fact, research tends to uncover the paradoxical and contested ways in which sites are experienced.

The exhibitions at heritage centres such as Wigan Pier, including the text used in interpretation, is written by professional local historians and not place marketers. Although more marketing-orientated in contemporary times, urban tourism attractions combine valuable conservation and education roles. In her study of two heritage sites in northwest England, Bagnall (1998, 2003) suggests that it is wrong to assume that urban tourists passively accept what is presented. Although in most cases personal and family memories were drawn upon to confirm what was presented, personal narratives were also drawn upon to reject the story. In this way, some visitors challenge the constructed nature of heritage sites, and there is a 'place for retelling' (Game 1991: 163 cited in Bagnall 2003). Contemporary education – both formal and informal – increasingly consists of easily consumed and interactive chunks. Although the causes of these phenomena are debatable, they are not exclusive to urban tourism and heritage. Education around the world has taken on a flexible, interactive and modular form, even in the institutions of materialist academics. The interactive approach to both formal and informal learning creates a place for contesting, as well as accepting, knowledge.

Materialist analyses also tend to assume that local people cannot benefit from urban tourism and place marketing. Quite apart from income and employment generation, urban tourism projects can improve the quality of life for ordinary inhabitants (including lower socio-economic groups). In cities such as Liverpool and Bristol, for example, access to considerable areas of waterfront has been regained with redevelopment schemes. Redevelopment has opened up large areas of public space, removing the barbed wire shrouding derelict buildings and docks. These areas are enjoyed by local inhabitants and are not merely enclaves for an urban elite. Qualitative research conducted at the Albert Dock, Liverpool, shows how the site is actively used by residents 'as the point of departure for their own memories of a way of life in which economic hardship and exploited labour were offset by a sense of community, neighbourliness and mutuality' (Mellor 1991:100).

Although the London Docklands communities remain a favourite example in the materialist literature, redevelopment has taken place on land left derelict and vacant by deindustrialisation in many cities. It is significant that the emotional engagement of visitors with maligned heritage sites is only possible through drawing upon experiences, memories and relationships through work, family and other social relationships (Bagnall 2003). In critiques of heritage, the lack of empathy with a process of reminiscence embedded in provincial rather than metropolitan culture is quite striking. Whilst critics are all too ready to express their opposition to romanticised representations within heritage centres, one could identify a certain romanticising of inner city areas by materialist writers.

It also tends to be assumed in materialist accounts that place marketers have no interest in the authentic and appropriate versions of local history and culture – in other words, no emotional attachment to the places they market. MacDonald (1997) shows how the establishment of a heritage centre on the Isle of Skye in Scotland was viewed as a way of strengthening, rather than diluting, Gaelic language and culture. In this case, the heritage centre is primarily for the people of the island, and far removed from any romantic account of Scottish history. It is not uncommon for heritage centres to develop out of a local inclination to tell an alternative story, rather than through the strategies of place marketers. In any case, personal communication with tourism and place-marketing practitioners suggests that many have lived in the locality since childhood, and have the same emotional attachments and sense of place

3.2: Mersey River Festival: celebrating or exploiting maritime history?

as the rest of the local population. Some are actually motivated in their choice of career by their attachment to their home town or city. Such urban tourism practitioners have had the benefit of a profound insight into the impact of globalisation and deindustrialisation on their communities, arguably considerably more so than materialist academics.

In the explanation of postmodern culture advanced by Harvey (1989a) there are serious contradictions in the conceptualisation of place marketing. On the one hand, place marketing is represented as a vain attempt to differentiate places in order to attract inward investment and tourists. This is a 'zero-sum game', as each city acquires a waterfront and heritage attractions, and no advantage can be gained. Postmodern urban culture, including urban tourism consumption is merely a response to the latest phase of capitalism – flexible accumulation. On the other hand, place marketing is a tool and agent of capital, a bourgeois project which enables the accumulation of capital by an urban elite. Place marketing, therefore, is represented as both a passive and vain response to globalisation and flexible accumulation, and a powerful agent of capital accumulation. If urban tourism is simply the cultural logic of late capitalism, it is surprising that it provokes such criticism.

CASE STUDY 3.1: THE CONSUMERS OF WIGAN PIER, ENGLAND

Bagnall's research (1998, 2003) challenges both the emphasis on the visual consumption of urban tourism (see chapter five) and the materialist critique of heritage. This case study shows how the performativity of both the employees and consumers of a heritage site in northwest England – Wigan Pier – is paramount to the heritage and urban tourism experience. It also demonstrates how the consumers of heritage do not passively consume 'inauthentic' history, as Hewison (1987) argues in his critique of the same heritage site. Instead, they invoke imagination, reminiscence and in many cases, memories in order to both confirm and reject what they encounter.

Wigan Pier was chosen for the study because it exemplifies the use of tourism by local authorities attempting to transform an area's image. With its use of live performances, simulacra and tangible reconstructions, Wigan Pier also epitomises many of the recent developments in heritage (Bagnall 1998:78). The site was opened in 1985 and is a registered museum. It is housed in historic industrial buildings in the town of Wigan, northwest England. Wigan Pier, the North West Tourist Board's Visitor Attraction of the Year award-winner in 1996, invites visitors to 'step back in time to Victorian England and rediscover life in a bygone age' (Bagnall 1998:79). Although the study used a variety of research methods, visitor interviews played a major role. An objective of the study was to capture the ways in which visitors 'read' and negotiate the site, and how they develop their own interpretations and meaning. The researcher wanted consumers to talk about their experiences using their own frames of reference. The semi-structured interviews were conducted not with individuals, but in the groups actually visiting the heritage site. While some questions were concerned with the reasons for the visit, others were more specific to the experience of the site itself, underpinned by theoretical debates. Visitors were also asked about their participation in other leisure activities, and socio-demographic details were collected. The interviews were complemented by non-participant observation, conducted at various points within the heritage site.

In terms of the composition of visitors to Wigan Pier, it is clear that visiting is very much a group activity. According to visitor surveys by Wigan Pier (cited in Bagnall 1998:184), only 7 per cent visited the site alone, with 67 per cent in a group of three or more. In Bagnall's interview sample, nearly two-thirds of parties did not contain any children. Data from both Wigan Pier and Bagnall's study suggest that the majority of visitors to the site are women (65 per cent), and visiting parties often consist entirely of women. The pier attracts a wide range of age groups, although the 31 to 50 age group is overrepresented. According to Wigan Pier's own data (cited in Bagnall, 1998:191), 20 per cent of visitors are over the age of 61. The occupations of visitors seem to be very diverse. Contrary to the critique of heritage sites, 50 per cent of visitors are in socio-economic group C1, representing 'supervisory or clerical and junior professional'.

The educational attainment of Pier visitors is also comparable with the general population. According to Bagnall (1998:198), only 9 per cent of visitors have a degree or higher qualification. Although people with professional qualifications are slightly overrepresented compared to the general population, visitors with no qualifications are also overrepresented.

The substantive findings of Bagnall's study, however, are not related to the visitor profile, so often the focus of traditional visitor surveys. A major insight concerned the ways in which visitors physically, emotionally and imaginatively map their consumption (see Bagnall 1996). This mapping process allows 'visitors to connect to personal and cultural memories and biographies, and to practice and perform a form of reminiscence' (Bagnall 2003:3). The consumption of Wigan Pier was an active and physical process, and not merely passive and cognitive. Not only did consumption satisfy bodily needs such as hunger and thirst, but the past was embodied by visitors in a multi-sensual experience.

It seemed to be the physicality of the experience which enabled visitors to use their imagination and emotions. This was an active process, with visitors using their memories and previous knowledge to either accept or reject what the site offered. The majority of visitors confirmed their experience as providing 'emotional realism', feeling that they really were consuming the past, or at least appreciating what life in the past was like. A minority of visitors, however, rejected the structured consumption that the site provided, as their personal memories contradicted what was on offer. Visitors related the heritage site to their personal experience and family histories, making comments such as 'I think it's tempered with what ... grandparents and that tell you'. Another visitor reflected upon representations of coal mining, and in the context of one particular process, commented that 'it was only for two years but I did that'. This confirmation or rejection of the heritage site according to personal memories challenges the discourse within the heritage literature representing heritage consumers as passive and uncritical. As Morley (cited in Bagnall 2003:6) suggests, there is a 'contested reading' of the site, whereby the visitor, 'by relating the message to some concrete or situated object ... may modify or partially inflect the given preferred reading'.

It is significant that personal and family memories played such a significant role in the visitor experience of the site. Visitors were found to employ their biographies as a key resource in order to engage emotionally with the site. Visitors used phrases such as 'now that's taken us back a bit', and 'yes, definite reminders of my youth'. Not only does the use of memories bring the past to life, but it enables visitors to explore the past for themselves. Likewise, when occasionally the constructed nature of the site is rejected, it is when personal memory has been drawn upon by visitors. As Bagnall (2003:10) argues, citing Game, there is thus a space for personal memory and a place for retelling. This reminiscence is not a nostalgic desire for that which never existed, but 'being in a place where you know what happened, know the ways, and know what cannot be seen (de Certeau cited in Bagnall 2003:10). This reveals the 'pensioners of Wigan Pier' to be very different from the passive and rather docile characters represented by Hewison (1987). This group of visitors are the most able to reminisce, and, drawing upon their personal and family memories, they both confirm and reject what the heritage site presents.

Bagnall's research also adds to the debate concerning the 'inauthenticity' of heritage. Some visitors found the Wigan Pier experience too emotionally resonant, and actually avoided this 'emotional closeness' during their visit. A female visitor, for example, used to work in a cotton mill and did not want her memories to resurface. Other elderly visitors preferred to look forward, rather than going back into times of sadness and hardship. Live performances did vary in their ability to engage visitors, at times invoking a strong sense of nostalgia, at others achieving less engagement. In most cases, the success of the performance was influenced by variations in the audiences themselves. The majority of visitors, however, experienced some degree of 'emotional realism'.

Following researchers such as Ang (1996), Bagnall argues that heritage consumers are aware of exaggerated and melodramatic features, yet they can still use sites to stir their own memories and emotions. As Bagnall (2003:8) puts it, 'visitors may have encountered real coal in a plastic mine, but there was no doubting the emotional impact it could engender, or the feelings that it could mobilise'. Meaning is thus created through presenting a plausible experience. This suggests that visitors do not simply soak up messages, as suggested by some heritage critics (e.g. Hewison 1987; Ascherson 1995). It is also striking that to the majority of visitors, authenticity is bound up in the ability of the site to encourage reminiscence, rather than provide historical 'facts'. The ability of heritage sites to bring the past to life is dependant on the representation being confirmed in relation to family histories and memories. This is surely a more salient sense of authenticity in the context of urban tourism.

The study demonstrates, therefore, that heritage consumption is an active, rather than a passive process. Reminiscing can enable 'the awakening of dreams and desires, and effect a connection between past and present' (Bagnall 2003:15). Urban tourism consumption is thus embodied by consumers who engage a range of senses, and experience the site on an emotional level. There is no simple transference of meaning between representations and the visitor, and visitors read the site in different ways. Most importantly, heritage consumption is closely related to individual and social memories, and the biographies of consumers (Bagnall 2003). Not only do the life histories of visitors play an important role in the consumption process, but these emotions and memories are actively engaged in order to experience the heritage site. It is significant that these 'landscapes of memory' are not constructed out of national historical facts, but out of the local, contextual, everyday life of visitors.

Acknowledging Culture

Lyotard's challenge to the meta-narratives of modernism has important implications concerning how one conceptualises the city and urban tourism. Lyotard is particularly interested in the way meta-narratives are challenged by vast increases in the amount and variety of information available. Using the term 'language games', he draws attention to the irreversible shift in the complexity and speed of information. For Lyotard, modernism is concerned with the universal theories of science, planning and economics – in fact 'any science that legitimates itself with reference to a metadiscourse, making an explicit appeal to some grand meta-narrative...' (Lyotard 1984:xxiv).

In the age of information technology, therefore, the volume and variety of messages sweeps away any universal sense of order and rationality. The fragmentation and plethora of images much commented upon by authors such as Harvey, and crucial to urban tourism, are actually attributed a more profound significance by Lyotard. The fact that we experience competing and contradictory images and messages prevents there from being any universal meta-language. In fact, the impossibility of any meta-language is the only truth and certainty in postmodern society. Any grand theory is therefore inconsistent with postmodernism.

Instead, Lyotard draws on narrative analysis to consider the ways in which science and technology controls and legitimises knowledge. Drawing on Wittgenstein, Lyotard focuses on 'language games', or the way 'various categories of utterance can be defined by a set of rules specifying their properties and the uses to which they can be put' (Lyotard 1984:11). In an influential contribution to the 'crisis of representation', Lyotard touches upon the concerns of Habermass (1976), yet rejects any totalising ambitions of a society-wide consensus. Recognising that certain traditional institutions 'are losing their attraction' (Lyotard 1984:14) in terms of information and decision-making, he also states that 'a person is always located at "nodal points" of specific communication circuits, however tiny these may be' (ibid.:15). Language is therefore conceptualised as an unstable exchange between different speakers, a conflict and act of trickery rather than a mutual 'passing of tokens from hand to hand' (ibid.:xi). Narrative thus becomes a legitimate and important way of thinking, as important as science and logic. Attention should therefore be devoted to these language games. This is relevant to urban tourism research in that attention is focused on the language and decision-making of actors in relation to particular destinations. Lyotard believes that 'the society of the future falls less within the province of a Newtonian anthropology (such as structuralism or systems theory) than a pragmatics of language particles. There are many different language games – a heterogeneity of elements. They only give rise to institutions in patches – local determinism' (ibid.:xxiv). These contributions have important implications for the contemporary city. If the legitimisation of master narratives no longer holds, whether in science or elsewhere, the focus should turn to small and local narrative units. This implies devoting attention to the local 'ground rules' and particular discourses within cities and in relation to particular phenomena. Social scientists have extended Lyotard's language games to considering different groups of people within localities – particularly cities – and in terms of characteristics such as gender, class, lifestyle, age and attitudes. Thus, Lyotard has been inspirational to researchers concerned with the 'local knowledge' (Geertz 1983; Rose 1988) of particular groups in particular places. It is worth noting that geographers also identify with Lyotard's critique of an obsession with history and a fidelity to the past at the expense of space. This includes the way in which narrative consumes the past and focuses attention on its control, objectification and ownership – a fundamental political issue in contemporary society.

Valuing space is an important theme running through Ed Soja's contributions to the debate, particularly *Postmodern Geographies* (1989). Of relevance to urban tourism research, Soja draws on a rich variety of authors and traditions to argue for a heightened awareness of space. Amongst the trends identified are the increasing centralisation and concentration of capital ownership, and a 'technologically-based integration of diversified industrial, research, and service activities' (Soja 1989:185). The substantive contribution of the text, however, lies in its discussion of theoretical developments which offer hope in reasserting space in place of the historicism of much of social theory.

Soja's journey takes him through the work of Marx, Lefebvre, Berger and Foucault, before reconsidering the challenges addressed by Giddens's structuration theory. Soja's main concern is that 'an essentially historical epistemology continues to pervade the critical consciousness of modern social theory' (Soja 1989:10). This concern with 'the making of history' is believed to 'occlude a comparable critical sensibility to the spatiality of social life…social being actively emplaced in space and time in an explicitly historical and geographical contextualisation' (Soja 1989:11).

In common with a number of human geographers (e.g. Gregory 1989), Soja engages with Foucault's critiques of historicism and meta-theories, emphasising that a postmodern attitude is necessary to capture the complexities of the postmodern city. Foucault offers insights into 'reasserting the interpretative significance of space' (Soja 1989:11), particularly through his sustained attacks on the order and universality of 'total history' (Foucault 1972:9). This includes any meta-theory which imposes order on a complex world through the use of *a priori* interpretations. Foucault believed that 'nothing is fundamental: this is what is interesting in the analysis of society' (Foucault 1980:18), and Soja identifies with this concern, including the need to engage with the chaos and complexities of space and place. Foucault's work relating to the spatialisation of power (Foucault 1980) is of great interest to geographers. Although he was at best a 'closet geographer', Foucault's more explicit references to space are also attractive to authors such as Soja. Foucault's development of concepts such as 'spaces of dispersion' (1980) and 'heterotopia' (1967) are particularly relevant to urban tourism, and will be discussed in chapter five.

Soja recognises in Foucault an affinity with Lefebvre's concern with capturing 'actually lived and socially created spatiality, concrete and abstract at the same time, the habitus of social practices' (Soja 1989:18). Soja argues that almost every variant of Marxism has been characterised by a neglect for space. Space has been conceived merely as a contingent factor, an abstract and generalised physical form and a container of social and economic processes. Attempts to 'people' and spatialise Marxism, from the contributions of Althusser (1969), to the more explicit statements of Mandel (1975) and Lefebvre (1970), have met with mixed success. Mandel considers uneven development between regions and nations to be 'on the same level as the exploitation of labour by capital' (Mandel 1975:43). Such statements have been influential in the long-term development of human geography, but have also caused acrimonious fragmentations of the Marxist tradition. A variety of materialist geographers, undoubtedly influenced by Lefebvre's contribution, later sought to occupy a middle ground between an aspatial Marxism, and what has been termed 'spatial fetishism' (e.g. Castells 1983, 1985; Massey 1984; Smith 1984).

It is Lefebvre who offers some of the richest yet neglected insights into conceptualising the contemporary city. Lefebvre has perhaps been more influential amongst Anglo-American human geographers (e.g. Gregory 1994; Soja 1985, 1989; Gottdiener 1995) than in his native France. It should also be acknowledged that Harvey has long been influenced by Lefebvre, including his contributions on the changing form of capital circulation (1973), changing representations of space (1989) and even the role of perception and imagination in the construction of place (1993). Lefebvre's engagement with Marxism has perhaps attracted a disproportionate amount of interest relative to his other valuable insights. While geographers such as Soja (1989) rightly find much in his work to support their quest for the spatialisation of social theory, his experiential approach to everyday life is undervalued.

It is interesting that Lefebvre considers the daily life of the majority of the population to remain largely untouched by the discontinuities associated with an endless succession of 'isms'. Rather than simply elevating space at the expense of time, Lefebvre is interested in the interplay of space and time, particularly in projects such as 'rhythm analysis' (1967). Massey and Meegan (1992) draws upon such approaches, highlighting the feeling of insecurity experienced by the most mobile and technology-literate in society. It is argued that experience of space and time is complex and heterogeneous, varying significantly between different groups of consumers.

Further developing his interest in the contradictions of everyday urban life, *Right to the City* (1968) emphasises the city as a place of encounter where differences come together. Rational analyses are not sufficient to understand the dialectical movement between form and content, thought and reality. Urban form, in particular, is conceptualised as an amalgam of people, events, perceptions and different elements. Improvements in communications have brought these together, yet also created divisions and inequalities within society. Again highlighting the complex relationships between space and time in urban tourism, Lefebvre shows how the theatre, sport, fairs and spectacles restore a sense of time. The *oeuvre*, which can be defined as a totality which assembles differences in one place and at one time, may not coincide with its official and institutional form (1967:161).

The need to consider the city as a totality, particularly in terms of everyday life, is a recurring theme. Lefebvre also comments on a long anti-urban tradition in academic work which refuses to recognise people's experiences of the city (1986). His calls for a sensitivity to everyday experience run through the majority of his work, and he asks why 'must Marxism evacuate the symbolic, the dream and the imaginary…the oeuvre?' (1976:268). It was perhaps these concerns which motivated Lefebvre to combine Marx with the writings of Nietzsche (1970). Lefebvre's conceptualisation of difference was thus concerned with conceptualising the contradictions of urban life, rather than reducing them within universal theories.

His engagement with time directs us towards intersubjective social experience (1970:204). The concept of 'moments' refers to modes of experience, such as work, rest and play (1959). He was also interested in the way the norms of different social groups influence such behaviour (1959:648). In his later work, Lefebvre was actually returning to his early phenomenological concerns, particularly relationships between the body, its rhythms and space. Production of space (1986) is fundamentally concerned with the body as a place of interaction of the biological, the physical and the social (1985:197). These ideas draw on phenomenology, starting analyses with the body in time and space, yet also demanding much more concern for social influences. This is seen as a way of overcoming artificial divisions between the components of a city (1986). Whilst critical of his oversentimentality, Lefebvre identified with certain of Heidegger's terms, such as 'habitus'. Rather than the rural, however, it was the being and consciousness of the city which was fundamental.

Conclusion

An attempt has been made to introduce the postmodern city, and to summarise the two predominant epistemological approaches to conceptualising the city. There is a degree of consensus concerning the 'soft' nature of the contemporary city, and the ability of cities to be differentiated by having identities created for them. The city is characterised by images, and the pace of contemporary life results in a montage of images and representations from a wide variety of sources. In addressing urban tourism, we are engaging with the concept of urban culture. The postmodern debate, however, is polarised around the issue of postmodern urban culture. While materialists view postmodern culture as merely a response to the latest phase of capitalism – flexible accumulation – other writers view urban culture very differently.

Some of the most critical contributions from materialist writers relate to the use of heritage in urban tourism development. Hewison (1987), in particular, is extremely critical of what he considers to be a lack of authenticity within heritage sites such as Wigan Pier in northwest England. Considerable attention is also devoted to the alleged appropriation and commodification of local working-class history and culture, in order to attract high income urban tourists. Authors challenging the position of writers such as Hewison dismiss the argument that there is a true and authentic history, and the assertion that authors such as Hewison have access to 'the truth'. There is also a surprising dismissal of heritage consumers in materialist critiques, despite the fact that they may have considerable knowledge and experience of local history and culture.

It has also been argued that although materialist writers offer a convincing discourse, they show a disregard for the experiences of place consumers, whether they be tourists or residents. It would also seem that the complex phenomenon of urban tourism poses some problems for the materialist epistemology. Materialist studies privilege global economic processes and accredit very little agency to either practitioners or consumers. Despite an apparent interest by some authors in 'other peoples' of the city, a materialist framework also prevents visitors or residents from being conceptualised as conscious, thinking and experiencing beings.

To those drawing on the contributions of writers such as Lefebvre, Lyotard and Foucault, postmodern urban culture has much more autonomy and agency. Researchers who acknowledge urban culture value the language and experiences of different groups of people, the way they perceive the city, and the way that they act in relation to the city. According to this approach, the city should be approached not through the meta-theories of materialism, but at the level of different experiences. The latter approach implies a concern for context, an interest in differences, and an emphasis on the everyday experience of groups of people in the city.

Chapter summary:

- The postmodern city is dominated by a contradictory and schizophrenic mixture of images, landscapes, signs, symbols and styles.
- Authors have characterised the postmodern city as 'soft', open to the manipulation and imposition of different identities.
- Materialist writers conceptualise urban tourism merely as a response to the latest phase of capitalism. Materialists are extremely critical of heritage and urban tourism, accusing them of appropriating and commodifying local culture for profit.
- The dismissal of urban tourists by authors such as Hewison (1987) has been challenged by researchers interested in the culture and experience of tourism. Authors interested in local knowledge, everyday experiences of the city and urban culture offer an alternative to materialist arguments.

Further Reading

Harvey, D. (1989) *The Condition of Postmodernity*, Blackwell, Oxford.

Hewison, R. (1987) *The Heritage Industry: Britain in a Climate of Decline*, Methuen, London.

Kearns, G. and C. Philo (1993) (eds) *Selling Places: The City as Cultural Capital Past and Present*, Pergamon Press, Oxford.

Lyotard, J. (1984) *The Postmodern Condition: A Report of Knowledge*, Manchester University Press, Manchester.

Soja, E. (1989) *Postmodern Geographies: The Reassertion of Space in Critical Social Theory*, Verso, London.

Urry, J. (1995) *Consuming Places*, Routledge, London.

Chapter 4
Place Image and Urban Tourism

The following topics are covered in this chapter:

- The theory and concepts of research into the image of urban tourist destinations.
- The potential of place image research as a tool for urban tourism practitioners.
- Methodological limitations of place image research.
- Theoretical limitations of the place image literature.
- Possible solutions to the limitations of place image research.

Introduction

The importance of images to urban tourism has been discussed in chapter two. Page (1999:170–71), for example, provides a model of 'the process through which individuals perceive the urban environment'. Oppermann (1996) identifies an important line of place image research developing within the context of urban tourism. Out of a sample of place image studies evaluated by Gallarza et al. (2001), seven directly address cities. Urban tourists imagine destinations when they do not have first-hand experience of visiting, and upon actually visiting they gain perceptions of the destination. This process is therefore crucial to tourist decision-making, and behaviour in the urban tourist destination. According to Page (1995), authors such as Lynch (1960) help us to understand key features of an image, common elements in mental maps of cities, and the way individuals collect information about the city. In recent years, there has also been an exciting and innovative advancement of place image research, providing useful policy-analysis instruments (see Jenkins 1999; Chon 1990; Ashworth 1987). Authors have built upon a useful conceptualisation of the existence of different place images relating to the stages of consumer decision-making (Gunn 1972). This has enabled researchers to develop methodologies to compare different types of image. There is little doubt that place image has important marketing and management implications for urban tourism, relating to destination positioning (Font 1996), product development (Ashworth and Goodall 1988), promotion (Bramwell and Rawding 1996) and branding (Pritchard and Morgan 1996).

It is argued in this chapter, however, that despite significant contributions, place image studies suffer from some common limitations. Methodological weaknesses include an overemphasis on statistical analysis at the expense of eliciting images that are salient to consumers. In terms of the theory of place image, there are clear similarities with the urban tourism literature. In particular, there is a poorly developed conceptualisation of urban tourist experience, social groups and culture. Very few place image researchers acknowledge the implications of the 'cultural turn' within the social sciences which so convincingly challenges claims to universal and objective knowledge. Only a minority of place image researchers discuss theoretical issues and provide justification for a behaviouralist approach (e.g. Goodall 1991). It is argued in this chapter that, despite the potential of the place image literature in understanding this aspect of urban tourism, tourism researchers cannot ignore the profound implications of contemporary conceptualisations of culture and experience.

The Concept of Place Image
The Significance of Urban Images

It has been argued that urban tourism is plagued by practical problems caused mainly by its complexity. Best-case examples of urban tourism suggest that an integrated approach to urban tourism development is essential, addressing both the demand- and supply-side, and focusing on the salient aspects of both the images and experiences of consumers. The obstacles to successful urban tourism development include the number and diversity of organisations involved and the risk of contradictory activities, the issue of political accountability, the inflexibility of cities and an ambivalent attitude towards tourism. Perhaps the greatest risk of all, however, is the possibility of discrepancies between experiences inside and images outside a locality. It is argued in this chapter that the monitoring of these – conceptualised in the marketing and tourism literature as demand- and supply-side images – is essential in both attracting visitors and maximising their satisfaction with the destination.

The process is not unidirectional, as a low level of satisfaction with first-hand experiences of the destination will prevent even short-term sustainability. Conversely, unfavourable images outside a city can seriously thwart even the small-scale development of urban tourism. It is precisely this paradox which bestows on place image an active role in mediating between urban tourism demand and supply. A substantive contribution of destination image studies relates to the crucial role of images and expectations in an individual's decision-making. Place image researchers are also interested in levels of satisfaction or dissatisfaction resulting from first-hand experience of the place product. It is assumed that a decision-maker initially acts upon their image of a locality, rather than the 'reality' of the destination. The image of a destination changes at different stages of decision-making, most significantly upon actually visiting the destination. Discrepancies between these different images have important implications for promotion, product development and destination positioning, and have been the focus of some innovative and valuable place image studies.

Place image has received increasing attention in the tourism and marketing literature, and there have been some significant advances in place image theory. From a marketing perspective, image is considered to constitute an integral part of a product, playing an important role in an individual's purchase decision. As Gallarza et al. (2001:56) point out, the importance of the tourist destination image is universally acknowledged, due to its effect on the consumer's perception, consequent behaviour, and destination choice. The complexity of the place product is considered to make image even more critical (Ashworth and Voogd 1990). If consumers do not have first-hand experience of the destination, marketing organisations and the travel trade are forced to sell images of towns and cities – bought on trust, and evaluated only upon visiting. Within the tourism and marketing literature, research has provided valuable insights into the importance of images to tourism products and destinations (see for example Ashworth and Voogd 1990; Pearce 1982).

A purchase decision is considered to be influenced less by a product's quantifiable performance characteristics than by the consumer's overall expectations regarding levels of satisfaction. Consumers are conceptualised as choosing products because of their perceived attributes, using their perceptions of attributes as input factors to estimate the utility they will derive from consuming the product. Market research can evaluate perceptions of a product, and strategies can be devised to strengthen, alter or create an image. Numerous pieces of research, including Pearce (1982) and Woodside and Lyonski (1990), indicate that the destination's image does influence travel behaviour, and that destinations with positive images are more likely to be chosen in the decision process.

Defining Place Image

As Gallarza et al. (2001:59) note, there are nearly as many definitions of place image as scholars contributing to its conceptualisation. Psychologists have defined image as a 'distinct way of processing and storing multi-sensory information in working memory' (Echtner and Ritchie 1991:4). Similarly, Embacher and Buttle, cited in Gallarza et al. (2001:60), define place image as 'comprised of the ideas or conceptions held individually or collectively of the destination under investigation. Image may comprise both cognitive and evaluative components.' Reynolds (1965) also emphasises cognitive processing with the elaboration, embellishment and ordering of impressions. Cooper et al. (1998:38) also draw upon psychology, stating that an individual's awareness of the world is made up of the cognitive evaluation of experiences, learning, emotions and perceptions. Goodall appears to attain a balance between psychological and marketing perspectives, defining place image as 'a function of holiday-makers' awareness of that product, attitudes towards the product, and expectations created by (limited) knowledge of that product' (Goodall 1991:63). Researchers have also provided more 'holistic' and qualitative definitions of what constitutes an image. An image is defined by Chon as the net result of the interaction of a person's beliefs, ideas, feelings, expectations and impressions about an object (Chon 1990). Dichter (1985:76) states that 'an image is not just individual traits or qualities, but the total impression an entity makes on the minds of others'. Kotler et al. (1993) appear to agree, emphasising the 'sum of beliefs, ideas, and impressions that a person hold of it'. Crompton (1979:20) also defines destination image in a holistic way, as the aggregate 'sum of all those emotional, and aesthetic qualities such as experiences, beliefs, ideas, recollections and impressions that a person has of a destination'. Although Pearce (1988:163) perhaps overstates the visual, he is more sensitive to the sense of 'place' of destinations, emphasising a 'search for the long-term memory for scenes and symbols, panoramas, and people'. This infers that a locality's image is more experiential and intersubjective.

Place Image and Urban Tourist Decision-making
Decision-making Models

Place image researchers contribute to our understanding of urban tourist decision-making. One of the first attempts to model consumer decision-making was by Wahab, Crompton and Rothfield (1976), based on the 'grand models' of the early consumer-behaviour textbooks. A more refined and tourism-orientated model was devised by Schmoll (1977), in which social and personal determinants of travel behaviour include motivations, desires, needs and expectations. The input factors in the model include travel stimuli, the traveller's confidence, previous experience and cost and time constraints. According to Mayo and Jarvis (1981), the consumer moves from general images to more specific information to make their decision. Mathieson and Wall's five-stage model (1982) emphasises unique characteristics of the place product, such as intangibility, heterogeneity and perishability. In most models of decision-making, there is also an important feedback loop which represents the learning process following a visit, and particularly the influence of first-hand experience on the individual's image.

Authors have used decision-making models to understand the relationship between destination image and a tourist's buying behaviour (Goodall 1991; Stabler 1988). As Jenkins (1999:2) argues, destination images influence both the decision-making behaviour of potential tourists and levels of satisfaction upon experiencing the destination. MacInnis and Price (1987) also stress that imagery pervades the whole consumption experience. Goodall (1991:63) argues that because consumers have only a limited knowledge of the attributes of destinations they have not visited, the image of the destination has a crucial influence on decision-making.

A widely accepted model of consumer decision-making consists of five stages: recognition, search, evaluation, purchase and post-purchase evaluation. Goodall (1991: 63) describes a process whereby activities and experiences are given mental ratings by the place consumer and, according to their personal tastes and dislikes, the individual has a preferential image of their ideal holiday. The individual's expectations are conditioned, creating an aspiration level or evaluative image, against which their actual visit is compared. As a result of limited information, the individual, at any one time, is aware of only part of the total opportunities available. Using information from a variety of sources, the consumer constructs a naive image of each destination, in the absence of first-hand experience.

Following Moutinho (1987), Goodall (1991:63) argues that a consumer concentrates on destination attributes most relevant to their needs, while also modifying information to suit their needs through a process of 'selective distortion'. The consumer compares naive images against their evaluative image. As Goodall (ibid.:63) puts it, 'perception is therefore more important than reality in conditioning choice'. Naive images which meet or exceed the evaluative image are believed to result in a destination being chosen, subsequently setting the expectations for the holiday. It is significant that images are conceptualised as changing throughout the holiday experience, as more information is acquired by the consumer (see Ashworth and Goodall 1988).

Initial Stages of Decision-making

Motivation forms the initial stage in most decision-making models. As Shaw and Williams (1994:74) point out, it is also extremely difficult to measure. Most authors agree that the decision to travel depends on both needs and desires. Needs are considered to be intrinsic, including emotional, spiritual and physical drives. Desires are therefore extrinsic, created through an individual's expectation that they will gain pleasure or satisfaction from an activity. Although appreciation of culture and social relations differs between authors, desires are generally considered to be conditioned by the value system prevalent in the society. Seemingly relevant to urban tourism, Crompton (1979) emphasises states of disequilibrium or homeostasis that are rectified by breaking away from routine life. Several of Crompton's seven motivations appear to be relevant to urban tourism, including escaping from a mundane environment, prestige and the facilitation of social interaction. Iso-Ahola (1982) further develops the notion of 'escaping' and 'seeking' dimensions. These are combined with 'personal' and 'interpersonal' dimensions, representing the degree to which interaction with other people creates both push and pull factors.

Gray (1970) emphasises just two dimensions, 'sunlust' which refers to the allure of coastal resorts, and 'wanderlust'. The latter is more relevant to urban tourism as it describes the search for unique and authentic experiences which differ from life at home. Authors such as Krippendorf (1987), however, stress the complicated and often misleading nature of an individual's motives. There is a degree of consensus that motivation consists of both push and pull factors, relating to the individual's home environment, and pull factors, relating mainly to the cultural and social benefits from specific destinations. Regarding specific motivational factors, however, there is a striking lack of agreement. It may be unwise to attempt to define universal tourist motivations, as motivations vary so much between different contexts.

In the information search and evaluation stages of decision-making, place image is conceptualised as a pull factor in the choice of destination. The potential visitor searches for information in order to find the destination which best satisfies their goals within time and financial constraints. There is, of course, variation between consumers with different planning horizons and levels of preparation. An impulse buyer, for instance, engages in very limited planning, whilst a meticulous planner will seek information from a range of official sources before carefully selecting a product. Information search may rely on primary sources such as previous experience, but is more likely to involve secondary sources. Although it is argued that external information search is relatively extensive for tourism products (Giletson and Crompton 1983), it is possible that the influence of sources such as family and friends is perhaps more significant (Walter and Tong 1977). It is believed that there is a preliminary filtering of destinations, and that existing spatial knowledge is important in ruling out certain destinations.

Gunn's Model

According to Gunn (1972:120), the different stages of the decision-making process result in a variety of place images, depending on the amount, source and objectivity of information available. Gunn, in a seven-phase decision-making model (figure 4.1), makes a useful distinction between the official 'projected image' of the tourism authorities, and the 'organic image' gleaned from non-tourist sources. The term 'organic image' is given to the formation of images based on non-commercial sources, such as art, literature, education, family and friends and the mass media. More commercial sources of information and representations are conceptualised as contributing to an 'induced image'. The induced image is formed from advertisements, brochures, guidebooks and the activities of intermediaries such as travel agents, tourist boards and marketing consortia. The 'modified induced image' is formed with the addition of first-hand experience of the destination, and may itself be changed by return travel and reflection following the visit.

Such models, therefore, consist of a hierarchy of images, consisting of initial perceptions based on organic sources and a modification of the image upon visiting the destination. This modification results in a much more 'realistic, objective, differentiated, and complex image' (Echtner and Ritchie 1991:4). It is extremely significant that first-hand experience is influential only in the final stages, emphasising the importance of images formed without first-hand experience. Naive images – the images of consumers who have not visited a destination – consist of representations from a wide variety of sources. While satisfaction with the place product is fundamental to urban tourism, the vast majority of place consumers will base their decision on naive images, without any first-hand experience of the locality.

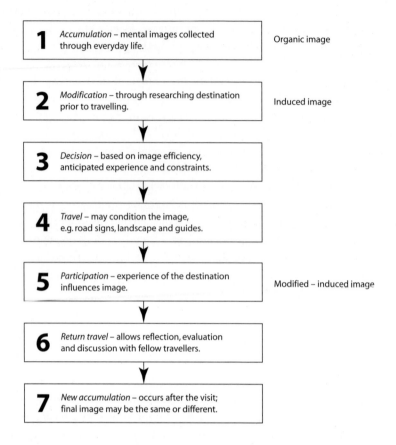

Figure 4.1: Destination image and consumer decision-making. Source: after Gunn (1972:120).

Place Image Research
Comparing Images

There has been something of a consensus amongst the various place image researchers concerning the significance of comparing images at different stages of the theorised decision-making process, and this has been a recurring theme in many studies (e.g. Ashworth and De Haan 1987). Satisfaction with the place product is the primary focus in studies by Gartner (1986), Mayo (1973) and Pizam et al. (1978). The methodological considerations of measuring images are of concern to Phelps (1986) and Scott et al. (1978). Surprisingly, the wider (and fundamental) relationship between images and tourism development are addressed by relatively few, although Gunn (1972) and Mayo (1973) are notable exceptions. Mill and Morrison (1985) and Pool (1965) are amongst the few researchers concerned with the influence of nationality and culture on image formation and change.

Although there is a degree of consensus on the importance of monitoring the image received by target groups, systematic research into the image modification process for any one destination is rare. A small-scale exception is Dietvorst's 1987 evaluation of the image held of the city of Nijmegen, Netherlands. Several studies have concluded that image reception is dependent on how the media used to communicate messages are perceived. Individuals appear to reject much of what they encounter, and, unlike organic images, the official images of promotional activity may lack the necessary 'active collusion' (Uzzell 1984).

Projected Images

As Bramwell and Rawding (1996:202) point out, most place image studies focus on the received images of tourists, including both organic and projected sources of information (e.g. Ashworth and Voogd 1990; Burgess and Gold 1995; Lawson and Baud-Bovey 1977). The projected images of tourism promotion have received more attention recently, however – particularly in relation to urban tourism (e.g. Watson 1991). Pritchard and Morgan (1996) provide an interesting comparison of Scottish, Irish and Welsh brochure images. Cohen (1993) uses a structuralist analysis of brochure images of island tourism in southern Thailand. Selwyn (1990) is notable for his socio-anthropological contributions, particularly his emphasis on 'postmodern myths'.

Bartels and Timmer (1987) found that out of 160 local authorities in the Netherlands, almost one-third of promotional expenditure was directed towards media advertising to create a favourable image. Although knowledge about the selection of media is incomplete, it is likely that public-sector attempts at transmitting favourable images are more effective in influencing large numbers of consumers in the early stages of the decision-making process. A dispersed market, therefore, may lead to highly generalised mass media advertising at a low cost per recipient.

According to Burgess (1982), the source of information and the style of present-ation significantly affect its credibility. Nolan (1976) also questions the credibility of some marketing media. Testing respondents' confidence in accuracy, objectivity, informational content and personal involvement, it was found that news media was seen as the most credible, while press and broadcasting advertising was perceived as the least credible. Giletson and Crompton (1983) also emphasise the importance of non-official sources, such as the advice of friends. They conclude that official sources regarded as authentic, accurate and informative may be used, but the final decision is legitimised by organic images. There may be some blurring of the organic-induced categorisation, however, due to the contemporary sophistication of public relations aimed at developing 'credible' media such as travel writing (see Urry 1995). Significantly, in one of the few integrated studies, Ashworth and De Haan (1987) compare the projected and received image of the Languedoc Coast in southern France, and stress that it is the monitoring of different destination images which provides an important tool in the development of a coherent tourism strategy.

4.1: 'Glasgow's Miles Better' campaign, Glasgow, Scotland. Courtesy of Department of Geography, Liverpool John Moores University.

Place Image Methodologies

Although one might expect to find a wide variety of approaches to researching place images, two distinct types of methodology are apparent. An important methodological distinction is between structured and unstructured techniques. Structured approaches, where the researcher provides the attributes or constructs, are by far the most common in place image research (see table 4.1). As Echtner and Ritchie (1991:9) describe, the attributes of destinations tend to be specified and incorporated into standardised instruments, often with the use of a ratings scale such as the Semantic Differential or Likert. Gallarza et al. (2001) found that out of their sample of quantitative place image studies, 15 used the Likert scale. The data from standardised scales, therefore, tends to be easy to administer, code and analyse.

In terms of analysis, there is an associated tendency for the use of multivariate techniques, such as principal components analysis, factor analysis, cluster analysis and multi-dimensional scaling. This is mostly due to the assumed multi-dimensional nature of place image, and the ability of these techniques to simplify the data into dimensions and groups of respondents. As Jenkins (1999:5) points out, although it is argued by some that destination images are holistic representations of places, in measuring images, most researchers feel compelled to analyse separate parts or attributes. The structured approach has been extremely popular with marketing and advertising professionals, due to the large-scale quantitative data produced.

Researchers such as Haahti (1986) have used a structured approach to examine the unique images of different localities using product attribute analysis. Other researchers have used techniques such as multi-dimensional scaling, overcoming some of the problems of generating the constructs to be used in the study (e.g. Gartner 1986). Gartner used previously collected data from the US states of Utah, Wyoming, Colorado and Montana to compare images of residents and non-residents in relation to recreational products. Of the numerous studies of destination images, very few have incorporated constructs which could be termed 'holistic'. Surprisingly, very few researchers use structured techniques involving consumers to generate the constructs used. This issue is discussed in more detail below.

The main alternative, according to the place-marketing and tourism literature, is to use an unstructured methodology. This may consist of free-form descriptions to measure images, exemplified by Boiven's study (1986). The attributes or constructs are not specified at the beginning of the research, and the respondent freely describes their impressions of the place product. This approach is used by researchers such as Reilly (1990), Dann (1996b) and Embacher and Buttle (1989). As Echtner and Ritchie (1991) describe, Reilly used open-ended questions for respondents to describe images of Montana. The study uncovered some useful holistic images, although it was acknowledged that the level of detail is highly variable, depending on the eloquence of individuals and their willingness to participate. Several researchers have used focus groups, such as Fakeye and Crompton (1991) and Driscol et al. (1994). In-depth interviews have been used by researchers such as Bramwell and Rawding (1996) and Selby and Morgan (1996). Other qualitative studies have used content analysis, such as Baloglu and McCleary's (1999) study of promotional material.

Destination Marketing Implications
Policy Analysis

The image of a locality can be considered to have a multi-faceted relationship with urban tourism development, representing both the focus of urban marketing and tourism strategies, yet often a serious obstacle to realising the objectives of marketing strategies. As early as 1975, Hunt recognised that images largely determine the success or failure of tourism development. An important development in place image theory has been the comparison of a destination's image at different stages of tourists' decision-making cycles, and the use of this range of images to form the basis of a policy-making tool.

Font (1996:126) suggests that destination marketers should begin by establishing whether consumers are familiar with a destination before considering whether or not impressions are favourable. Perceptions of a city, relating to both first-hand experience and representations, have important policy implications. This is particularly the case where there are significant differences between first-hand experiences of the destination, and perceptions based upon experiencing representations of the locality from outside. In the language of place image studies, there may be significant discrepancies between the demand-side 'naive image', consisting of the organic and projected image, and the supply-side 're-evaluated image', which includes perceptions of the place product itself. Furthermore, discrepancies can have their roots in either the demand- or supply-side. Weaknesses on the supply-side may result in expectations not being met upon experiencing the destination. Weaknesses on the demand-side may cause negative stereotypical perceptions, deterring potential visitors and resulting in non-purchase decisions.

Market Segmentation and Positioning

Successful urban tourism development is virtually impossible without rigorous, sensitive, and periodic image research. Destination marketing requires the development of a place product which meets or exceeds the expectations of target-market segments. Furthermore, the benefits of place image studies in segmenting the tourism market have been demonstrated by numerous researchers, including Ahmed (1996), Baloglu and Brinberg (1997) and Sternquist Witter (1985). Place image – particularly discrepancies between different types of image – plays a crucial role in service quality. A knowledge of discrepancies between consumers' naive images of a destination and the re-evaluated images of actual visitors, can help marketers to close the gap between the expected and perceived destination (see Ahmed 1991). The place marketer may take action to improve the place product, addressing weaknesses identified by visitors whose expectations were not met. The promotional mix may be used to address unfavourable naive images, or to alter the expectations of potential visitors.

Data on the image of the destination is also crucial to positioning. Place image studies focusing on positioning include Ahmed, (1991), Alford (1998) and Calantone et al. (1989). To position a product, marketers develop and communicate a product's attributes and benefits, relative to those of competitors. As Font (1996:127) argues, 'positioning involves creating the desired image in the minds of consumers'. Indeed, the sustainability of a destination depends on marketers differentiating a destination from competitors. This process has been represented as a transition of the destination from a commodity area, competing on price, to a status area, with unique and attractive attributes (Font 1996:128–29). To communicate the unique selling proposition of the destination to potential consumers, place marketers increasingly need to be innovative in their use of the promotional mix.

Place Promotion and the Place Product

An interesting conclusion of many recent place image studies is that the official image projected is rarely the most important source of ideas about the destination. Conflict between sources, particularly in relation to the news media, often prompts defensive promotion to counteract images from other sources. It would seem that the selection of projected images and promotional media in relation to the organisation's objectives, is critical. The objective of 'remarketing', for example, may not be consistent with the need for clarity, simplicity and the avoidance of dissonance. It also appears to be important to maintain consistency between the images of a locality projected by different organisations and on different spatial scales.

Significantly, destination images are influenced by a much wider spectrum of information sources than other products. Post-industrial cities are even more likely to be influenced by naive images, as derogatory economic, political and social represent-ations can be significant. Some cities, for example, may be subject to negative media reporting of unemployment, crime and dereliction, and these negative organic images are incorporated into the destination's naive image. Madsen (1992:635), for example, illustrates both the creation of negative stereotypes by the national press and their influence on the purchasing behaviour of place consumers. He cites an article in the *Independent* newspaper, about Liverpool Close in Grantham, southeast England. It was claimed that houses remained unsold for three years due to the street's association with the city of Liverpool. Unfortunately, such representations further contribute to the negative stereotypes (naive images) which influence the decision-making of potential visitors and investors.

The majority of potential visitors to a destination will not have visited the locality recently, and may not even have been exposed to the more commercial sources of information. The vast majority of potential visitors to a destination will decide not to visit, and this decision is based mainly on their organic sources of information. Naive images are believed to be extremely stable over time, and slow to adapt to product development (Gartner and Hunt 1987). As authors such as Bramwell (1998:37–38), Jenkins (1999:2), Selby (1995) and Selby and Morgan (1996) argue, it is imperative that marketers include these 'non-visitors' in image research, comparing naive images to the experiences of actual visitors.

There are few other products for which such strong emotions exist before the product has been experienced first hand. The need to separate, compare and contrast the images of different social groups of consumers becomes apparent. Different groups of consumers are likely to have intersubjective experiences of representations of a locality, or the place product itself. As Ashworth and Goodall (1988) argue, place image has a vital mediating role between consumers and the supply factors of the tourism product. The complexity of the place product, particularly its short-term inflexibility, together with the significance of images formed without direct contact with the place product itself, make the matching of urban tourism supply and demand even more critical. The evaluation and analysis of both demand- and supply-side images, therefore, offers hope in avoiding 'vague, generalised, and thus ineffective geographical marketing of which there are too many examples' (Ashworth and Goodall 1988:11). Separating the visitor and non-visitor images, then, becomes an invaluable exercise, enabling the salient attributes of the naive or demand-side image, and the supply-side image to be acted upon. This process also has the potential to identify the groups of place consumers with particularly positive or negative images, enabling informed and targeted action by destination marketers and urban tourism practitioners.

CASE STUDY 4.1: CONSUMING CARDIFF: RESEARCHING URBAN IMAGES
AND EXPERIENCES

The potential of comparing the images and first-hand experiences of visitors is apparent in a study focusing on Cardiff, the capital of Wales. The survey used in the study was informed by an initial phase of more qualitative research, using repertory grid analysis (see case study 6.1). Like the first phase of the study, the sample was designed to capture both the first-hand experiences of visitors to the city of Cardiff and the naive images of urban tourists who had not visited the destination. As the repertory-grid analysis had hopefully uncovered salient constructs, the survey was more tightly structured. It was desirable to use a scaling system which would subsequently enable responses to be coded, into 'naive images' and 'first-hand experiences', both 'positive' and 'negative'. The sample, therefore, actually consisted of two sub-samples, one for eliciting experiences of Cardiff, and one for images among non-visitors. This would then allow constructs exhibiting significant discrepancies to be identified, and analysed through a statistical method such as factor analysis.

The core of the survey consisted of 11 constructs elicited through the initial phase of research using repertory grid analysis. Although the study used a seven-point scale, the 'consensus repertory grid' should be distinguished from semantic differential studies. As authors such as Phelps (1986) have argued that numerical scales are not always understood by respondents, it was decided to use a seven-point scale with labels, and include a 'neutral' option to accommodate respondents who felt unable to respond to a particular construct. An attempt was made to mix the constructs randomly so that those with either positive or negative construct poles were not bunched together. This has been shown to encourage the respondent to think about each construct individually.

It was also intended to elicit some less conventional social and role-related data in the personal information section, as well as the more typical demographic and socio-economic data. In addition to geographical and demographic data, the survey also elicited data relating to membership of any societies and professional bodies, educational attainment and hobbies and interests. They were also asked how they would describe their social class, and where they thought that they had heard or read or watched things about Cardiff. The full survey was piloted among six respondents, testing the clarity of instructions and the ease of use.

The data collection took place over a period of a year. Access was gained to Cardiff Castle, Cardiff Civic Centre, Cardiff Bay Visitor Centre, Bristol Tourist Information Centre and Edinburgh Tourist Information Centre. One additional site was chosen in both Edinburgh and Bristol, in Princes Street Gardens and on the Broad Quay respectively. It was decided to use a convenience sample of visitors exiting the tourist information centre or attraction. By the end of the data collection phase, 335 usable surveys had been completed. Although the response rate was slightly disappointing, the quality of the responses was considered to be high.

To analyse the data, a bar chart was initially useful in enabling general observations and identifying interesting or problematic constructs. The graphical representation assigned the unfavourable or derogatory constructs a negative image score, whilst the favourable constructs had a positive score. It is significant that the sub-sample of experiences is considerably more positive than the sub-sample of images. This would seem to indicate that the place product generally meets or exceeds expectations, whilst the image of Cardiff is problematic.

Particularly significant are the strongly negative images for certain constructs. The images sub-sample is particularly negative for the constructs 'industrial' and 'inaccessible'. These constructs are important because they represent the aspects of Cardiff where images (and expectations) are particularly low in relation to first-hand experience. Not only do a significant minority of potential visitors expect Cardiff to be industrial and inaccessible, but these perceptions are very different from visitors' experiences of Cardiff.

Among the positive constructs for experiences, 'historical' and 'friendly' scored particularly highly. It is noteworthy that Cardiff is perceived as being 'accessible' by actual visitors, yet 'inaccessible' is one of the strongest negative images amongst non-visitors. In terms of negative experiences, unfavourable constructs with high negative scores include the construct 'congested'. Together with 'dirty', these constructs represent the negative experiences of visitors to Cardiff.

The data was also subjected to factor analysis, a statistical technique for analysing the multiple correlations within the data, and arranging variables into associated groups. The correlation coefficient, termed factor loading, is considered acceptable if it is at least 0.3. The factor-analysis extraction for negative images produced three factors. One factor, for example, had high loadings for the constructs 'industrial' (0.56) and 'unsafe' (0.45), and the variables 'television and radio' (0.68) and 'newspapers' (0.62). This data suggests an association between negative images of Cardiff and representations of the city in the mass media. As Cardiff's images seemed to be its main weakness as an urban destination, these findings would seem to have policy implications concerning place promotion and media relations.

The factor analysis on 'negative experiences' reveals a high loading for 'congested' at 0.47, and high loadings for 'professional' (0.82), 'groups and societies' (0.43), 'high income' (0.53) and 'higher education' (0.78). Although some caution is necessary in interpreting such factor-analysis output, when supplemented by the qualitative data also collected during the study, the data appears to identify a group of discerning and fairly critical urban tourists, likely to be professional, educated and to belong to special interest groups and societies. It is interesting that the qualitative data collected adds clarity to this picture, indicating areas of the city where congestion does indeed detract from the experience of such visitors.

Factor analysis on positive images reveals a factor with the construct 'arts and culture' (0.66), 'friendly' (0.66) and 'historic' (0.70). Other variables with high loadings are 'past visit' (0.35) and 'promotion' (0.38). Although hardly surprising, these results suggest that the respondents outside Cardiff who have positive images of the city tend to have either experienced promotional material or visited before (although not in the last five years). In terms of positive experiences, the analysis produced a factor with high loadings for 'accessible' (0.37), 'past visit' (0.61) and 'female' (0.41). As 'inaccessible' is one of the most serious negative images of Cardiff, it would appear that visitor perceptions are revised upon visiting Cardiff, and that the city's accessibility, particularly from London and southeast England, is actually perceived as a strength of Cardiff as an urban destination.

It would seem that studies which compare naive images with first-hand experience have important policy implications in terms of developing the place product and place promotion. Even simple graphical methods of analysis can help to reveal where the most serious discrepancies between images and experiences lie. Powerful techniques such as factor analysis, however, allow the researcher to focus on the groups of tourists with particular images and experiences, enabling a considerably more sophisticated contribution to urban tourism policy analysis. Whilst caution is always necessary in interpreting the output of factor analysis, it would seem that it is possible to identify both the types of consumer and types of representations and landscapes associated with particular images and experiences of an urban tourist destination.

Limitations of Place Image Studies
Methodological Problems

In practical terms, it is possible to identify some methodological problems associated with place image research. Even when studies have seemingly offered useful insights, the techniques used to generate the attributes or constructs used in structured studies have somewhat invalidated their findings. As Gallarza et al. (2001) argue, the complexity of the tourism product causes severe problems, and this is exacerbated by the fact that place image is multi-dimensional in nature. Not only are images held by many different groups, including potential tourists, actual tourists, excursionists, residents and retailers, but the intangibility of the urban tourist experience makes for an even more subjective area of study. In place image research, it is possible to identify a degree of trade-off between structured and unstructured techniques. Despite their flexibility, suitability for coding and ease of use, structured techniques may use constructs which are not salient to respondents. As table 4.1 indicates, few published studies use consumers to elicit the constructs used in structured methodologies (see also Jenkins 1999:7). The ratings of constructs revealed may therefore bear little relevance to urban tourist decision-making. A comprehensive review of place image studies by Echtner and Ritchie (1991) reveals that out of 14 structured place image studies, only four used consumer research to elicit the constructs used in the main study. Calantone et al. (1989) and Kale and Weir (1986) do not even discuss the issue.

Among the researchers who do divulge their methods of generating constructs, the emphasis on 'tourism experts' and 'researcher's judgment' is common (e.g. Gartner and Hunt 1987). Um and Crompton (1990:438) use 'an interacting panel of five individuals whom the authors believed to be knowledgeable of this literature'. The same authors state that 'when situational constraints are specified and integrated into consumer choice models, their predictive power is enhanced' (ibid.:433). The heterogeneity of contemporary markets, and the inherent subjectivity of place image, raise important questions about the salience of attributes or constructs used in surveys. Gallarza et al. (2001:65) also point out that the categorisation of destinations used in comparative image studies is often set by the researcher. The place consumer, however, may not categorise destinations or attributes in the same way or at the same level of abstraction as the researcher. By contrast, Jenkins (1999:7–12) provides a convincing argument for conducting place image research in two stages. Qualitative consumer research, such as interviews or repertory grid analysis can be used to generate salient constructs, followed by the use of rating scales to measure consumers' perceptions.

In light of the proliferation of what Parrinello (1993:237) terms 'almost obsessive forms of methodological sophistication', perhaps more attention should be directed towards the specific contexts of place image formation. Even in terms of the respondents of place image studies, there is often a concern with *a priori* variables, such as demographic or socio-economic characteristics. It is possible that place image research is characterised by a disproportionate emphasis on statistics and sophisticated methods of analysis. Dann et al. (1988) produce a diagram with four quadrants representing the relationship between the methodological sophistication and theoretical awareness of tourism research. The majority of urban tourism and place image studies can still be considered to fall into a quadrant representing a lack of theoretical underpinning, despite sophisticated analytical techniques. In the context of place image, Schroader (1984) argues that simpler statistical techniques tend to be just as effective as complex ones, and that place images are best summarised by graphical techniques.

As Gallarza et al. (2001) note, there is lack of agreement amongst place image researchers over whether place image is multi-dimensional or a holistic construct. Most researchers conceptualise place image in terms of different attributes, and this informs their methodology. As we have seen, this does not mean that the attributes are actually salient to respondents. A minority of researchers conceptualise place image as holistic, focusing on overall impressions of the destination. While the latter conceptualisation usually necessitates qualitative research, several researchers attempt to

Table 4.1: Methodologies used by destination image researchers

Reference	Type of Methodology	Technique for the Generation of Attributes
Hunt (1975)	Structured (20 attributes, semantic differential scale)	Tourism experts, researcher's judgment
Crompton (1977)	Structured (18 attributes, semantic differential scale)	Consumer interviews (36), general reading material, brochures
Goodrich (1977)	Structured (10 attributes, Likert scale)	Tourism experts, travel brochures
Crompton (1979)	Structured (30 attributes, semantic differential scale)	Consumer interviews (36), general reading material, brochures
Pearce (1982)	Structured (13 attributes, Likert scale)	Repertory grid analysis with consumers (10)
Haahti and Yevas (1983)	Structured (10 attributes, Likert scale)	Literature review, focus group
Crompton and Duray (1985)	Structured (28 attributes, semantic differential scale)	Consumer interviews (100), general reading material, brochures
Kale and Weir (1986)	Structured (26 attributes, Likert scale)	Not discussed
Phelps (1986)	Structured (32 attributes, checklist)	Researcher's judgment
Tourism Canada (1986–89)	Structured (29 attributes, Likert scale)	Not discussed
Gartner and Hunt (1987)	Structured (11 attributes, semantic differential scale)	Tourism experts, researcher's judgment
Richardson and Crompton (1988)	Structured (10 attributes, comparative scale)	Tourism Canada Survey
Gartner (1989)	Structured (15 attributes, Likert Scale)	Not discussed
Calantone et al. (1989)	Structured (13 attributes, Likert scale)	Not discussed
Reilly (1990)	Unstructured (open-ended questions)	Not applicable

Source: After Echtner and Ritchie (1991:8).

derive a global score; while the holistic view of place image has advantages, quantitative studies which produce 'a pondered sum of the perceptions of components' (Gallarza et al. 2001:70) are not so convincing.

Theoretical Limitations
Acknowledging the Complexity

In the early 1990s it was acknowledged that 'although such studies have become the staple of the tourism research agenda, invariably they have been atheoretical and lacking in any conceptual framework' (Fakeye and Crompton cited in Gallarza 2001:57).

Gartner (1986:57), states that 'most tourism image research is piecemeal without a theoretical basis for support'. In general, it would seem to be very rare for place image researchers to reflect upon the theoretical assumptions underpinning their research. Related to this problem, place image researchers rarely acknowledge important theoretical debates which have taken place in the social sciences. Squire (1994) presents an interesting review of the lack of mutual co-operation and interest between the disciplines of tourism and human geography, concluding that the cost is borne by both.

Echtner and Ritchie (1991), following their perceptive discussion, proceed to deliberate on the dimensions of place image which should be included in place image studies. Despite advocating the use of qualitative consumer research, Jenkins (1999:5) also attempts to define the dimensions of place image. More recently still, Gallarza et al. (2001) review a large sample of the image literature. First it is arranged into just three 'dimensions', suggested by Mazanec (1994). It is then classified into four 'features'. Although Gallarza et al. (2001) make some perceptive comments, it is likely that such classifications will always be rather arbitrary. It is also of concern that in applying such dimensions, 'studies using qualitative techniques, although contemplating attributes, are not considered ... due to the difficulty of homogenizing attribute names' (Gallarza et al. 2001:62). It is uncertain how the endless creation of dimensions and taxonomies benefits tourism research in such diverse contexts. Place image research appears to suffer from what Franklin and Crang (2001:6) call 'the obsession with taxonomies and 'craze of classification'. Citing Lofgren (ibid.:6), they argue that these lists 'represent a tradition of flat-footed sociology and psychology driven by an unhappy marriage between marketing research and positivist ambitions of scientific labelling'.

The Culture of Decision-making

It is important to question the theoretical assumptions made by researchers, as these determine the methodologies used, and consequently the knowledge of urban tourism produced. In the context of tourism motivation studies, Parrinello (1993) makes some points which are also salient to place image research. The anticipation stage of tourist decision-making is influenced by a complex amalgam of 'tourist culture', with increasingly widespread and intensive channels of communication (Parrinello 1993). Recent motivational theories are based on complex interactive models, including situational factors relating to specific contexts. There have been advances in incorporating social context into motivation studies, and a move away from a behaviouristic conception. Pearce (1982) identifies the difficulty of assuming the same cognitive process in different cultures. This includes the culture-specific nature of language. Perhaps more significant are calls to begin any motivational study from everyday life in different contexts. Parrinello (1993), for example, suggests that researchers should look to phenomenologists such as Schutz (1972) and Berger and Luckmann (1966).

Despite the progressive refinement of decision-making models, it is possible to identify common features and assumptions. The emphasis is on the individual consumer, with little or no consideration of social relations. The consumer is assumed to be rational and actively seeking internal and external, official and unofficial information. There is a sequential movement from general and implicitly inaccurate information towards more specific and realistic images. Information, therefore, is considered to be the key to decision-making, fundamental to the search and evaluation activities of the consumer once they have been motivated to travel. Further complicating the existence of different 'rules' of decision-making, it is far from certain whether the consumers in a specific market segment should be considered as satisficers or optimisers. While satisficers will select the first destination that satisfies their goals, an optimiser will choose the one that best satisfies their goals (Goodall 1991:67).

Although there is extremely contradictory evidence concerning the significance and timing of different sources of information in decision-making, researchers tend to assume that the process of decision-making is universal. It would seem that research can be flawed if it is assumed that consumers always progress towards more official, realistic, and differentiated information. MacInnis and Price (1987) suggest that official sources of information are important in the initial stages of information search, followed later by unofficial 'holistic' images. By contrast, Echtner and Ritchie (1991) suggest that organic sources are important in the initial stages of decision-making and official sources are significant in the later stages. Pritchard and Morgan (1995) describe research by the Wales Tourist Board which suggests that brochures are often used to confirm decisions already made, decisions based mainly on organic sources.

Place image researchers acknowledge that there are significant variations in decision rules. There is little evidence, however, that such differences in consumer behaviour are considered by place image researchers in their choice of methodology. In general, there has been very little attention paid to the given choice context. Baloglu and McCleary (1999) argue that most studies present a static version of the image-formation process, rather than a more realistic dynamic model. The image-formation process itself, however, is likely to vary between different contexts. The social environment, in particular, is likely to be significant in the process of decision-making, particularly through the norms and value systems of different groups. Despite a limited recognition of the importance of social context (e.g. Goodall 1988), there has been little success in incorporating social relations into decision-making research.

Limitations of Behavioural Research

Behaviouralist approaches dominate the place image literature, although the limit-ations of the epistemology are very rarely discussed. As discussed in chapter two, both place image and urban tourism researchers draw upon the work of Kevin Lynch (e.g. 1960). The mental-map research discussed by Page (1995, 1997, 1999), is also advocated by Pearce and Fagence (1996) and Walmsley and Jenkins (1992:270). In the latter study, cognitive maps of tourists visiting Coff's harbour in Australia are developed, and a similar approach has been used by Pearce (1977, 1981). Ankomah and Crompton (1992) focus on the influence of distance on tourists' perceptions of urban destinations.

Behaviouralist approaches assume that consumer decision-making is bounded, the result of imperfect knowledge. Despite human geography's general indifference towards tourism (Squire 1994), there was actually a wave of interest in tourist images in the late 1970s and early 1980s. This included mental-map research (e.g. Gould and White 1974), differences between the images of tourists and inhabitants (e.g. Belanger and Gendreau 1979), and a proliferation of 'repetitive travel' studies relating to tourism (e.g. Leiber 1977). Such behavioural approaches brought a number of benefits. They introduced the subjective element, arguing that an understanding of individual cognition of the ordinary environment is vital in predicting behaviour. Researchers were also concerned to contribute directly to policy-making, not unlike many urban tourism researchers.

Behavioural research has been faced, however, with some convincing criticism. An obvious problem is the association of behavioural approaches with behaviourism. While some critics were perhaps a little harsh in linking behavioural geography to Skinnerian or Pavlovian psychology (Cullen 1976; Ley 1981a), fundamental problems were highlighted. These were related to 'the old questions of sensation and image, of feeling and emotion' (Richards 1974). Theoretical work was limited to searching for 'universal claims about the subjective processes of environmental cognition' (Phillips 1993:23). The focus is the individual rather than social groups, conceptualising images as the result of psychologically determined processes of perception and cognition. Mental images were thus considered to be natural, non-political distortions of an objective reality.

It is also important to question the relationship between cognition and behaviour. Despite the widespread acceptance of the link between behaviour and images, the relationship has long been challenged (e.g. Sack 1980). As Werlen (1993) argues, too few researchers appreciate the differences between 'action' and 'behaviour'. Tourist decision-making models, despite adopting the cognitive form of behaviourism which includes perception and cognition, conceptualise socio-cultural factors as merely an input into the psychological conditioning of the individual. Even cognitive studies, which conceptualise information as the stimuli, suffer from the contradiction of describing the observed reaction of an individual as a 'decision'. If an individual is reacting to stimuli rather than being involved in purposeful activity, they can not be considered to be making a 'decision'. The cognitive-behavioural tradition in tourism research conceptualises the reaction of individuals to tourist decision-making in terms of psychological conditioning factors. It can only relate, therefore, to individual consumers. As even Goodall (1991:73–74) indicates, tourism is a social phenomenon, with the collection of information, decision-making and participation occurring in social groups.

There are fundamental and largely unresolved arguments relating to the atheoretical nature of behavioural research. The contributions of more radical critics represent behavioural approaches as dehumanising, governed by 'psychologism' which obscures the social and economic conditions that operate independently of the individual. According to this view, behavioural approaches lead to an atomistic form of explanation that relegates social action. As Werlen (1993:15) argues, 'the theoretical concept of behaviour is inadequate for an understanding of social relations'. The behavioural approach relies on the reduction of all social phenomena to the psychological factors of perception, learning and thinking. It is difficult to maintain, however, that any human activity can be explained 'without reference to our social surroundings, to social institutions and to their manner of functioning' (Popper 1969:90). It is not possible to reduce the social to the psychological, and take society as 'given' (Werlen 1993:16).

What is significant from such critiques, therefore, is the way in which a combination of the positivist origins of behavioural approaches, together with an atheoretical subjectivism, raise considerable doubts about the ability to incorporate and conceptualise experience or culture. This implies the dismissal of everyday experiences, common-sense meanings of agency and the social relations of structure. Most place image studies display at least some of these limitations, attributing relatively little importance to the culture and social context of studies.

Significantly, in many place image studies, images are seen as 'false understanding', '...not just nonsense or error, but...a coherent, rule-governed system of errors' (Mitchell 1986:172). In line with the 'new' cultural geography, Phillips (1993)

4.2: Tourism as a social phenomenon (Chinese Festival, New York). Courtesy Jan Rath, University of Amsterdam.

discredits the unreality of place images through a discussion of the tendency within society to privilege certain types of images as reality. Maps, for example, have commonly been accepted as a realistic, credible and neutral likeness of the world. It is possible, however, to read such representations in different ways, uncovering political influences on their creation and maintenance (Cosgrove 1984). Behavioural approaches naturalise images, denying the existence of a struggle between different representations to convey the 'truth'. The language of behavioural approaches, therefore, privileges elite and detached representations over the representations of everyday life to which context is fundamental. By contrast, cultural studies focus on the differences between representations, exploring their form and context, as well as identifying those which are salient to consumers.

Conclusion

Place image studies offer considerable insights into the images of urban tourist destinations, and the decision-making of urban tourists. There has been an encouraging development and consolidation of theory and research relating to decision-making and place image. Particularly useful is the conceptualisation of a range of place images, related to stages of the decision-making process. This enables place image to be used as a policy-analysis instrument. The comparison of images at different stages of decision-making over a range of constructs has been demonstrated by a number of authors, and enables the identification of weaknesses of the destination on the demand-side amongst potential visitors, and on the supply-side amongst actual visitors.

While progress has been made, decision-making models and place image studies also display methodological and theoretical problems. Methodological problems, for example, relate to a lack of salience of constructs used in research to place consumers, and a lack of comparability between different images. The more fundamental epistemological problems relate to the theoretical limitations of behaviouralist research. Despite the emphasis on cognitive processes, there is still a strong positivist influence in these studies. Place image studies are often unable to capture social context and social relations, despite their significant influence on tourist decision-making. Particularly inconsistent with contemporary social science, images are conceptualised as distortions of an objective reality. Together, these epistemological problems suggest that many urban tourism and place and image studies would greatly benefit from alternative conceptualisations of culture, experience and action. It is now necessary to expand upon these initial observations relating to the potential contribution of cultural studies.

Chapter summary:

- There have been useful developments within place image research, particularly when different types of urban image are compared.
- Place image is closely related to the different stages of tourist decision-making.
- Place image studies can provide data useful for the promotion, product development and positioning of a destination.
- The structured approach to place image research is by far the most common, and this type of methodology has limitations.
- Many of the limitations of place image research have their roots in the theoretical underpinning or epistemology.
- Although the behaviouralist epistemology dominates the place image literature, it fails to incorporate culture, experience and social relations into place image studies.

Further Reading

Ashworth, G.J. and B.Goodall (1988) 'Tourist Images: Marketing Considerations', in B.Goodall and G.J.Ashworth (eds) *Marketing in the Tourism Industry*, Croom Helm, Beckenham, 215–38.

Echtner, C.M and J.R.B.Ritchie (1991) 'The Meaning and Measurement of Tourism Destination Image', *Journal of Tourism Studies* 2 (2), December.

Font, X. (1996) 'Managing the Tourist Destination Image', *Journal of Vacation Marketing* 3 (2), 123–31.

Jenkins, O.H. (1999) 'Understanding and Measuring Tourist Destination Images', *International Journal of Tourism Research* 1, 1–15.

Morgan, N.J. and A.Pritchard (1998) *Tourism Promotion and Power: Creating Images, Creating Identities*, John Wiley and Sons, Chichester.

Pritchard, A. and N.J.Morgan (1995) 'Evaluating Vacation Destination Brochure Images: the case of local authorities in Wales', *Journal of Vacation Marketing* 2 (1), December, 23–38.

— (1996) 'Selling the Celtic Arc to the USA: A Comparative Analysis of Destination Brochure Images Used in the Marketing of Ireland, Scotland and Wales', *Journal of Vacation Marketing* 2 (4), 346–65.

Selby, M. and N.J.Morgan (1996) 'Reconstruing Place Image: A Case Study of its Role in Destination Market Research', *Tourism Management* 17 (4), June, 287–94.

Chapter 5
The Culture of Urban Tourism

The following topics are covered in this chapter:

- An introduction to cultural analysis, and its potential in the context of understanding urban tourism.
- A review of studies of tourism which use cultural analysis.
- The application of key concepts from cultural analysis by urban tourism researchers and practitioners.
- A critique of the cultural analysis of urban tourism, particularly relating to the lack of attention to consumers.
- Approaches to cultural analysis that include the experience of urban tourists.

Introduction

Despite greater attention in recent years to the culture of tourism, there is only a limited dialogue between urban tourism researchers and cultural researchers. While 'travel' and 'the tourist' have become popular metaphors amongst cultural researchers for the postmodern condition, this does not imply a widespread interest in tourism itself. Urban tourism studies were criticised in chapter two for their lack of interest in epistemological and methodological developments within the social sciences. As authors such as Squire argue, 'tourism research has been somewhat isolated from wider disciplinary trends; first from humanistic geography and more recently from the theoretical and methodological questions that have revitalised social and cultural enquires' (1994:1). The last chapter ended with a consideration of the great potential of the 'new cultural geography' in urban tourism studies. This chapter aims to critically review the application of cultural approaches to studies of urban tourism.

There are signs that tourism researchers are finally engaging more with cultural studies. Traditionally, however, there has been a failure amongst tourism researchers to engage with theoretical developments within the social sciences, and a reticence amongst cultural researchers towards tourism. The last decade has seen a proliferation of tourism and travel metaphors used in cultural analysis (see Jokinen and Veijola 1997).

Tourism, however, represents a significant cultural phenomenon *per se*, fundamentally related to the ways in which 'people assess their world, defining their own sense of identity in the process' (Jackle 1985:xi). As Rojek and Urry (1997) argue, tourism has come to occupy centre-stage in understanding contemporary culture.

Urban tourism is therefore closely bound up with the concerns of the new cultural geography – particularly the relationships between culture and social life, and the way meaning is produced, communicated and interpreted. As Ringer (1998:1) argues, 'tourism is a cultural process as much as it is a form of economic development, and the destination of the tourist and the inhabited landscape of local culture are now inseparable to a greater degree'. Tourism as a cultural phenomenon is dominated by the central concern of cultural geography – representation. In the context of marketing the post-industrial city, it is representation which ascribes meaning to particular localities. The reading of landscapes and representations is also central to the tourist experience, and socially constructed meaning is mediated through a range of institutions. Although representation remains the core concept within cultural studies, researchers have more recently embraced the embodiment and performativity of tourism, which are also discussed in this chapter.

It is argued, however, that the complex nature of contemporary consumption – particularly tourism – has not always been tackled convincingly by cultural researchers. In contrast to retrospective cultural studies, there are inherent problems in reading contemporary landscapes and representations on behalf of consumers. In the context of contemporary consumption, the landscapes and representations which are read by the cultural researcher are also read by place consumers in their everyday lives. The lack of attention in cultural studies to the everyday readings of tourist representations and landscapes raises serious questions regarding the reception and embodiment of cultural meanings. This is despite recent studies emphasising the performativity of consumption, which still tend to conceptualise culture on behalf of consumers.

Whilst 'cultural tourism' has received considerable interest amongst academics and practitioners in recent years, rather than focusing on culture as a product, the emphasis is on the cultural analysis of urban tourism. This chapter begins with an overview of cultural studies of consumption, including contributions both in the tourism literature and within human geography. The aim is to initially indicate the scope of cultural studies of consumption, before devoting more attention to the key concepts and methods underpinning the cultural approach. The potential contribution of cultural studies to researching the city is explored. The discussion then identifies limitations of cultural studies revealed in the context of place consumption. Drawing on this critique of cultural studies of consumption, the discussion turns to possible solutions.

Cultural Analysis
Introducing Cultural Studies

Before considering the culture of urban tourism in more detail, it is useful to outline the potential of cultural analysis. The 'cultural turn' refers to a reappraisal and re-emergence of cultural approaches within the social sciences. The origins of cultural geography can be traced to the North American Berkeley School and the work of Carl Sauer. In 'Morphology of Landscape', landscape was defined as 'the unit concept of geography' (Sauer 1925:25), and the 'impress of the works of man upon an area' (Sauer 1925:30). The early forms of cultural geography attributed causality to culture itself, asserting that 'culture is the agent, the natural area is the medium, and the cultural landscape is the result' (Sauer 1925:46).

Although early cultural analysis was influential, the new cultural geography is more likely to draw on the work of Raymond Williams (e.g. 1977) and the Centre for Contemporary Cultural Studies. Authors such as Duncan (1980) argue for the rejection of a reified notion of culture, and the development of a more sociological approach. Sauer's superorganic approach (Sauer, 1925) is seen as encouraging an obsession with objects and artefacts, at the expense of social processes. Contemporary approaches are more likely to recognise the importance of the non-material and symbolic aspects of culture, and the social relations and power underlying them. Researchers have increasingly considered 'the way cultures are produced and reproduced through actual social practices that take place in historically contingent and geographically specific contexts' (Jackson 1989:23).

Authors such as Stuart Hall, therefore, paved the way for a reformation of the cultural approach which sees culture as 'the way, the forms, in which groups "handle" the raw material of their social and material existence' (Clarke et al. 1976:10). In this conceptualisation, culture refers to the codes by which meaning is constructed, conveyed and understood, or as Williams puts it, 'a realised signifying system' (1981:207–9). As Cosgrove and Jackson (1987:96) argue, the latter conceptualisation of landscapes as 'configurations of symbols and signs' implies the use of interpretive approaches rather than morphological techniques. Central to this genre of cultural geography is the 'landscape as text' model, drawing on post-war work in the field of semiotics and linguistics. In a similar way to the conceptualisation of anthropology by authors such as Clifford Geertz, the metaphor of 'text' is used to conceptualise the act of reading landscape as if it were a social document. Geertz (1983) argues that social life involves the interpretation and negotiation of meaning among a group of social actors, but that social scientists introduce another layer of meaning in their writing. As Ringer (1998) argues, although the concept of landscape may be somewhat ambiguous, in the context of tourism it is crucially important. This is due to its emphasis on 'the manner in which the visible structure of a place expresses the emotional attachments held by both its residents and visitors, as well as the means by which it is imagined, produced, contested, and enforced' (Ringer 1998:6).

Landscapes and Representations as Text

One of the most significant readers of landscape, and a major influence on the new cultural geography, is Barthes. In one of the first cultural studies directly referring to tourism, 'The Blue Guide' (1986), he evaluates the Alps and parts of Spain as represented in the Hachett World Travel Guides. This work is particularly notable for its illustration of the process through which meanings become buried under layers of 'ideological sediment'. Central to this view of culture is the belief that social reality is composed of many signifying systems, of which the landscape is one. Myth is also important, as it involves the appropriation of objects suitable for communication, including landscape and various representations.

In 'The Blue Guide', Barthes argues that the travel guide acts as 'an agent of blindness', focusing the traveller's mind on a selected range of landscape features, and replacing inhabitants with 'ideal types'. In this work, and essays such as 'The Eiffel Tower' (Barthes 1984), he refuses to accept landscape or culture as natural or neutral, showing how myths appear to depoliticise the world. His work pays relatively little attention to social processes, however, and there has been some concern over his attempts to contrast representations with 'reality'.

The allure of the poststructural approach is perhaps better illustrated with Barthes' later work, which concentrated more on the text, and the power associated with it. In *Empire of Signs* (1987) he argues that landscape is a text which employs an endless chain of metaphors. Actors are seen as writing their own 'landscape poetry' as they interact with one another and the landscape, this social interaction termed 'erotic discourse'. Although Barthes has been inspirational to contemporary cultural geographers, there has been a subsequent attempt to combine literary theory with social theory, changing the emphasis towards social relations. As Duncan and Duncan (1988:117) argue, literary theory provides ways of examining the text-like quality of landscapes, and the ways in which they are transformations of ideologies.

Literary theory also provides theories of reading and authorship which can shed light on the ways in which landscapes are incorporated into social processes. According to Ringer (1998:6), 'tourism is essentially about the creation and reconstruction of geographic landscapes as distinctive tourist destinations through manipulations of history and culture'. As Shurmer-Smith and Hannam (1994:13) argue, 'places do not exist in a sense other than culturally ... places then have no objective reality, only intersubjective ones'. According to the new cultural geography: 'space, place and landscape – including landscapes of leisure and tourism – are not fixed but are in a constant state of transition as a result of continuous, dialectical struggles of power and resistance among and between the diversity of landscape providers, users, and mediators' (Aitcheson cited in Pritchard and Morgan 2001). In the textual model, which is fundamental to cultural studies, text is taken to mean not merely print on a page, but a range of cultural productions such as paintings, maps, landscapes and even social, economic and political institutions. Consistent with the postmodern view, these are seen as constituting reality, rather than mimicking it (Cloke et al. 1991).

Such practices of significations are intertextual, in the sense that they embody a range of other cultural texts. Significantly, as Riccoeur (1971) argues, texts often have an importance beyond the context in which they were originally written. Social events, festivals, institutions, as well as literary texts, are interpreted and reinterpreted as circumstances change. Both literary texts and cultural texts have meaning and consequences unintended by their author, with the text effectively escaping its author (Cloke et al. 1991). The meaning of texts is unstable, as it is subject to a wide range of interpretations by various readers. As the text becomes detached from its original authorial intentions, the social, psychological, and material consequences of landscape are closely related to the various possible readings.

Analysing Texts

Semiotics, the basis of much cultural analysis, is concerned with the mechanics of how language uses signs to produce meaning. As Echtner (1999) illustrates, semiotic analysis has considerable potential in the field of tourism research. Cultural objects and practices are believed to convey meaning in the form of signs, and these signs can be read by the researcher (Manning 1997). As Gale (1996) argues, semiotics was effectively pioneered by de Saussure, in his *Course in General Linguistics* (1966). According to de Saussure, the sign consists of two components, the signifier and the signified. While signifiers are the expressions carrying a message, the signified is the concept that it represents. The relationship between signifier and signified is determined within a particular culture by language. In the context of urban tourism, it is possible, for example, to identify signifiers within the brochure images of a destination. The signifiers may include groups of visitors, heritage attractions, street performers, cafe terraces, food, drink and water sports. The signifieds may relate to a high-quality lifestyle, an upmarket destination, a thriving yet historical area and plentiful leisure opportunities. Accordingly, the researcher may then explore the ideology behind the signifieds.

As Echtner (1999) demonstrates, semiotics has considerable potential in understanding the meaning of tourism representations. The study of systems of signs is useful for analysing the meaning within a wide range of representations of urban tourist destinations. Drawing upon de Saussure, researchers may focus on language, and particularly the relationship between particular patterns of words (Echtner 1999:48). As the sign is conceptualised as the relationship between a signifier (the word itself), and the signified (a concept), it is possible for researchers to analyse the meaning created in texts. A more socially orientated genre of semiotics, however, was inspired by Peirce (1931). As Echtner (1999:48) notes, Peirce introduced the 'interpretant', conceptualising the 'semiotic triangle'. The semiotic triangle conceptualised the way in which meaning is created through a triadic relationship. This includes the sign and the designatum, which is the concept signified. The triangle also includes the interpretant, or one interpreting the sign. The system of signification can only be understood, therefore, by examining all of the possible relationships between the points of the triangle. Peirce also differentiates between three different types of sign (Echtner 1999:48). An icon resembles an object, such as a postcard or a map of an urban tourist destination. An index has a causal relationship to its designatum, such as a suntan. A symbol relies on an arbitrary social agreement, understood within a particular culture. Echtner (1999:49) provides the example of the Statue of Liberty, signifying freedom and the 'American dream'.

Although Peirce was an early pioneer of semiotic analysis (see Sless 1986), Barthes (1972) developed a particularly useful distinction between the denotative and connotative function of the sign. Whilst denotation is the simple or literal description of signs, connotation allows the sign to be interpreted in terms of social, political and ideological processes. In the case of urban tourism, for example, it is common for promotional material to use connotations aimed at challenging the negative stereotypes developed during times of industrial and economic decline. The approach has inspired researchers such as Gottdiener (1995), who are eager to develop a socio-semiotics, capable of linking symbolic processes to the material world.

The potential of semiotics in the analysis of tourism has been noted by authors such as Urry (1990a) and Culler (1981), who point out that all tourists are, in effect, amateur semioticians, eagerly consuming the representations and landscapes of contemporary tourism. According to Rojek and Urry (1997:8), semiotic skill involves the 'ability to move forwards and backwards between diverse texts, film, photographs, landscape, townscape and models, so as to "decode" information'. Ringer (1998:8) argues that landscapes of tourism are 'articulated and made visible though the expression and acquisition of experiences'. As Culler notes, 'all over the world the unsung armies of semioticians, the tourists, are fanning out in search of the signs of frenchness, typical Italian behaviour, exemplary Oriental scenes...' (1981:127).

There have been several contributions within the tourism literature aimed at advancing the method of cultural analysis in the context of tourism. Approaches to textual interpretation have been explored, particularly through semiotics (Adler 1989; Evans-Pritchard 1989). In a special edition of *Annals of Tourism Research*, for example, MacCannell (1989) introduces a collection of articles advocating the use of semiotics, claiming that semiotics offers hope in rectifying a major fault in tourism research. In a departure from his early work, he criticises both the assumption in tourism research that culture is homogeneous and attempts to explain differences as 'individual and personality differences'. Bennett's analysis of Blackpool Pleasure Beach (1983), and Albers and James' (1988) analysis of postcards are noteworthy examples of the technique. Many of the contributions in the volume, however, are again concerned with defining the relationship between host and guest, at the expense of more original insights.

In poststructural work there is an effort to 'go beyond linguistic and literary theory in order to deal with the socio-historical processes through which meaning arises' (Duncan and Duncan 1988:118). This involves questioning the naturalisation of meaning, and any claim by academics of deciphering the true and authentic meaning. Texts are conceptualised as a web of complex and unstable meanings, and this is considered to be the key to the application of the textual metaphor to landscape. The potential of the textual metaphor in place consumption studies, and a convergence with phenomenological approaches, is revealed in Eagleton's view of reading, in which

> our initial expectations generate a frame of reference within which to interpret what comes next, but what comes next may retrospectively transform our original understanding, highlighting some features of it and backgrounding others...each sentence opens up a new horizon which is confirmed, challenged, or undermined by the next [Eagleton 1983:77].

According to this conceptualisation, texts have 'backgrounds' and 'foregrounds', which appear as 'alternative layers of meaning between which we are constantly moving' (Eagleton 1983:77–78). The texts of tourism can be analysed in terms of linguistic characteristics, such as the use of cliche, understood as overworked and overfamiliar phrases. Voase (2000), for example, evaluates the use of cliche in travel journalism. Voase concludes that the travel journalist uses cliches in order to assume the advance agreement of the reader, without the possibility of them challenging the author's assertion. It is also significant that the tourist plays a major role in 'self-authoring' the tourism product, through projecting their expectations and experiences onto the deliberately bland text. Texts, therefore, are both the product of the society which creates them and the result of the intertextual creations of the reader.

Discourse

It is possible to use the textual metaphor on a larger, more open-ended basis, referring to discourse (Cloke et al. 1991). Discourse is understood as a framework which contains sets of concepts, narratives, signs and ideologies, underlying social action (Barnes and Duncan 1992). A discourse is seen as constituting the limits within which ideas and practices are seen to be natural, although they are always open to negotiation and contest. It is, therefore, through the medium of discourse that power relations are communicated and resisted. In the context of tourism, for example, it is possible to identify a discourse which represents the people of Africa, South America and Eastern Europe as primitive and static (Morgan and Pritchard 1998:37). Closer to home, an anti-Welsh discourse represents the Welsh as antiquated, primitive and untalented (ibid.:153).

Discourses, and the 'truth' they supposedly represent, are seen to vary between different cultural groups, classes, genders and other interest groups. Different groups may generally support the hegemonic discourse, or there may be open clashes between different groups. In Wales, for example, whilst the London-based national press is argued to have been instrumental in an anti-Welsh discourse, the Welsh Language Board, and the Wales Tourist Board have worked to foster a positive cultural identity (Morgan and Pritchard 1998:153). Foucault (1967) shows how representations themselves are a form of power: discourses have a 'naturalising' power whereby certain types of knowledge become 'common sense' or scientific fact. Foucault (1967) argues that it is the association of discourse with institutions which legitimises the 'truths' they produce. The contemporary emphasis on travel writing as a form of tourism promotion is an indication of the significance of national media institutions. These 'truths' have a material basis in institutions and practices, and in this way, discourse exercises great power.

The power of discourse in relation to different groups also depends on the reception of this knowledge. The meaning of a text is unstable, and depends on the range of interpretations of different discourses made by a great variety of readers. If we introduce social relations into this process, however, it is soon apparent that interpreters are subject to the discursive practices of their particular social groups. In other words, they are subject to the practices of different textual communities. A textual community can be defined as 'a group of people who have a common under-standing of a text, spoken or read, and who organise aspects of their lives as the playing of a script' (Stock 1983:294).

Stock (1983) believes that, despite the inherent instability of meanings, textual communities create some consistency or intersubjectivity within particular groups. In the same vein, intertextuality is taken to refer not only to different texts, but also the relationship between texts and social practices. The concept of textual community, in the context of the discussion above, implies that landscapes and a range of repre-sentations are read 'inattentively at a practical or nondiscursive level...inculcating their readers with a set of notions about how society is organised: and their readers may be largely unaware of this' (Duncan and Duncan 1988:123). It follows that if such information is received as if it were neutral and accepted unquestionably, the knowledge reinforces the institutional structure producing the representations. The representations, therefore, are not only linked to the action of the individuals within the textual community, but they are also naturalised and rendered 'innocent' in the process. In tourism, it is clear that consumers act upon the 'truths' of localities encountered through various sources, and in doing so they reinforce such repre-sentations. Studies such as Duncan's evaluation of attitudes and practices in an exclusive suburb of New York (N.Duncan 1986), illustrate the way in which ideologies can become concretised in the landscape and reinforced by readings. They are seen as 'contributing to a structuration process to create and maintain landscapes' (Duncan and Duncan 1988:124).

Whether landscapes exist as a conscious application of written texts or are the unintended consequences of social practices, they tend to naturalise social relations. Many see the cultural geographer's role as denaturalising the landscape. This is most often achieved through an 'attempt to "approximate" and subject to critique the inter-pretations which particular people attach to specific landscapes at particular times in particular places' (Duncan and Duncan 1988:125).

Although somewhat outside of the scope of this book, this endeavour has far-reaching consequences for writing social science itself. Whereas geographical writing has long been influenced by a philosophy of naive realism and considered unproblematic, writing is now seen as extremely problematic. Under the banner 'crisis of repre-sentation', researchers have increasingly recognised that the world is not given, but represented. As there is no reason why academics should be exempt from the textual model, it is impossible to maintain that there is a preinterpreted reality about which to write.

Academic texts draw upon a range of other texts. This intertextuality means that we can no longer privilege one text over another. To authors such as Clifford, this is a 'tectonic' shift, and 'there is no longer any place of overview (mountaintop) from which to map human ways of life' (Clifford 1986:22). Even economics and physical science must be re-evaluated in terms of the ideological influences behind their metaphors. It is clear that, in addition to providing a model of great relevance to urban tourism, cultural approaches raise fundamental questions relating to the whole research process.

Culture and Urban Tourism
The Culture of Tourism

Within the tourism literature, various attempts have been made to define and concept-ualise the culture of tourism. To Cohen tourism is about seeking difference (1972), or escaping from the alienation of everyday life (1979). To MacCannell (1973), tourists are on a sacred journey in search of authenticity, consuming the 'staged authenticity' provided by the tourism industry. MacCannell (1976), in particular, inspired a pro-liferation of work engaging with the theme of authenticity (e.g. Pearce and Moscardo 1985; Littrell et al. 1993). Offering an alternative conceptualisation, Urry (1990a) focuses on the 'tourist gaze' emphasising both the visual consumption of the destination itself, and the consumption of images outside the destination. In conceptualising the 'tourist gaze', Urry adds an important dimension to studies based on authenticity. The reflexive nature of the tourist gaze means that the images created by the tourism industry, together with unofficial organic images, link representations of localities to the first-hand experience of tourists. In this way, a more significant form of 'authen-ticity' concerns whether or not first-hand experience authenticates the images and representations of the destination.

It is encouraging that Urry (1990a:2) urges researchers to evaluate 'the typical contents of the tourist gaze... to make sense of elements of the wider society with which they are contrasted'. Urry maintains that the tourist gaze is socially organised, and the way of looking differs between different social groups. Urry (1990a, 1992, 2001) draws on Foucault (1977), likening 'sight-seeing' at tourist destinations to a form of surveillance. Tourism thus treats local people as if they are 'the mad behind the bars' (Urry 1992:183), and this is an intrusion into local lives. Not only do local people feel under the gaze even when they are not, but authentic experience is denigrated, resulting in the staged authenticity of shows and events produced for the tourists.

The majority of contributions concerned with authenticity, however, foster only universal classifications and typologies. Authors tend to conceptualise authenticity in terms of 'the genuine, the real, and the unique' (Sharpley 1994:130), relying on the researcher's judgment rather than the experiences of tourists. Given the size and diversity of contemporary tourism, there are significant dangers in developing universal conceptualisations. According to Thurot and Thurot (1983:188), MacCannell, who inspired so much tourism research, 'told his readers about a society which had virtually disappeared. Because he lacked an actual picture of tourism, he never discovered the present social reality.'

As Morgan and Pritchard (1998:12) argue, 'there is an undeniable tendency to undervalue the actual experience of tourists in the pursuit of some all-encompassing framework'. Selwyn (1996:6) notes the lack of ethnographic research underpinning typologies and classifications. Urry (1990a, 1992) has also been accused of over-stating the significance of the visual in a rather universal conceptualisation of tourists (see Jokimen 1994). Although tourism researchers devote considerable effort to developing universal *a priori* conceptualisations, relatively little is expended on exploring the culture of actual tourists, in the context of both its production and consumption.

It is significant that the new edition of *The Tourist Gaze* (Urry 2001b) emphasises more the embodiment of tourist experience and culture, rather than merely drawing upon the visual metaphor. The ways in which tourist sites are structured around the visual are still considered important, but Urry also recognises the interaction of different senses in the tourist encounter. Although tourist destinations may be organised around sight, tourists also move around the destination in different ways – sometimes resisting the socially constructed destination. The additions to *The Tourist Gaze* (Urry 2001b) focus particularly on globalising the gaze. Urry argues that globalisation has resulted in reconfigurations of the tourist gaze, for both the mobile bodies of tourists and the hosts. There has therefore been a shift from a more singular gaze in the nineteenth century to numerous discourses, forms and embodiments of the gaze in contemporary times. Mobility is seen as being central to life in general, creating the 'diasporas' of people constantly on the move which contradict simple notions of 'home' and 'away'. Urry argues that an array of developments, in aspects as diverse as technology, academic work and place marketing, are taking tourism from the margins of global order to almost the centre of the world of 'liquid modernity' (Urry 2001b:2).

Landscapes and Representations of Tourism

A relatively early sign of the increased interest in cultural studies amongst tourism researchers is Dann's *The Language of Tourism* (1996a). In an earlier work, Dann (1992) analyses representations of destinations by UK travel writers and tourism promoters. He shows how representations reassure potential consumers that overseas destinations are 'just as civilised as England'. Dann (1996a) argues that the language of tourism is used in a variety of forms of social control. The decisions, experiences and conduct of tourists are therefore regulated by the 'norms, values, prescriptions, and proscriptions' of this language (ibid.:3). Despite applying such concepts to various aspects of the tourist experience, it is interesting that Dann ultimately draws upon Boorstin (1964). Tourists are represented as fairly passive, and the effectiveness of the language of tourism as social control is taken for granted. Although Dann (1996a) increases the accessibility of cultural analysis to tourism students and researchers, the psychologism of the tourism literature is still apparent.

Although the subject of heritage tends to have the effect of polarising episte-mologies and arguments, it is encouraging that cultural geographers are adding to the literature, providing an alternative to the discourse characterised by authors such as Hewison (1987). Addressing themes such as the strengthening of local identity and residents' sense of belonging and the generation of local heritage, authors such as Clifford and King (1993), Cooper (1994), Crow (1994), Rose (1994) and Willems-Braun (1994) go some way towards redressing the balance. The Celtic heritage of Wales is addressed by Gruffudd et al. (1999). The study examines the presentation of Celtic themes at Welsh heritage sites, and shows how such presentations are based upon myth and nostalgia rather than a dynamic view of Welsh culture. In addition to attracting tourists, however, the heritage sites offer visitors the possibility of relating the past to their own identity, and examining their roots. Willems-Braun (1994) directs us along an alternative route to conceptualising and researching fringe festivals, emphasising intersubjective experience. The way in which heritage is a complex amalgam of spatial identity, time, memory and history is illustrated in a study which emphasises 'temporal imagining'.

The contradictory relationships between heritage and national identity have been explored in the context of Ireland (Graham 1994; Innes 1994), Australia (Saunders 1994), Cyprus (Papadajis 1994), and England (Pick 1994). National and regional identity has long been of interest to cultural geographers, and this features in work such as Taylor's study of photography and Englishness, *A Dream of England* (1994). The cultural approach is used by Lafant (1995) to explore representations and identities in the context of international tourism. Representations of developing-world desti-nations are also the focus of studies by Silver (1993) and Mellinger (1994). Women's travel writing has inspired work such as Blunt (1994) and Monicat (1994). The rather questionable distinction between the 'sympathetic traveller' and the 'voyeuristic tourist' is developed in an article by McDowell (1994). A thought-provoking discussion of the rhetorics of 'travel' over 'tourism' in 'the new middle class' is provided by Munt (1994).

The tourist postcard has been analysed by Whittaker (2000), revealing its role as a 'historical text of popular attitudes'. Photographic images of indigenous people captured on postcards serve as a barometer of prevailing thought and ideology. The tourist map also plays an important role in the production of tourism spaces, as demonstrated by Del Casino and Hanna (2000). Tourist maps, tourist spaces and identities are seen as interrelated processes, and the ambiguities of these processes are not apparent if maps are merely conceptualised as products. The novel *Lost Horizon* by James Hilton provides the focus for an intriguing insight into the role of literature in constructing tourism spaces (Cater 2001). The fictitious lamasery of the Shangri-La was so evocative that it entered the English Language, defined as 'an imaginary earthly paradise'. Although it is claimed that the inspiration came from a monastery to the north of Zhongdian, Yunnan, Cater discusses the tendency for international tourism to create 'mis-taken identities'.

Selwyn (1996) edits a comprehensive analysis of the use of tourism images. Addressing both the production and consumption of tourist myths, he explores the ideology underpinning representations. Dann (1996a), for example, addresses the images of tourist brochures, focusing on the relationship between tourists and residents. Edwards (1996) analyses the 'exoticization' of non-Western peoples in postcards, and Meethen (1996) analyses the promotional images of Brighton. One of Selwyn's most useful contributions concerns his conceptualisation of authenticity. He distinguishes between the 'cool authenticity' of objective approaches and the 'hot authenticity' in a more experiential sense. Whilst cool authenticity is concerned with the authenticity of knowledge in relation to the 'real world', hot authenticity is salient to the experiences of place consumers.

In a valuable collection of essays, Urry (1995) uses a variety of contexts to examine the relationship between tourism and the way that localities adopt local, regional and international identities in the process of place consumption. Voase (1999) uses a cultural approach to consider the use of two different metaphors to understand tourism in the historic city of York in northern England. A business metaphor conceptualising the city as a consumable product is contrasted with a cultural perspective emphasising the reading of the urban landscape by tourists. The latter conceptualises the tourist-historic city as 'a multitextual narrative which is used by the tourist as a stage on which to create their own personal drama' (Voase 1999:293). Ringer (1998) also emphasises the social construction of tourist destinations: contributions in the collection range from the 'Cybertourism' analysed by Rojek (ibid.:33), to the landscapes of the Pacific addressed by Hall (ibid.:140). As Ringer (1998:2) argues, the contributions in this volume engage with

> ... a localised, socially constructed environment often overlooked; simultaneously, they address the lack of study on tourist destinations in the cultural landscape work of geographers, who until recently concerned themselves primarily with descriptive studies of movement and the broader utilization of space, rather than the recognition of tourist places.

Place Promotion

Another emergent genre of cultural studies of tourism focuses on promotional imagery and representations. Uncharacteristically, both pioneering work (Burgess 1982) and recent contributions (Morgan and Pritchard 1998), are concerned with urban tourism. As early as 1982, Burgess was concerned with urban images in the context of inward investment. A range of authors appear to have been influenced by the work of Burgess, and a substantial body of literature on the promotion of towns and cities has developed.

Studies focus on attracting inward investment and tourism, including individual case studies (e.g. Burgess and Wood 1988; Watson 1991; Goss 1993; Bramwell and Rawding 1996), edited collections (Ashworth and Voogd 1990; Kearns and Philo 1993) and more theoretical contributions (Urry 1995).

Pritchard and Morgan (2001) present a critical evaluation of tourism representations of Wales. Analysing marketing campaigns of the Wales Tourist Board and Welsh local authorities, they identify both repressive and liberating discourses which explain why the marketing of Wales differs between the UK and overseas markets. Pritchard and Morgan (2001:168) demonstrate how the tourism advertisement becomes a self-fulfilling prophecy, as it 'directs expectations, influences expectations, and thereby provides the preconceived landscape for the tourist to discover'. Using a similar culturally informed approach, the same authors (Morgan and Pritchard 1998) analyse the social construction of black heritage attractions in the US, and reflect upon changing power structures within the country.

Although researchers have largely avoided conducting research to evaluate the reading of tourism texts by place consumers, a notable exception is McGregor (2000). The study examines the dynamic relationship between guide-books and tourists in Tana Toraja, Indonesia. A reliance on a limited number of guide-books has the effect of directing the tourists' gaze towards particular aspects of the landscape, objectifying the exotic 'other'. This dynamic process of reading texts which is so often overlooked, commodifies the Tana Toraja landscape, and socially constructs the destination itself. Although not concerned directly with tourist readings, D'Arcus (2000) takes up a similar theme. The study of Gallup, New Mexico, examines the regional discourse inherent in a place to create a National Indian Memorial Park. He shows how the discourse representing the region as a 'Land of Enchantment' is challenged by American Indian activists. A study more specific to urban tourism is Stevenson's (1999) examination of the discourse used to promote the regional city of Newcastle, Australia. The discourse, developed in the context of deindustrialisation, is concerned with selling the 'ideal' of redevelopment of the inner city to local residents. This discourse of images and identities is inherent to the process of urban redevelopment, yet it is also contested and negotiated by local residents who experience the city in their everyday lives.

Recent years have also seen human geographers engaging with representations of advertising. This is despite the fact that, as Gregson (1995:137) puts it, 'advertising texts differ so markedly from the Gainsboroughs and Constables so beloved of cultural geographers'. The advertising industry itself has been examined, including the use of space by television advertising companies (Clarke and Bradford 1989). Sack (1988) devotes considerable attention to advertising imagery, including the analysis of a range of advertisements. One of the few authors to consider the audience of representations, Jackson reminds geographers of the folly of purely academic readings of landscapes and representations (Jackson 1994; Jackson and Taylor 1996). Jackson and Taylor (1996) argue that it is necessary to analyse both the content of advertising messages and their reception by groups of consumers.

The Culture of Consumption

Since the beginning of the 1990s, human geographers and sociologists have been concerned with issues of consumption, exemplified by texts such as Clarke (1991), Knox (1991) and Miller (1996). Consumption is also a dominant theme in some of the broader discussions of economic and social change, such as Glennie and Thrift (1992) and Wrigley and Lowe (1995). A growing interest in consumption has been apparent as early as the late 1980s, with international conferences devoted to the field. One such event, Creation of Myth, Invention and Tradition in America, included contributions on the planning profession (Rees 1988), built form (Domash 1988) and representations of the American city (Krim 1988; Letendre 1988; Shapiro 1988).

Although cultural geography has tended to be fairly retrospective, attention has increasingly turned to the emergence of new urban landscapes and representations. The Pacific Rim, the sunbelts of the US and post-industrial cities in Europe have all attracted attention. These newly created consumption spaces feature heavily in Ley's work (1987, 1989; Ley and Olds 1988), and Mill's (1988) study of a new class of gentrifiers named 'lifestylers'. The theatrical nature of the consumer's world has emerged as a particularly attractive area of cultural research since it was introduced by authors such as Sack (1988).

Crang also provides an innovative and amusing personal account of working in Smokey Joe's restaurant whilst completing his doctorate, illustrating how consumption and the service sector blurs the boundaries between the social, the cultural and the economic (Crang P. 1994). A similar (although less personal) approach is used by M. Smith (1996) in an analysis of Starbuck's coffee bars. This study explores the local and global relationships involved in consuming the product. Recent cultural studies of consumption have taken a more political perspective, sensitive to inequalities and labour processes (Crewe 2000) or the embodiment of consumption (e.g. Probyn 1999; Valentine 1997). Whilst embodiment is discussed below, work relevant to urban tourism tends to focus on spaces of consumption. Although this was a preoccupation throughout the 1990s, recent work includes studies on the city as a space for the consumption of fashion (Gilbert 2000) and the fetishism of the shopping mall through magic, memory and mystique (e.g. Backes 1997).

Landscapes of Consumption

Cultural studies have often drawn upon Foucault's *Discipline and Punish* (1977) concerned largely with morals, control and exclusion. Foucault's later work (1980), however, has generated interest in the field of leisure and consumption. This includes a report on contemporary leisure landscapes (Clarke and Purves 1994), which emphasises conflict and social tensions between different groups of place consumers. Foucault's concept of 'Heterotopia' (1980, 1986), understood as a heterogeneous site which juxtaposes many incompatible places, has also been influential and will be examined later in the chapter. The concept inspired a proliferation of studies of the shopping mall, which has been read as a new representation of the spatial and as the ultimate postmodern consumption site.

Authors such as Shields (1989, 1992), Hopkins (1990, 1991) and Goss (1993) have drawn upon Foucault to understand the combinations of retail and leisure activities and their sense of utopia and fantasy. The attention lavished upon the shopping mall is partly due to its apparent appropriation of representations of distant places, and the sense in which they replace 'real' places. It would seem that the epitome of these postmodern sites has been West Edmonton Mall, Canada, inspiring work by Hopkins (1990), Shields (1989), Fairburn (1991), Butler (1991) and Jackson and Johnson (1991). The few attempts to evaluate consumers of shopping malls tend to draw upon Benjamin's '*flâneur*' (Benjamin 1979), discussed in more detail below. This approach to researching place consumption advocates a 'prowling' observation of the everyday life of the city from street level. Although focusing on everyday experience, the voyeuristic nature of the approach has been criticised by feminist writers.

The concept of 'hyperreality' (Eco 1986), and Baudrillard's 'simulation' (1983), have been influential in emphasising the superficiality of postmodern consumption, and the erosion of the distinction between the real and the imaginary. Authors such as Baudrillard (1983), Jameson (1984) and Sorkin (1992) provide an alternative to 'heterotopia', emphasising the erosion of public space in Disney-style simulations. According to Sorkin's concept of 'ageographia' (1992), the real social order of the city is concealed by the simulation of an image-driven postmodern culture. Lees (1997) applies the contrasting concepts of heterotopia and ageographia to explore Vancouver's new public library. She concludes that elements of both are apparent, although the library may move further towards the ageographia model in the future.

Performativity

An insight into (or rather an encounter with) operationalising the concepts of embodiment is provided by Crouch (2000a). Crouch argues that tourism is something that people 'do', in terms of actively practising something. This approach to cultural analysis, which is examined in more detail later in the chapter, has been demonstrated by only a small minority of tourism researchers. Until recently, it has mainly been confined to researchers concerned with the interplay between sexuality and tourism, and the creation of gay city spaces (Aitcheson 1999). A noteworthy example is Pritchard et al. (1998), which analyses the Canal Street gay village in Manchester, northern England. Crouch (2000a) makes an important point concerning the need to treat tourism as a cultural process, rather than a product.

Adler (1989) has been influential in conceptualising tourism as performance, describing tourism as 'performance art'. In particular, she draws attention to the ways in which guide-books 'served as a means of preparation, aid, documentation, and

5.1: Performativity of urban tourism in Sydney. Courtesy of Tourism New South Wales.

vicarious participation' (Adler 1989:67–68). Feminist theory has inspired approaches concerned more with the encounters and interaction of urban tourists. Wearing and Wearing (1996) and Grosz (1995), for example, draw upon the concept of 'chora' – a place where people interact and are reflexive. Arguing that tourism is an important means by which people are reflexive – making sense of their lives – Crouch (2000a) presents a project in northeast England which develops an alternative narrative, writing a heritage trail which draws upon 'groups of people and the places they know and value' (ibid.:97). In a rare example of cultural research concerned with everyday experience and the reading of the landscape by place consumers, Crouch elicits intriguing feelings and emotions. These everyday readings of the rural landscape contrast with the official and academic language of ecology and sustainability.

A convincing analysis of the perfomativity of urban tourism is provided by Edensor (2000), who points out that too much tourism research has been concerned with over-generalisation, functionalism, defining tourism *per se* and developing tourist typologies. He then focuses on the stages on which tourism is performed, drawing on research carried out at the Taj Mahal in India. Concentrating particularly on modes of walking, he demonstrates 'the various dispositions and conventions which people bring to particular contexts' (Edensor 2000:341). He argues that, in contrast to tourist typologies, urban tourists fulfil a variety of roles. One role identified is as part of disciplined rituals, ranging from reading the Quranic text inscribed on buildings, to participating in guided tours. Conversely, tourists were observed participating in partly improvised performances, displaying an almost ironic approach to taking photographs and buying souvenirs. Furthermore, these roles conform to cultural norms, exemplified by a degree of the criticism of the behaviour other nationalities. Edensor (2000:341) cites a British tourist who comments 'I think the Indians are really crap tourists. They just don't know how to be tourists, rushing around, talking all the time and never stopping to look at anything – even here at the Taj Mahal'. Edensor argues, therefore, that the culture of urban tourism is as much about the tourist's everyday life at home, as it is about the destination itself.

A groundbreaking book on the performativity of tourism is *Destination Culture* (Kirshenblatt-Gimblett 1998). Not only is it argued that tourism provides an important means for understanding society past and present, but a convincing case is made for the analysis of tourism through performance studies. Criticising the dominance of visual approaches to tourism culture, the book analyses a wide range of tourist destinations and 'attractions', from exhibitions of Jewish history to an analysis of 'kitsch'. Recent examples of the approach include a study of the performative nature of Goathland, a destination which is the filming location for the Yorkshire Television series *Heartbeat* (Mordue 2001).

M. Crang (1997) provides a refreshing approach to addressing the tourist gaze – through the photographs of tourists. Crang is one of the few researchers interested in the touristic practices by which representations are simultaneously produced and consumed. This is a useful alternative to the numerous studies which merely analyse representations themselves. Crang advocates the use of phenomenological approaches, in order to capture 'the future perfect experience' (ibid.:359), embodied in social relations. As Crang points out, 'in this sense images are not so much counterposed to reality as a route through which worlds are created' (ibid.:362). The theoretical concepts used in studies of place consumption and the various methods of cultural analysis are considered in more detail below.

Urban Culture
Understanding Urban Culture

The 'cultural turn' profoundly affects the way the city is conceptualised and researched. Recent years have seen an intensification of debate concerning the postmodern aesthetic, the socio-economic aspects of postmodernity and the postmodern attitude as a paradigm of knowledge. Images and representations of the city are central to the majority of discussions of postmodernism and place consumption.

In terms of aesthetics, postmodernism has been linked to the rise of reproductive media such as photography and global electronic communications systems (Bishop 1992:5). It has been argued that there has been a fragmentation of time and space and, in effect, reality has been transformed into images (e.g. Featherstone 1991; Sack 1988). This image-making process is argued to occur in numerous spheres, with the appropriation of a profusion of styles from earlier periods. The creation of this pastiche, from art to academic disciplines, has even been represented as a change from consuming beliefs to endlessly consuming images. Sontag (1978:24), for example, argues that 'industrial societies turn their citizens into image junkies; it is the most irresistible form of mental pollution'. Images have therefore been linked to fragment-ation, irrationalism and even schizophrenia (Foster 1983).

As discussed in chapter three, several influential materialist writers have taken up the issue of urban culture, seeking to locate it firmly within the global economic process of flexible accumulation. Harvey emphasises a bewildering collection of signs and images in *The Condition of Postmodernity* (1989a:3), drawing upon Raban's *Soft City* (1974). Emphasising a mistrust of the artificial and ephemeral nature of urban life, Jameson uses an analysis of the Bonaventure Hotel in Los Angeles to conclude his account of the postmodern condition. Reading architectural peculiarities such as unmarked entrances and reflective exteriors as the 'latest mutation in space... transcending the ability of the human body to locate itself...', Jameson addresses the 'imaginary city' (1991:45).

Somewhat ironic considering his obsession with appropriation, however, Harvey is accused of flattening the nuances of Raban's account to set the scene for his own meta-theory (Patton 1995:115). Whilst Harvey's city is merely a reflection of a deeper reality, Raban does not believe in a distinction between the real and the imaginary. Instead of concentrating on the accumulation of capital, *Soft City* can be read as emphasising the changing relationships between people. If the contemporary city is a community of people who are strangers, it is because members of that community increasingly rely on fragments of knowledge, images and stereotypes. These cues are socially conditioned, and there is an intersubjective nature to this process. If 'in cities people are given to acting, putting on a show of themselves' (Raban 1974:37), not only is there a culture of theatricality, but there is a constant striving for identity. As Eco (1986) demonstrates, the boundary between the sign and reality has been dissolved. According to Baudrillard (1983:83), the 'contradictory process of true and false, of real and the imaginary, is abolished'. This dissolution of the real and imaginary, subject and object, in the deconstructive sense, plays a crucial role in the experience of urban tourism.

In both materialist and behaviouralist accounts of place consumption, the discovery (rather than construction) of a reality is only possible by denying the existence of true subjectivity. This involves rejecting other viewpoints, dismissing the discursive nature of objects, and elevating oneself to a privileged and unconflicted place (Deutsche 1991:7). Harvey, for example, reveals that he prefers to climb to the highest point in a city and look down at 'the city as a whole' (Harvey 1989b:1). The cultural approach, however, has profound implications for how researchers concept-ualise the real and the imagined in the context of urban tourism.

Views of the City

The visual metaphor is well developed within cultural studies of tourism, exemplified by Urry (1990a). Of inspiration to contemporary cultural geography, de Certeau (1988:92) believes that disembodied viewpoints produce 'imaginary totalisations' and a 'fiction of knowledge'. According to de Certeau, imagination and knowledge are far from neutral, always having a social function. Using the example of the CN Tower in Toronto, de Certeau considers the way the planner's objectifying 'bird's eye' view leaves behind the realities of everyday life in the city. It is, therefore, when 'Icarus can ignore the tricks of Daedalus in his shifting and endless labyrinths' that the 'fiction of knowledge' is created (de Certeau 1988:122).

As Shields (1996:229) argues, 'a shroud of representations stands between us and even the concrete objects which are the elements of the city'. Everyday life involves the conception and reception of numerous different representations, although some are accepted as more official and therefore more realistic than others. The everyday 'noise' of difference, which is so problematic to both materialists and behaviouralists, is argued to be the very lifeblood of the city. To rid the city of this is to 'interdict the possibility of a living and "mythical" practice of the city', leaving '... its inhabitants only the scraps of programming produced by the power of the other and altered by the event' (de Certeau 1988:203).

Representations of localities can actually replace the locality so that one's social interaction is more often than not mediated through signs. Shields (1991) develops a useful account of material and imaginary places, using the phrase 'social spatial-isation'. He shows how places become accepted as suitable for particular activities and practices, acquiring 'connotations and symbolic meanings' (ibid.:60). Places are therefore labelled by their place images, and the constancy of place images can lead to the formation of 'place myths' (ibid.:61). In this way, cities can become inseperable from the images created by urban tourism. The mere mention of Monte-Carlo, Las Vegas or New York conjures up a place myth which has been produced and repro-duced in order to sell the city to place consumers.

Authors such as de Certeau (1988) and Benjamin (1979) provide inspiration to cultural researchers concerned with exposing the treachery of representations accepted as neutral. Shields comments that the non-resemblance of representations to everyday experience is rarely considered, due to the 'bustle of everyday activities – including the pressurised atmosphere of city councils' (Shields 1996:229). Plans of cities, for example replace the complex interactions and social processes, 'freezing' them and removing differences and idiosyncrasies. The city itself as a physical entity can be treated as a representation of the society which constructed it; yet there are also 'unofficial texts' (Shields 1996:231) linked to myths, self-identity and typical roles. These are bound up with the landscape of the city, and with power in the form of domination and repression, but certainly not in any universal or deterministic way.

The notion of memory as embodied is a theme in the work of Bachelard (1964). The house, for example was used to show how memory is inherently spatial. Spaces are not merely physical, but are imbued with meaning and memory. The embodied and spatial nature of memory is largely consistent with the emphasis on space in the formation of identity and stereotypical roles. Increasingly, cultural researchers are recognising the need for more sophisticated conceptualisations of place image. As Urry comments, 'phenomenology is concerned with experiencing image in its reverberations' (Urry 1995:27).

Hyperreality

Disneyland has been used as the ultimate example of 'hyperreality' by Eco (1986), and 'simulation' by Baudrillard (1983). Eco (1986) has been inspirational to authors concerned with the use of fantasy and imagination to construct a place which is actually more 'real' than 'authentic' places. In Disneyland, 'the lines between the real and the fake are systematically blurred' (Fjellman 1992:225). Following Baudrillard (1983), Marin (1984:240) states that the 'distorted and fantasmatic representations of daily life' obscure the 'violence and exploitation' used to acquire such values. Despite the contrived origins of Disneyland, E.Cohen (1995) suggests that it now has deep structural meaning within American culture.

Although tourism has been represented as a quest for authenticity (Krippendorf 1984; MacCannell 1989), tourist destinations increasingly rely upon dramatically inauthentic attractions. Venturi et al. (1972 cited in Rojek and Urry 1997:11) demonstrates how Las Vegas creates the ultimate hyperreality: the Las Vegas landscape mixes replicas of Egyptian temples, reconstructions of the Wild West and Victorian England. Hyperreality is also an important feature of heritage sites such as Wigan Pier (see case study 3.1), which recreate various cultures, places and histories.

Defined as 'the unique manifestation of distance' (Benjamin 1983:148), aura denotes 'remote' objects which inspire awe, compliance and identity amongst particular social groups. Auratic objects can be people, such as the Pope or George Washington. Often they are landmarks such as the Eiffel Tower, the Statue of Liberty or Sydney Opera House. Arguing that their auratic status is due to the role of the imagination and the 'internal journey' that people make, Benjamin argues that technology and consumerism diminishes this aura. Replicas of the Acropolis in shopping malls, Eiffel Tower keyrings and virtual tours on the Internet all reduce the aura of urban tourist attractions. As Rojek (1997) argues, there is a corruption of the hierarchical structure determining the authority of the object. It can then seem as if the representation is 'closer to everyday life than the original object' (Rojek 1997:59). Ritzer and Liska (1997) use the term 'McDisneyization' to describe the search for the inauthentic – the perfect simulation. They argue that the closer that life in the destination resembles 'play', the greater the attraction to tourists. They point out that there is a form of inflation occurring, whereby everyday places of consumption at home such as restaurants and shopping malls also recreate Mediterranean villages, Mexican saloons and the Taj Mahal. This leads to the tourism industry in the places

5.2: The 'hyperreal' Las Vegas landscape. Courtesy of Las Vegas New Bureau.

represented striving to attract tourists by creating even more contrived environments. However, Morgan and Pritchard (1998:26) point out that while Main Street, Disneyland may be the epitome of 'inauthenticity', to place consumers it is just as real as any American street.

The Flâneur

Benjamin (1979) has been influential to cultural geographers in his attempt to introduce ethnographic approaches, getting back to the everyday level of the street. The wandering, prowling approach of the *flâneur*, although not exactly popular with feminist writers, draws attention to the ways in which different groups of people read the city. This theme, taken up by Buck-Morss (1989), reveals the city as 'the repository of people's memories and of the past' and 'a receptacle of cultural symbols' (Urry 1995:24). The memories embedded in buildings, for example, can have both a significance very different from that intended by the architect, and form part of a collective myth which is socially conditioned.

In his work on the nineteenth-century city, Benjamin (1989) classifies people according to their spatial activities, including groups as diverse as people wearing sandwich boards, and prostitutes. He writes of the experience of wandering through shopping arcades, collecting objects, being a tourist, taking photographs and even using hashish. He concentrates particularly on the shopping arcades of Paris, pointing out that they are an important attraction to foreign tourists. He is primarily interested, however, in revealing 'the psychology of consumer culture' (Rojek 1997:36). Benjamin emphasises the ideal-typical figures on which people based their own identity and action. Through his flaneurial approach, he seeks to uncover the impulses, aspirations and meanings motivating social interaction. Benjamin's approach also has potential in understanding groups of tourists based on their experience of the locality, rather than universal and *a priori* classifications.

In addition to aura, Benjamin (1979, 1986) has developed a number of concepts and metaphors that have been taken up by cultural researchers. A more general contribution has been the metaphor of the labyrinth to describe modern culture – multi-layered, with numerous turnings and false perspectives, always changing and never ending (Rojek 1997). The term 'phantasmagoria' has also been influential, meaning a combination of real and imaginary experiences which defy the existence of a fixed and stable reality. The Paris arcades are thus represented simultaneously as simulated places of escape from industrial society and places of seduction and commodification. Benjamin's analysis of the arcades revealed how they taught the consumer to associate consumption with pleasure, a crucial aspect of contemporary urban tourism.

Despite some sensitive insights into the culture of the city, Benjamin has been criticised by feminist writers for the male bias in his conceptualisation of the *flâneur*. As Wolff (cited in Wearing and Wearing 1996:232) points out, 'there is no question of inventing the Flaneuse...impossible by the sexual divisions of the nineteenth century'. The *flâneur*, taking pleasure in possessing the city, is seen by many feminist writers as embodying the 'male gaze', representing men's 'visual voyeuristic mastery over women' (Wilson cited in Wearing and Wearing 1996:233). Researchers such as Wearing and Wearing (1996) and Grosz (1995) therefore suggest alternative concepts such as 'chora'. Defined as 'a space between being and becoming', in urban tourism chora are places where interaction with other tourists and the hosts takes place. This process (rather than product) allows tourists as chorasters to construct their own meanings and identities rather than objectifying a destination through their gaze.

Difference

Lyotard's influential challenge to meta-theories in his discussion of postmodern epistemologies advances a model based on difference (Lyotard 1984). It is argued that consensus is accepted, not in any universal way, but in terms of a local consensus limited in space and time. Lyotard borrows from Wittgenstein (1968) in emphasising language games. Because of the variations in these language games and their rules, there cannot be any meta-prescriptions or universal rules. This 'hetero-morphy' of language games cannot be accommodated or smothered under a grand materialist (or any other) theory.

Derrida's theory of deconstruction is particularly useful for conceptualising the way that official and rational representations dismiss contradictory phenomena as anomalies (Derrida 1978). This has obvious applications in the study of both induced and organic representations of tourist destinations. As Spivac comments, '… we exclude the possibility of the existence of things so radically different that they can't be explained within our system of rational thought' (Spivac, 1990:80). As Shields (1996) argues, this implies devoting attention to dualisms such as urban–rural, public–private, and developed–undeveloped. Difference refers to the way in which these constructs are generated and defined. It is argued that it is necessary to examine the systems which underpin such definitions. It would seem that such ideas have important implications for both the language of place marketing and research into the images and experiences of tourists.

Derrida (1978) also influences feminist work questioning public–private dis-tinctions (e.g. Wilson 1991; Stansell 1986), and 'postcolonial' work focusing on racial difference (e.g. Spivak 1987; Said 1991). A useful line of enquiry therefore is to ask how and through what institutions language becomes accepted as neutral. This implies a concern for alternative representations of the city, and how they frame the possi-bilities for action within a particular textual community (see Shields 1991). The emphasis on difference in terms of texts alone would appear to encourage a rather partial treatment of urban culture, actually directing attention away from the spatial context which is so crucial to the meaning of such differences (see Werlen 1993). Derrida's theory of difference, however, has been influential in cultural studies of the city due to its emphasis on questioning hegemonic 'world-view' representations.

Foucault, Truth and Power

Cultural studies of cities have been heavily influenced by the work of Foucault (e.g. 1986, 1979), which also provides useful insights into urban tourism. In particular, we are encouraged to treat the image not as indicative of a deeper reality, but as being substantive and constitutive in itself. Not only are images central to contemporary culture, but they are closely bound up with the distribution of power in society. In relation to landscape, too, Foucault has been influential in a conceptualisation emphasising meaning rather than quantifiable physical matter. In arguing that the representation should be considered as constituting reality rather than reflecting it, the notion of truth itself is challenged (Foucault 1986:60). Foucault was particularly concerned with 'seeing historically how effects of truth are produced within discourses which in themselves are neither true nor false' (Foucault 1986:60).

The Foucaultian conceptualisation of power emphasises how it 'produces reality … produces domains of objects and rituals of truth' (Foucault 1979:194). Power, therefore, can be enabling and positive, despite the disproportionate attention generated by *Discipline and Punish* (see Philo 1989; Driver 1985a, 1985b; Dear 1981). The potential of such an approach to power, not unlike Deleuze and Guattari's notion of desire (1983), lies particularly in linking power to knowledge, as 'relations of power are not static...they are matrices of transformations' (Foucault 1981:99). Truth is conceptualised as power, linked in a 'circular relation with systems of power which produce and sustain it, and to effects of power which it induces and which extends it' (Foucault 1986:74). Crucial in this process are the fine capillaries of power, focusing attention on the systems of transmission and the geometry. Indirectly, Foucault offers alternative insights into researching images of localities. Instead of treating images as distortions of reality, researchers are encouraged to uncover the politics, ideologies and structure behind particular representations.

This reading of Foucault draws upon *The Archaeology of Knowledge* (1972) and *Death and the Labyrinth* (1986a), particularly his discussion of Roussel's writing, to emphasise an existential quality in which there is no deeper truth beyond existence, nor a hierarchy of objects or qualities. This again draws attention to 'the local, changing rules' (Dreyfus and Rabinow 1982:55) in a particular locality and in relation to a particular phenomenon. This implies a methodology which avoids '*a priori* constructs not rooted in the empirical materials at hand' (Philo 1992:150). Linked to Foucault's concepts of truth and history, this approach also convincingly challenges the discourse dismissing heritage as 'bogus history' (Hewison 1987:144).

Urban Heterotopia

As Philo (1992) argues, a major contribution of Foucault lies in him seeing only spaces of dispersion: 'spaces where things proliferate in a jumbled up manner on the same "level" as one another – one where advanced capitalism and the toy rabbit beating a drum no longer exist in any hierarchical relation of the one being considered most important or fundamental than the other' (Philo, 1992:139). Perhaps Foucault's most explicit engagement with space has resulted in a range of studies developing and drawing on the concept of 'heterotopia'. Theorists have drawn upon a lecture entitled 'Of Other Spaces' (1986) to discuss socially constructed 'external' sites which have a function which is different to all others. First mentioned briefly in *The Order of Things* (1980b), heterotopia have important methodological implications in terms of focusing on the local in order to understand the workings of society's institutions. Foucault defines heterotopia as 'a set of relations...capable of juxtaposing in a real place several spaces, several sites that are in themselves incompatible' (Foucault 1986: 23–25). Drawing on phenomenology, Foucault emphasises the experience of places which are collections of several spatio-temporal sites and the relations between them. Supplying a diverse range of examples, including brothels, churches, hotel rooms, museums, asylums and Scandinavian saunas, *Of Other Spaces* is largely concerned with imaginary places. This is not to say that they do not have a concrete existence, but that they add up to more than the sum of the parts in terms of meaning. The Trafford Centre near Manchester, northwest England, serves as a useful example. Despite its function as a large, popular shopping centre, the landscape created draws upon references to a wide range of cultures and places, ranging from Ancient Greece to the Orient. In heterotopia, real existing sites are 'simultaneously represented, contested, and inverted' (ibid.:24). Heterotopia change with time according to the 'synchrony of the culture' (ibid.:25), and they often incorporate different slices of time, appearing to both abolish and preserve time.

It is apparent that the notion of 'other places' – a plethora of fragmented and contradictory representations – has had a pragmatic influence on researchers concerned with particular landscapes (e.g. Shields 1989). Authors such as Soja (1989), however, draw upon such ideas in a more fundamental effort to reassert space into social theory. A useful illustration of the contradictory nature of such places, and the way in which they challenge all notions of universal truth, reality and coherence, appears in the introduction to *The Order of Things* (Foucault 1980b). Quoting Borges' recollection of a Chinese encyclopaedia, all animals are to be classified as:

> a) belonging to the Emperor, b) embalmed, c) tame, d) suckling pigs, e) sirens, f) fabulous, g) stray dogs, h) included in the present classification, i) frenzied, j) innumerable, k) drawn with a fine camel-hair brush, l) et cetera, m) having just broken the water pitcher, n) those that from a long way off look like flies [Borges, 1988 cited in Genocchio 1995:103].

Embodiment of Urban Tourism

Despite the proliferation of visual metaphors in cultural studies of tourism, attention has turned to the way in which the landscapes and representations of tourism are encountered, rather than gazed upon. Crouch (2000a) points out that tourism representation tends to have a limited language as either the object of the gaze, or special pursuits such as in adventure tourism. He argues that there is considerable potential for 'relating representations and the content of those representations in terms of peoples lives and the environments they use, celebrate, endure' (ibid.:95). This shifts the emphasis away from merely sight towards a greater appreciation of multi-sensual encounters with tourist destinations.

More features of bodily encounter are therefore evaluated, capturing the sensuous (and sometime sensual) nature of tourism (ibid.). Embodiment can be defined as 'a process of experiencing, making sense, knowing through practise as a sensual human subject in the world' (Crouch 2000b:68). Crouch (2000b) explains how embodiment concerns how the individual grasps the world multi-sensually; how the body is surrounded by space encountering it multi-sensually; and also how individuals express themselves through space, changing it in the process. Embodiment is more than just adding to the concept of the tourist gaze, as it also implies a more active engagement with space and place. This 'non-representational theory' also challenges the emphasis of cultural studies which 'often seems to have taken representation as its central focus to its detriment' (Thrift 1999:318).

Urry (2001b) argues that there are complex connections between bodily sensations and the 'sense-scapes' of destinations which are mediated through discourse and language. The body senses as it moves, and the tourist can smell, touch and hear the urban tourist destination. In fact, it is common for urban tourists to value and savour the 'atmosphere' of the cities they visit. Urry (2001b:9) argues that the tourist also has sixth sense – kinaesthetics – which informs the tourist what their body is doing in space, in terms of their feet on the pavement or their hands on the steering wheel. The kinaesthetic sense is facilitated by various objects and technologies that have the effect of changing the nature of vision. The tourist gaze therefore varies, framed by the car windscreen, the railway carriage or the camcorder. Much urban tourism, however, also involves a 'compulsion to proximity', whether at a live performance such as a concert, a sports event such as the Olympic Games, or a unique moment in history such as Princess Diana's funeral (Urry 2001b:4).

As Rojek and Urry (1997) argue, the cultural analysis of tourism necessitates the evaluation of the different senses used to experience tourism, challenging the traditional privileging of the visual in theories of tourism and travel. Rojek (1997) conceptualises the tourist in a more active role, reading tourist destinations by 'dragging' representations, particularly media images, from the files containing their accumulated knowledge. As Veijola and Jokinen (1994) point out, amongst all of the discussion of 'the tourist', it is easy to forget that tourists are lumpy, fragile, aged, gendered and racialised bodies.

The urban tourist destination, therefore, is experienced by people, whether visitors or residents, who actively make decisions about how to position themselves in relation to the city. Individuals draw upon their imagination and memories to reconfigure the urban tourist destination, and the landscape is not grasped through a unified existence, but through a 'kaleidoscope' (Crouch 2000a:96). As Crouch (ibid.:99) argues, tourism involves 'encounters with people, rather than flat-views and "landscapes" detached and dis-embodied of lives'. It is therefore possible for researchers to gain a 'feel' for the destination as 'both a kaleidoscope and a patina, not a perspective or a picture. The place surrounds you, the senses are aware and alert ...' (ibid.:101). Significantly, however, for both visitors and residents, this process is a social one, and this leads to both shared encounters, and the 'presence, or absence, of other human beings and their activities' (Crouch 2000a:96).

Performativity and Urban Tourism

A source of inspiration for researchers engaging with the embodiment of space and place has been feminist work on the performance of gender and sexuality (Butler 1993). Butler is particularly concerned with finding more embodied ways of understanding the relationships between social structures and human agency. This relates particularly to the sedimented forms of gendered social practices, which appear natural according to gender norms. According to Nash (2000:655) some researchers have been concerned with denaturalising performance differentiated by gender, class, sex and ethnicity. Others have been concerned with a more generic and celebratory understanding of the embodied nature of human existence.

As Thrift (cited in Nash 2000) explains, 'non-representational theory' is about mundane everyday practices that shape the conduct of human beings towards others and themselves in particular sites. Drawing upon authors such as Deleuze (1991), non-representational theorists argue that these practices cannot be conveyed by either texts or cognitive processes, as they are embodied in everyday multi-sensual practices and experiences. This moves attention away from texts that can only convey what is written or spoken. In the context of urban tourism, this focuses attention on the practices that cannot easily be put into words by tourists or residents. The perceptions of tourists and residents are 'tangled up with specific possibilities of action – so tangled, in fact, that the job of central cognition ceases to exist' (Clark cited in Thrift and Dewsbury 2000:423). The encounters between tourists and residents in the city, therefore, may be better understood using the metaphor of dance and examining the complex styles, rhythms, steps and gestures of different groups of people.

The images and experiences of the city are therefore dynamic rather than static, yet there are certain places in the city where practice is acted out. Roach (cited in Thrift and Dewsbury 2000:425) uses the term 'vortex' to refer to the places in cities where everyday practices are celebrated and reinforced. Thrift and Dewsbury cite leisure as a prime example, with performance artists and buskers in the street, karaoke in bars and raves in clubs. Whether the performativity is at heritage sites (Bagnall 2003), theme parks or tourist attractions, urban tourism plays an important role in the emerging 'experience economy' (Pine and Gilmore 1999). Although in its infancy, the study of the performativity of consumption has great potential for understanding urban tourism, and contemporary society in general.

Implications for Understanding Urban Tourism

Donald draws upon such insights and states that 'there is no such thing as a city', instead: 'the city constitutes an imagined environment…the discourses, symbols, metaphors and fantasies through which we ascribe meaning to the modern experience of urban living – is as important a topic for the social sciences as the material determinants of the physical environment' (Donald 1992:427). This conceptualisation clearly provides alternatives to both materialist approaches and the behaviouralist methodologies common in tourism and place-marketing research. The endless intertextuality through a plethora of media is enough for some authors to claim that 'the boundary between social reality and representations of that reality has collapsed' (Jacobs 1993:830). Donald's conceptualisation of the city (repeated in Donald 1999) asserts that the relationship between 'the real city, the discursive city and the disappearing city' (Wolff 1992:553) has been fundamentally blurred. The deterministic approaches permeating the place-marketing and tourism literature therefore become even more difficult to justify.

It is worth summarising the main avenues of enquiry opened up by cultural studies. The textual model is useful not only in terms of objects of study, but also in the transposition of 'texts' for 'space'. We thus have a model consisting of the agent, the text and the researcher, so that the various forms of space are analogous to the literary theorist's understanding of 'text'. This enables an analysis of the text in terms of not only linguistic aspects, but also social, political and institutional influences. Attention is also focused on the textual communities who interpret the representations according to their assumptions and horizons of expectation (see Fish 1980). If the city can be read as a text it would seem that attention should be devoted to these textual communities, rather than groups or classes defined on *a priori* grounds such as social class.

As Derrida aims to 'pay the sharpest and broadest attention possible to context' (Derrida 1977:136), the concept of intersubjectivity, rather than objectivity, is highlighted. There is potential, therefore, in utilising notions of difference to examine the differences between both various representations, and the reading of representations in different textual communities. It would also seem that the full spectrum of representations should be treated with equal importance by researchers, avoiding the privileging of a particular representation or discourse. Overcoming rigid distinctions between the 'material' and the 'representational' recognises their mutual determination, and should prevent any one from being privileged. The rejection of meta-narratives implies that it is the researcher's task to apply these approaches in uncovering the local ground-rules in relation to a particular phenomenon. In the context of urban tourism destinations, these local ground-rules should also concern the way in which people encounter the locality, including the differences in the way ordinary people read landscapes and representations. This latter approach implies research into the embodied and performative nature of urban tourism.

Overlooking Consumers
The Practice of Consumption

The developments within cultural studies have created potential in terms of studying urban tourism, offering alternatives to both the materialist and the behaviouralist approaches which dominate much of the literature. Cultural studies of place consumption are not without their problems, however, and voices of dissent ultimately point towards a rather serious shortcoming in the context of both tourism landscapes and representations. Perhaps the most sensitive (and perceptive) critics have been feminist geographers. Whilst their objections are convincing and valuable *per se*, they point to a more general omission from textual studies of place consumption – people.

As Gregson points out, in the context of shopping malls, 'amid all the talk of the ludic and the carnivalesque, of iconization and simulation, there is one gaping absence: nowhere here is anything more than a passing reference made to the activity of shopping and to the skills of the shopper' (Gregson 1995:136). Gregson notes that the majority of cultural studies of shopping malls are by men, while the overwhelming majority of retail consumers (see Moore 1991), and retail employees are women (Lowe and Crews 1991). There is also understandable concern amongst feminist writers over the use of Benjamin's voyeuristic concept of the *flâneur* (see Wilson 1995). This concern over the masculine representations masquerading as the universal is well founded, particularly as authors such as Shields (1989) suggest that *flâneurie* is a universal activity. Whilst not wishing to appropriate these arguments, there is a strong sense in which they are indicative of a more fundamental problem within cultural geography, revealed by contemporary consumption.

The appeal of landscapes of consumption such as shopping malls, theme parks and festivals, to commentators of the postmodern, is not difficult to understand. They exhibit in one site a plethora of characteristics of the postmodern, and they lend themselves easily to the application of concepts such as 'heterotopia', 'hyper-reality' and '*flâneur*'. However, despite an interest in everyday experience by influential authors such as de Certeau (1988), the everyday experience of place consumers rarely figures. As Gregson argues, 'the mall is about the Santa Maria experience, dolphinariums, Metroland and the Spanish Village' (1995:136). It is not about Marks & Spencer, Asda, Ikea and Toys "R" Us. The shopping mall of Sack (1988) and Hopkins (1990, 1991) is a 'communicative text', yet there is no regard for how this text is read by place consumers. This lack of interest in the place consumer is not confined to the shopping mall. World fairs are read as 'heroic consumption' and 'spectacle' (Ley and Olds 1988), irrespective of the experiences of different groups of consumers, and Stonehenge is read on behalf of place consumers by Hetherington (1992). In contrast, Crouch (2000a:95) points out that practice is 'much more active, complex, and in ways of multiple encounters'.

The Production of Texts

As Jackson and Taylor argue (1996), even some of the more subtle and perceptive studies of advertising texts (e.g. Miller 1991), have little regard for how those texts might be read by contemporary consumers. It would seem that exactly the same problems pertain to both landscapes and promotional representations. Advertising texts themselves are certainly of interest, but it is unclear why so little attention is given to the everyday lives of the consumers, and how such promotional material is related to their decision-making. The audience's culturally constructed knowledge obviously plays a major role in 'decoding' media messages, with great variations between places and contexts.

It would seem that only limited progress has been made in escaping from the conceptualisation of audiences as 'passive dupes' and victims to be manipulated (e.g.

Adorno and Horkheimer 1972). The affinity of Dann (1996a) with Boorstin (1964) is indicative of this problem within the context of tourism. Although the view of the uncritical recipient of messages has been convincingly challenged by authors such as Hall (1973), it persists in advertising literature and appears to be accepted by many cultural geographers. Jackson and Taylor (1996) argue that advertising is still regarded as the lowest and most ominous aspect of the 'culture industries' (see Young 1990; Myers 1986). As Glennie and Thrift (1992) argue, much of the contemporary consumption literature relies on a myopic and rather simplistic history of modern consumption.

It would seem that many of the problems inherent in cultural geographical studies of consumption stem from an overemphasis on the production of texts rather than their consumption. This not only prevents a full understanding of the texts themselves, but it misses the process of interaction between the producer and consumer of the text. As Crang (1997:360) argues, 'there are limitations in looking solely at cultural products without looking at how they are taken up and used'. A number of studies (e.g. Morley 1986) indicate that audiences are far from passive, and readings are far from homogeneous. Advertising has increasingly used parody and irony, and any simplistic relationships between representations of place, gender and race have been called into question.

More Metaphors

While the recent attention to embodiment and performativity within cultural studies might be considered a step in the right direction (particularly by the metaphor-makers), urban tourism remains problematic within 'non-representational' studies. Although the performativity of tourism is claimed to be 'radically contextual' (Thrift cited in Nash 2000), for the metaphor of dance to be pre-linguistic, it is often elevated above the social and cultural world. As Nash (2000:658) points out, dance is actually 'mediated by words...scripted, performed and watched' and it is also highly formalised and stylised. The emphasis on precognitive performances raises important questions, particularly in urban tourism contexts. Visual and textual forms of representation are practices in themselves, yet non-representational studies seem to exclude them. Although performativity is a part of urban tourism, the core business of the tourism industry is still producing texts, whether in the form of promotional representations or the landscapes of destinations.

If practice is non-verbal and precognitive, Nash (2000) asks how it can be known by researchers. It seems that the most likely way is through abstract theorising of the non-representable, emphasising individualistic 'sovereign subjects' rather than specific contexts. If the concern shifts to what cannot be expressed, rather than what can, we seem no closer to understanding the experience of ordinary people. As Nash puts it: 'The energy spent in finding ways to express the inexpressible...seems to imply a new (or maybe old) division of labour separating academics who think (especially about not thinking and the noncognitive) and those "ordinary people" out there who just act' (Nash 2000:662). What is certain is that, with one or two notable exceptions (e.g. Edensor 2000), current applications of the concept of performativity and embodiment do little to bring us closer to the experiences of urban tourists. Despite developing a new metaphor, cultural geographers continue to ignore the everyday meanings consumers attach to activities such as shopping, visiting tourist attractions and sight-seeing. It seems that cultural analysis is moving on, playing with new words, without having addressed the ways in which texts are read by ordinary people such as tourists and residents.

Interpretation of Texts

Parkin (1971) was one of the first to consider the differential reading of media texts, developing the concept of 'codes' and meaning systems. Morley has also emphasised the 'socially governed distribution of codes across different sections of the audience' (Morley 1992:57), whilst others have emphasised the dynamic nature of socialisation (Giddens 1991). O'Barr (1994) focuses on representations of 'foreign places', and suggests that the audience is effectively divided into 'insiders' and 'outsiders' depending on the market segments targeted. In the context of place marketing, the process is even more complex, with promotional messages understood differently by various groups of place consumers. These perspectives raise serious questions regarding the lack of interest amongst cultural researchers in the reception of cultural texts by consumers.

In the context of urban tourism, it is clear that the significance of cultural texts is related to 'not only transmission [but] also reception and response' (Williams 1958: 313). Tourism involves patterns of social and cultural communication which are mediated by the meanings created by different groups of consumers. This process involves a dynamic and interactive process of creating, transmitting and receiving tourism representations. This overwhelming concern with 'how social meanings are made' (Corner 1986:61) ignores a large part of tourism, including its social significance.

The cultural study of tourism raises questions about context and the positionality of producers and consumers. As Squire perceptively argues, industrial restructuring alters 'not only the tourist services created, but also the relationship between producers and consumers of tourism products, and how meanings of the tourist experience are negotiated by various agencies' (Squire 1994:8). Johnson reminds us that 'the individual text is only a means to cultural study, a raw material for the part of practice' (Johnson 1986:8). It is possible that the persistent retrospective bias of cultural geography (see Cosgrove and Jackson 1987), causes cultural geographers to overlook what happens following production. As Burgess noted at the start of the last decade, 'few geographers seem willing, as yet, to undertake empirical research with the consumers of post-modern meanings' (Burgess 1990:140). Despite the importance of understanding the ways in which visitors read the texts of post-industrial tourism, the researcher still 'retains the position of power, telling readers what tourism means' (Squire 1994:8).

The Peopling Prognosis
The Process of Communication

The lack of attention paid to the experience of consumers by cultural geographers would seem to be a major blow to the endeavour of introducing concepts and methods from cultural geography into urban tourism studies. Despite the emphasis on images, representations and imaginary places, there is still some way to go in understanding the culture of urban tourism. Returning to Duncan and Duncan (1988), we are instructed to maintain contact with 'textual communities', defined as people 'who have a common understanding of a text, spoken or read, and who organise aspects of their lives as the playing out of a script' (Duncan and Duncan 1988:117). Overly scriptocentric and logocentric approaches marginalise textual communities and abolish the relationships between author and audience.

In a powerful and convincing challenge to cultural studies of consumption, Squire (1994) suggests that cultural geographers would do well reconsider the process of communication. Jakobson's model of linguistic communication (Jakobson 1960) is particularly useful in this respect. As Squire (1994) points out, the model incorporates both the addresser or producer of the text and the addressee or consumer who receives it. The code of the text comprises the rules structuring the message itself. The model emphasises the relationship between the producers and consumers of cultural texts, and the fact that meaning is transformed during the process of communication. In the same way that Natter and Jones (1993) substitute 'space' for 'text', it is argued here that Jakobson's original model is useful for conceptualising the producer and consumer of urban tourism texts (figure 5.1). The model can be further adapted to conceptualise both individual producers and consumers, and market segments.

The Circuit of Culture

The importance of negotiation and dialogue in the case of urban tourism texts, however, would seem to limit the value of linear models of cultural communication. It would seem that a number of authors have chosen a similar path (or circuit) in attempting to solve this problem (e.g. Jackson and Taylor 1996; Squire 1994; Morgan and Pritchard 1998). Johnson (1986:284) provides a description of the fragmentation of cultural studies into three main forms: production-based studies, text-based studies

Figure 5.1: Jakobson's model of linguistic communication.
Source: after Jakobson (1960:353), cited in Squire (1994).

and research into lived cultures (figure 5.2). Johnson argues, however, that 'cultural processes do not correspond to the contours of academic knowledge as they stand' (ibid.:279). This is because each approach is 'theoretically partisan, but also very partial in its objects' (ibid.:279). This framework helps to transgress the divisions, in terms of both developing new skills and seizing upon the inner connections between the moments. Johnson argues that in analysing cultural phenomena 'we must not limit ourselves to particular kinds of text, or specialised practice or institutional site. All social practices can be looked at from a cultural point of view' (Johnson 1986:282–83). Along with authors such as Burgess (1990), Johnson emphasises the transformation of meaning as representations that are encoded and decoded over time and in different contexts. Meaning is therefore transformed at each stage of the circuit of culture, including the incorporation of texts into larger symbolic systems, the transformation upon reading (which depends on the social characteristics of the audience) and the changes the text makes to lived cultures. Meaning can be further transformed in subsequent circuits.

In the framework (figure 5.2), each box represents a 'moment' in this circuit, each depending on the other. Preoccupation with any one moment prevents the others from being recognised. If the researcher is interested in the text alone, they will not be able to understand either the complex acts of production or the consumption of the text by readers. As cultural texts are read by people other than cultural researchers, the forms of reading may differ significantly between different groups of readers. While academics consider themselves exclusively equipped to read texts, it may be the 'mis-readings' (ibid.:284) which are more significant. To understand texts as trans-formations of meaning, it is necessary to 'grasp the specific conditions and practices through which the product was "consumed" or "read". These include all the asym-metries of power, cultural resources and knowledge that relate readers to both producers and analysts, as well as the more fundamental social relations...' (ibid.:284). Johnson also emphasises the need for researchers to have a knowledge of the cultural elements already encountered by the reader. The act of reading a cultural text makes an impression on lived cultures, – 'reservoirs of discourses and meanings' (ibid.:285). These lived cultures, underpinned by social relations, in turn shape the environment in which fresh cultural texts are produced.

Returning to the framework itself (figure 5.2), it is significant that the circuit involves a movement from private to public forms and back again (represented by the poles to the left and right of the diagram). In general, production is a process of rendering a cultural object public and consumption is a process of rendering the cultural object private again. More specifically, production consists of a transition from the private concepts of producers to public representations. Consumption involves a transition from an abstract and public form of cultural object to a concrete yet subjective form.

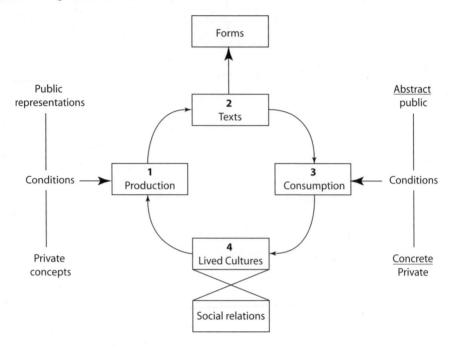

Figure 5.2: Circuit of culture framework. Source: after Johnson (1986:284).

CASE STUDY 5.1: THE CIRCUIT OF CULTURE OF CARDIFF BAY, WALES

To illustrate the changes which take place during the circuit of culture, it is useful to use an urban tourism example. At the beginning of the nineteenth century, Cardiff, the capital of Wales, was dominated by the coal and steel industries. In the 1920s, nearly half the male population of Wales was employed in mining, steel, shipping or on the railways (Middleton 1991:120), and the docks of Cardiff played a major role in this industrial economy. The scale of deindustrialisation, however, was equally striking. Between 1970 and 1990 the coal mining industry lost over 70,000 jobs (ibid.:126). By the 1980s, the only sign of this once-dynamic economy was a wasteland stretching along the Cardiff waterfront.

The regeneration of Cardiff Bay began in 1986, when a consensus emerged between the City Council, the County Council, the Welsh Office and the Welsh Development Agency. The Welsh Office had secured agreement for £2.4 billion of central government funding over a period of 10 years, and the area had already received Assisted Area Status (Babalikis 1998). A four-month report commissioned by the then Secretary of State concluded that extensive regeneration and the construction of a barrage would not only substantially increase land values, but foster 'new pride, new wealth, and a totally new image in the outside world' (cited in Middleton 1991:132). The vision was of a 'superb environment which will have few if any competitors in Britain' (ibid.:133).

The Cardiff Bay Development Corporation (CBDC) was created in April 1987. The planning authorities retained their designated powers over the area, and all land had to be purchased. There was a consensus from the start on the need to build a barrage and a peripheral road, and to link the area with the city centre. The 'regeneration strategy' was presented by Llewellyn-Davies Planning a year after the corporation had been set up, outlining the longer-term vision. Having assembled a Design and Architecture Review Panel, the board designated each of the nine sectors of the area to developers. These included Benjamin Thompson and Associates of Boston, who emphasised the importance of attracting people into the inner harbour area.

According to CBDC (1997), 'Cardiff Bay is planned to create 4 million sq. ft of office space, 5 million sq. ft of industrial space, 6,000 new homes and up to 30,000 new jobs'. In terms of tourism, Cardiff Bay aimed 'by the millennium to attract 2 million visitors a year, the majority visiting the arc of entertainment in the inner harbour'. The corporation also estimated that it would attract £1 billion of private investment by the year 2000, representing a ratio of 2.4:1 in terms of public-to-private investment (CBDC 1997). In terms of urban regeneration in the UK, Cardiff Bay has become something of a best-practice example. Numerous offices and large areas of housing have been built along with some successful visitor attractions.

As with any regenerated urban area, however, the experiences of consumers will vary. Contributing to possible variations in experience are factors such as Cardiff Bay's relative isolation from the city centre and the extent to which the disadvantaged Tiger Bay community has benefited. In contrast to other UK cities, and with the exception of the Pierhead Building and Bute Street, the area has been built rather than redeveloped. It is therefore more difficult to create a tourist-friendly 'honey pot' of attractions and architecture.

It is possible to apply the circuit of culture framework to the development of Cardiff Bay, illustrating the transition of the 'Cardiff Bay Cultural Text'. For a particular destination, both the place product itself and promotional activity can begin life as the private idea or concept of a developer or marketer. The partnership forming the CBDC, for example, brought together many 'private' concepts, ideas and aspirations. The concepts themselves were developed in the course of practical activities, whether in the boardroom or on the golf course. By giving the ideas and concepts the name 'Cardiff Bay', even before development took place there was a change in form, as the 'product' is subjected to the glare of publicity and becomes a public issue (Johnson 1986:286).

In terms of consumption, the change is towards a more concrete and particular form of cultural object. Cardiff Bay is initially consumed as a news item, a topic of discussion and debate and part of a discourse emphasising the benefits to residents, visitors and inward investors. To consumers, the development is initially an idea and a plan, claiming to offer benefits to the whole region. Once the product is actually consumed by individuals, however, it becomes a concrete phenomenon, yet consumers also gain subjective and private experiences. To actual visitors or inward investors, the Cardiff Bay product simultaneously becomes a concrete yet private reality.

Cardiff Bay can therefore be seen to occupy different 'moments' of consumption. Initially, the Cardiff Bay text has to be produced by the CBDC, in terms of both the physical landscape and representations. Once production is ongoing, the texts take on a certain form, and it is possible to analyse the content, messages and codes of the text. The consumers of the Cardiff Bay text – including residents, visitors and investors – read the text in different ways, producing different subjective experiences of Cardiff Bay. In turn, the different subjective experiences of consumers influence lived cultures. Groups of consumers with similar experiences may emerge, be they residents, visitors or investors. Crucially, such consumption has an impact, however minor, on social relations, as the identity of groups within society is reproduced by their experiences. It is possible for one group of consumers to gain a more positive image of Cardiff, while another may feel marginalised and excluded. It is significant, however, that the existence of such contested terrains influences social relations amongst consumers.

Johnson's conceptualisation has both theoretical and methodological implications for researching urban tourism. Theoretically, texts should not be separated from their social production and reproduction, as they have always been given meaning in some other social practice. It is by researching the different versions, therefore, that the transformations across the representational practices can be charted. The reading of texts should be as multi-layered as possible, incorporating different sets of common-sense knowledge which produce meaning. This implies also using the 'amateur knowledge' of different groups of consumers. Johnson (1986) argues that the methodological implications point towards ethnographic studies and possibly action research.

As Crouch (2000a:95) argues, there is potential for 'exploring the complex dimensions of tourism practice … relating representations and the content of those representations in terms of peoples lives and the environments they use, celebrate, endure'. It would seem that there is plenty of room for developing ethnographic studies of urban tourism, conceptualising urban tourism as cultural communication. Dann makes a similar point, recognising the potential of such interpretative techniques as semi-structured and open-ended interviews (Dann 1988). Eyles and Smith (1988) illustrate the potential of such techniques, particularly in the context of the city. Jamal and Hollinshead (2001) also demonstrate the unfulfilled potential of qualitative tourism research, using the term 'forbidden zone' to convey the positivistic tendencies of tourism research. In the context of tourism, very little attention has been devoted to understanding the social and cultural meanings of the tourism experience amongst different groups of tourists. Meanings have often been constructed *a priori* by the researcher. This is whether or not the meanings have any salience to the tourists themselves. Burgess once more leads the way in her study of the dialogue of different groups of inner-city residents, focusing on their experience of the countryside (Burgess 1990:160). Johnson (1986) concludes by implying that the study of culture would be considerably more fruitful if it began with everyday lived (inter)subjectivities, before moving around the circuit framework.

Conclusion

It is apparent that urban tourism studies can benefit from an engagement with developments within the new cultural geography. By reconceptualising the city as 'imaginary', consisting of landscapes and representations, cultural studies provides some profound opportunities. Methods such as semiotics and linguistic analysis, and concepts such as *difference* and *heterotopia*, introduce powerful yet sensitive avenues of analysis. Tourism, always tending to be marginalised within the social sciences, has the potential to play an important role in the cultural literature, representing an important form of cultural communication. Despite the encouraging signs and potential, however, place consumption reveals an overemphasis on the linguistic structure of the text itself, at the expense of consumers. This dramatically reduces the potential of incorporating cultural perspectives into place marketing and tourism studies.

It is apparent that a 'peopling' manoeuvre of some sort is needed. The adoption of a model which incorporates the addressee enables the interactive nature of cultural texts, or dialogue, to be captured. Rather than a linear model, the circuit of culture framework establishes everyday lived experience as a crucial element. Together, these lines of discussion, to use another spatial metaphor, point towards the incorporation of qualitative interpretative research within the analysis of the culture of urban tourism. To further develop this perspective, chapter six engages with a humanistic perspective.

Chapter summary:
- Cultural analysis has a long pedigree and offers great potential for analysing urban tourism.
- Cultural studies of tourism are now becoming more common, including some useful studies of urban tourism.
- Cultural studies draw upon a wide range of concepts and techniques, and have not yet fulfilled their full potential in the field of urban tourism.
- Despite the potential of cultural studies in understanding urban tourism, limitations relate to the lack of interest in place consumers.
- Authors such as Squire (1994) help to overcome some of the limitations, by drawing upon Johnson (1986) in order to incorporate the consumption of landscapes and representations into the model.

Further Reading

Donald, J. (1991) 'The City as Text', in R. Bocock and K. Thomson (eds) *Social and Cultural Forms of Modernity*, Polity Press, Cambridge, 417–61.

Duncan, J.S. and N. Duncan (1988) '(Re)reading the Landscape', *Environment and Planning D: Society and Space* 6, 117–26.

Echtner, C.M. (1999) 'The Semiotic Paradigm: implications for tourism research', *Tourism Management* 20 (1), February.

Jackson, P. and J. Taylor (1996) 'Geography and the Cultural Politics of Advertising', *Progress in Human Geography* 20, 365–72.

Johnson, R. (1986) 'The Story So Far and Further Transformations?', in D. Punter (ed.) *Introduction to Contemporary Cultural Studies*, Longman, London, 277–313.

MacCannell, D. (1989) 'Introduction, Special Issue: Semiotics of Tourism', *Annals of Tourism Research* 16, 1–16.

Manning, P.K. (1997) *Semiotics and Fieldwork*, Sage, London.

Mellinger, W.M. (1994) 'Towards a Critical Analysis of Tourism Representations', *Annals of Tourism Research* 21 (4), 756–79.

Morgan, N.J. and A. Pritchard (1998) *Tourism, Promotion and Power: Creating Images, Creating Identities*, John Wiley and Sons, Chichester.

Ringer, G. (ed.) (1998) *Destinations: Cultural Landscapes of Tourism*, Routledge, London.

Selwyn, T. (ed.) (1998) *The Tourist Image: Myths and Myth-Making in Tourism*, John Wiley and Sons, Chichester.

Shields, R. (1992) *Lifestyle Shopping*, Routledge, London.

Squire, S.J. (1994) 'Accounting For Cultural Meanings: The Interface Between Geography and Tourism Studies Re-examined', *Progress in Human Geography*, 18 (1), 1–16.

Watson, S. and K. Gibson (1995) *Postmodern Cities and Spaces*, Blackwell, Oxford and Cambridge, MA.

Chapter 6

The Experience of Urban Tourism

The following topics are covered in this chapter:

- A review of the use of humanistic research focusing on urban tourism.
- The contribution of alternative genres of humanistic research, investigating the meanings, values and emotions of individuals in relation to places.
- The limitations of humanistic approaches which concentrate on individuals rather than groups within society.
- The potential of 'existential' approaches to understanding the experience of people in a city.
- The potential of approaches which are concerned with the experience of social groups, how they acquire knowledge of places, and how they make decisions.

Introduction

Urban tourism has so far been examined from the perspectives of place marketing and tourism management, postmodernity, place image and culture. In the last chapter, despite the great potential of cultural studies in the study of urban tourism, we encountered certain limitations. There seemed to be a risk that cultural studies of consumption would drown in a sea of metaphors, while on dry land the experiences of people would be ignored. It is necessary, therefore, to find ways of incorporating the experience of place consumers into studies of urban tourism. As Franklin and Crang (2001:8) argue, 'we need both to consider the doing-knowledge of tourists and the academic knowledge of studies'.

There are relatively few contemporary studies of urban tourism which use an experiential approach, concerned with the knowledge, meanings, emotions and memories of urban tourists or residents. This is despite a recognition that both tourists and residents have views and feelings, develop values and make choices based on these values which effect and change the landscape (Kaplan and Kaplan cited in Ringer 1998). There are positive signs, however, that researchers are beginning to engage with the embodied nature of tourism, conceptualising tourism as an encounter. Under the banner of 'Non-representational Geography', or 'lay geographies' (Crouch 2000b), researchers have begun to find alternatives to both the visual metaphors which dominate our understanding of tourism, and research into representations and landscapes in isolation from the people who encounter them. Whilst psychoanalytical approaches have been popular, geographers and tourism researchers are beginning to re-examine the potential of phenomenology in capturing the experiences, knowledge and action of tourist encounters. It is argued that phenomenology offers a valuable contribution to understanding urban tourism. As Li (2000:865) explains, the term 'phenomenology' refers to 'reasoned inquiry that discovers the inherent essences of appearances' – in short, anything that appears to human consciousness.

Incorporating experience into geographical studies was also the aim of the humanistic geography which developed in the 1970s. This chapter acknowledges the limitations of the 'pure' and strict humanistic studies which are usually associated with the term 'phenomenology'. The emphasis on individuals attracted considerable criticism, and should also be avoided in contemporary studies. It is argued in this chapter, however, that alternative versions of phenomenology can make fundamental contributions to studies of urban tourism. Humanistic approaches relevant to urban tourism are discussed, drawing particularly on the constitutive phenomenology of Schutz (1972; Schutz and Luckmann 1974). It is argued that conceptualising the intersubjective experience of representations of a locality provides an essential link between representations and landscapes, images and experiences and the action of tourists.

The chapter begins by reviewing the limited application of humanistic approaches to studies of urban tourism. Generally, experiential studies of urban tourism are rare and tend be scattered amongst several different traditions of research. Recent attention to the embodiment of tourism is encouraging, however, and the chapter reviews the emergent body of literature concerned with the experience, knowledge and action of tourists. Previous attempts to develop humanistic geography are reviewed, and the chapter presents a discussion of the limitations of humanistic research, particularly individualistic approaches. The chapter explores the application to urban tourism of both 'existential' approaches and the 'social phenomenology' of Alfred Schutz. It is argued that the latter, in particular, offers important insights into the experience of urban tourism, through the concepts of 'intersubjectivity' and 'stock of knowledge' (Schutz and Luckmann 1974), and through his theory of action (1970). It is argued that Schutz provides a way of incorporating both first-hand and mediated tourist knowledge into studies of urban tourism. These concepts are useful in understanding the embodiment of urban tourism practice and the ways in which urban tourists and residents encounter the city.

Experiential Urban Tourism Research
Tourist Experience

As suggested in previous chapters, humanistic studies of urban tourism which focus on experience are relatively rare. Studying tourist experience implies an understanding of tourist behaviour from the tourist's own frame of reference, rather than one imposed by the researcher. As Jamal and Hollinshead (2001) argue, although there has been scant regard for tourism in general amongst social theorists, the experience of tourism is particularly neglected. As they argue, tourism study 'turns out not to be an objective, value free search for tourism knowledge' (Tribe cited in Jamal and Hollinshead 2001:74).

Authors such as Selwyn (1996) and Urry (1995) have challenged the objectivity and scientism which the tourism literature has clung onto for so long. Such authors have embraced postcolonialism, poststructuralism, and postmodernity, and new theoretically informed tourism journals are emerging. However, there is still a paucity of studies which 'locate the situated particularity of body and emotion in tourism, whether that of the tourist or the host' (Jamal and Hollinshead 2001). Veijola and Jokinen (cited in Jamal and Hollinshead 2001) demonstrate the loss of the situated body in tourism research, and Ryan (1997) also notes the positivist tradition within tourism studies. Much tourism research has been concerned with analysing relationships between quantifiable variables, often with the use of hypotheses to be proved or disproved. As Ryan (2000) explains, positivist assumptions relate to both ontology and epistemology. The positivist ontology assumes that an external reality which can be discovered exists in the form of laws of cause and effect. The positivist epistemology assumes that this discovery is both dualist (the researcher is outside the reality), and objectivist (only objectivity will enable the researcher to make the discovery).

Authors such as Veijola and Jokinen (1994), however, recognise that tourists are dynamic social actors, interpreting and embodying experience, while also creating meaning and new realities through their actions. The tourist destination is 'a negotiated reality, a social construction by a purposeful set of actors' (Ley 1981:219 cited in Ringer 1998:5). While positivism in tourism research leads to a search for methodologies to discover reality, researchers such as Jamal and Hollinshead (2001) recognise that the tourist is an agent of seeing, being, experience, cultural invention and knowing. In a pragmatic sense, interpretive research uses qualitative methods and tools that focus on interpreting (ibid.:67). Interpretive research analyses the meanings and constructions of various texts such as participant narratives, media constructions and socio-historical and political discourses. Rather than quantifiable variables, the emphasis is on the way that human beings actively contribute to knowledge constructions. Interpretivism, however, is also a paradigm. Although theoretical contributions are numerous and varied, the work of European philosophers such as Husserl, Heidegger and Merleau-Ponty have been particularly influential.

MacCannell (2001) draws upon interpretive traditions in his critique of Urry's (1990a) influential conceptualisation of the tourist gaze, calling for an alternative view of the human subject and agency in tourism research. Urry's conceptualisation is argued to be deterministic, particularly due to his use of Foucault's narcissistic subject to represent the tourist. MacCannell argues that despite the fact that Urry emphasises the 'freedom' of tourism, he actually conceptualises the tourist as conforming to 'a visual field marked off in advance in terms what is worth seeing and what is not' (MacCannell 2001:29). Whilst the tourism industry does structure the tourist gaze through tour operators' brochures, guide-books and travel writing, the process is not unidirectional or universal. Tourists remain free to 'look the other way, or to not look at all. And we can disrupt the order of things' (ibid.:24). Furthermore, tourists are not necessarily travelling to compensate for a life which relative to the tourist destination, is dull and unpleasurable. This not only creates a universal tourist, but also dismisses the many theorists from Marx to Freud who demonstrate the importance of 'everyday life'.

Whilst Urry (1990a) draws upon Foucault's *Birth of the Clinic* (1989), MacCannell points towards existentialists such as Sartre and Merleau-Ponty to conceptualise 'the second gaze'. The second gaze conceptualises the tourist, rather than the host, as 'caught, manipulated, captured in the field of vision' (ibid.:30). Tourists know that looks deceive, and that a purer unadulterated vision does not exist. They also know that sight is inseparable from the sign, and that the visual field cannot be separated from the linguistic field (ibid.:31). For everything which is seen, there is the unseen, and 'everything that attracts the gaze, every representation, has its own beyond' (ibid.:31). MacCannell points out that the desire to escape the limitations of the tourist gaze and the awareness of the false promises of the tourism industry structure the second gaze.

This second gaze is illustrated by MacCannell through the use of Stendhal's *Memoires of a Tourist*. Through the character of Mr L., Stendhal characterises the tourist as travelling 'in order to have something new to say', avoiding the 'fake astonishment and smiles for the hundredth and fortieth time' at mundane anecdotes recounted to friends and family (ibid.:32). Stendhal's character recognises the textual nature of the landscape, whilst seeking out not so much the extraordinary, but the unexpected. In both everyday life and through travel, Mr L. seeks the unseen behind the details. From the cobblestones in a street to statues and paintings, he finds unexpected and hidden meaning. The second gaze actually avoids typical tourist sights, and it sometimes rearranges the objects to make what is being seen more interesting. MacCannell (2001) argues, therefore, that tourists should be aware of the difference between primary experience and institutionalised versions of the tourist gaze. The anti-tourist is aware of the aggressive tourism industry, and moves to see that which is missing from the institutionalised gaze.

Researching Tourist Experience

Textual studies of tourism were discussed in some detail in the last chapter, but it is important to recognise that interpretations of the representations and landscapes vary significantly amongst both tourists and residents. Thus, in analysing features of the Las Vegas landscape such as the tomb of Tutankamun at the Luxor Casino (Cohen cited in Ryan 2000), it is also important to know how tourists themselves perceive and interact with the landscape, and what knowledge they develop and draw upon. Among the minority of tourism researchers advocating experiential approaches, Ryan (2000) demonstrates the potential of phenomenography – the study of the way people understand the world. Ryan argues convincingly that it is important to avoid dichotomising the subject and object when analysing tourism, in order to avoid 'a fictional non-existing world constructed by the scientific observer' (Schutz cited in Ryan 2000).

This ethos is central to M. Crang's (1997) discussion of 'research through the tourist gaze'. Crang focuses on the practice of tourist photography and, perhaps surprisingly, demonstrates the corporeality of experience rather than the purely visual characteristics. The circuit of culture framework (Johnson 1986) is seen by Crang as focusing attention on the consumption of representations. He points out, however, that the framework should not encourage the artificial separation of the production and consumption of cultural texts. Tourist photography is used to examine the interrelated nature of tourism production and consumption and the ways in which photographic images act as a route through which worlds are created. Crang draws upon Merleau-Ponty (1962) to show how tourist photographs enframe the tourist sights, shaping the knowledge of different social groups.

Crang argues that it is important to avoid separating the experience from the representation of tourism. He demonstrates the ways in which tourist photographs embody tourist knowledge and become part of the practice of tourism. Images, sight and activities become linked through such tourist practices. It is also significant that events are framed for the future perfect, for tourists to prove that they have been to famous sights. Tourists are seen as binding sights into a series, using photography and 'the anxious accumulation of souvenirs and demonstrations of doing' (Bourdieu cited in M. Crang 1997:365). Crang suggests, therefore, that urban tourism could be understood through the way the destination is captured in photographs, as embedded within them is the practice and experience of tourists. Tourist photographs complicate simple models of subject and object, image and reality. Furthermore, much of this self-presentation takes place when the tourist is back home, using 'holiday snaps' to structure anecdotes of 'being there'. Whilst this can become tedious for family and friends after the sixth film, the practice is firmly embedded within the culture of mass tourism. Noting that the process of tourist photography varies between different cultures, Crang (1997:368) advocates the use of tourist photographs as a 'luminous transcript of life'.

Photographs form the focus of another experiential approach to understanding urban tourism, namely the Q method. As Fairweather and Swaffield (2001) explain, the individual sorts photographs into a continuum ranging from their favourite to their

6.1: 'Us in Sydney!': exploring urban tourism through tourists' photographs. Courtesy of Tourism New South Wales

least favourite photograph. A nine-point scale is used, and the elements are placed in piles on the scale. An interpretive version of the Q method often uses in-depth interviews to elicit attitudes and values underlying the ways in which individuals sort their photographs. Individual Q sorts can also be subjected to factor analysis to identify common patterns. This technique is used as part of an urban tourism study by Middleton (forthcoming). Middleton used 30 photographs of the tourist landscape in the city of Manchester, northwest England, and a sample including both overseas and domestic visitors. The photographs consisted of indoor and outdoor scenes, both during the day and at night. The research followed the experiential paradigm for the Q method, seeking an insight into 'the holistic experience of visitors through in-depth interviews'. Rich insights were gained into the attitudes of visitors to different components of the urban tourist landscape. Particularly interesting data was elicited from overseas visitors who found it useful to contrast cultural differences between Manchester and their home regions. Factor analysis also revealed salient experiences of the tourist landscape, involving the full range of senses.

An early demonstration of the potential of ethnographic research in the context of tourism is Cohen's study of life in the slums of Bangkok (1982). In particular, Cohen reveals the fleeting yet complex relationships between Thai girls and male tourists. Such studies provide a depth and subtlety which can only really be provided by ethnographic research. More recently, Hebditch (cited in Ryan 1995a) has used participant observation to research places commodified by British television series. Jardine (1998) uses ethnographic research in his existential evaluation of bird-watching with friends in southern Ontario, a place where he spent much of his childhood. An ethnographic approach is used by Bruner to understand the relationship between native people and tourists in both Indonesia (1995) and Ghana, East Africa (1996).

An experiential study of urban tourism in China is presented by Li (2000). The study is a phenomenological exploration of Canadian tourists on two separate package tours. Data was gathered using a combination of unstructured long interviews and survey questionnaires completed before and after the trips. Significantly, the participants were considered to be 'co-researchers', rather than merely respondents. The data revealed a degree of consensus or 'intersubjectivity' amongst the tourists. Common experiences were related to themes including understanding difference, broadening the mind through tourism, the need for mutual understanding and the way in which tourism is both of global importance yet also a personal need.

Perhaps more significantly, the study revealed some subtle and idiosyncratic urban tourism experiences. One co-researcher, for example, readjusted her views of the media at home, which she believed had led to her misjudging the local people she had encountered on the trip. Another commented on the paradox concerning contact with the tourist infrastructure, of relevance to MacCannell's 'second tourist gaze' (2001). He commented that 'without the tourist infrastructure, I wouldn't be able to find my way...But I need some space away from the group.' In this case, the space allowed the tourist to experience the subtleties of the city, such as 'the policeman coming home taking off his belt' and 'a shop assistant coming home putting a jacket over her uniform dress'. The study demonstrates how these seemingly mundane encounters make a profound impression on tourists. Furthermore, urban tourists actively seek situations which facilitate the 'experiential learning' which is inherent to urban tourism.

Phenomenography is defined by Marton (cited in Ryan 2000:123) as 'a research method adapted for mapping the qualitatively different ways in which people experience, conceptualise, perceive, and understand various aspects of, and phenomena in, the world around them'. According to Marton, this differentiates phenomenography from phenomenology, which is concerned with what people perceive. In advocating the application of phenomenography to tourism research, Ryan (2000) points out that phenomenography does not adapt a dualistic ontology, separating subject and object. Drawing on Husserl (1970), Ryan points out the folly of analysing the objective tourist destination, separated from the subjective tourist experience of the destination. The two are fundamentally related, and only the phenomenon as a whole can be analysed. Phenomenography focuses on the process of learning. Enquiry is often concerned with content within a particular context. Researchers might evaluate, for example, the knowledge and understanding of a tourist visiting the city of Rome. Alternatively, the approach could be applied to more general investigations into how urban tourists construct their realities.

Phenomenographic research will tend to use in-depth interviews in the form of a structured dialogue. The dialogue, however, is non-directive, with the researcher asking a very limited number of questions aimed at encouraging the interviewee to clarify their thinking. Questions such as 'what do you mean by that?' encourage the

6.2: The more public side of Shanghai. Courtesy of Department of Geography, Liverpool John Moores University.

respondent to focus on the context, whilst avoiding privileging details which only the researcher considers relevant. Phenomenography recognises that things can be experienced on different levels. In the context of urban tourism, this might vary from what place consumers consider superficial or insignificant encounters in the destination, to profound insights provided by travel. According to Ryan (2000), phenomenographers have been drawn to software packages such as NUDIST (Non-numerical Unstructured Data Indexing Searching and Theorising) in order to analyse the qualitative data produced by interviews. A recent innovation is to use 'artificial neural software', which clusters words according to their closeness with other words within the text. Ryan and Sterling (1997) demonstrate the use of such software in a study of attitudes of visitors to Litchfield National Park, Northern Territory, Australia. Although the software only provides an aid to understanding and analysis, in this case indicating the perceived beauty of the park, and fears about commercialisation, Ryan (2000) argues that phenomenography helps to foster a closer relationship between the researcher, and the transcripts produced through interpretive research.

Visitor Satisfaction

It is indicative of the nature of urban tourism research that the majority of experiential frameworks are found within the recreation literature in the US. Prentice et al. (1998) draw upon hierarchical models of experience deriving from the work of authors such as Driver et al. (1987) and Manning (1986). Contributions from the outdoor recreation literature include the *Recreation Opportunity Spectrum*, in which it is recognised that 'the end product of recreation management is the experiences people have' (Prentice et al. 1998:2). Authors have tended to emphasise either benefits-based management focusing on improved conditions (Driver et al. 1987), or experience-based management, where the focus is on subjectively experienced outputs (Bengston and Xu 1993). Another approach within the recreation literature which avoids *a priori* conceptualisations of experience, is the 'means-end chain' (Prentice et al. 1998:3). This approach is concerned with linking reasons for undertaking activities into a hierarchy, from the more concrete to the more intrinsic.

According to Graefe and Vaske (1987), the experience of tourists is influenced by 'individual, environmental, situational and personality-related factors as well as communication with other people' (Page 1995:24). Significantly, such authors argue that it is vital for the tourism industry to constantly evaluate tourist experience to establish the benefits gained by consumers, and whether their expectations are being met. Authors such as Sheenan and Ritchie (1997) stress the importance of developing non-financial measures of the effectiveness of urban tourism development in destinations. These include visitor satisfaction with both the services and information provided by tourist boards.

Bowen (2001) presents a rare interpretive study of tourist satisfaction and dissatisfaction, using participant observation. As the author notes, the vast majority of studies into consumer satisfaction or dissatisfaction are quantitative, and use surveys to evaluate the 'antecedents' that supposedly have an effect on satisfaction. It is far from certain, however, whether questionnaires can capture the 'consumer voice' and, according to Bowen's research, many managers also appear to doubt their effectiveness. To address some of these problems, the study of a long-haul tour to Singapore and Malaysia uses 'a phenomenological and qualitative approach' (ibid.:32), based on participant observation and semi-structured interviews. In particular, Bowen is concerned with increasing the validity of satisfaction research, overcoming the limitations of the positivistic studies which dominate tourism research. Most consumer-satisfaction research denies consumers the opportunity to speak of their experiences in their own words, and also assumes that all respondents interpret questions in the same way.

Having recognised the power of qualitative research in providing an in-depth understanding of tourist experience, Bowen focuses on the words of tourists, tour leaders and managers. Participant observation proved to be particularly suited to understanding the underlying processes, relationships and patterns within specific socio-cultural contexts. Aiming for 'analytical generalisations', the researcher accompanied the participants on a 'two-week, small-group, soft-adventure long haul tour' (ibid.:34). In contrast to quantitative studies, the whole 'vacation sequence' was studied, from checking in before the outbound flight, to the disbanding of the group in the arrivals lounge. The resulting narrative, totalling 32,000 words, provided some intriguing insights into tourist experience.

The performative nature of the tourist experience was particularly apparent, whether it was the individual or group performances of tourists, tourism personnel, or the host population. It was significant that on occasions, the entertaining nature of performances compensated for products and services that were poor in objective terms. For example, the theatrical preparation of a meal in the cramped kitchen of a pontoon restaurant in Malaysia increased satisfaction, despite the very poor quality of the food. It also emerged how the intensity of judgment concerning satisfaction varied temporally, increasing towards the end of the tour when there had been sufficient events with which to compare experiences. Individual tourists also varied in their propensity to judge experiences, exemplified by 'Donald', who offered an evaluation 'event-by event but also on a day-by-day basis' (ibid.:38). Bowen (2001) concludes both that participant observation has great potential in researching tourist satisfaction, and that marketing in general would benefit from a less myopic approach towards social science disciplines.

The benefits of research into the satisfaction of visitors is stressed by Bramwell (1998). Satisfaction surveys can be used to evaluate users' expectations of a destination, and whether those expectations are met by the actual experience (Bramwell 1998:37). As only selected aspects of the city are being sold to the visitor, surveys can help to improve both the product and images projected by tourism authorities. Bramwell suggests that it is important to establish the attributes of a destination which are salient to the overall satisfaction of consumers and consumer decision-making (ibid.:37). To this end, it is possible to compare data on visitor satisfaction with the images of potential visitors to a destination (see also Selby and Morgan 1996).

Addressing such concerns, Bramwell (1998) describes research into the satisfaction of visitors to the city of Sheffield. Seeking to elicit the perceptions of both visitors and residents, the research enables comparisons between different groups of place consumers. An interesting finding relates to differences in satisfaction between various types of place consumer. These were most notable not between residents and visitors, but between visitors attending sports events and those visiting for other purposes (Bramwell 1998:41). It is also found that the leisure setting – including the city-centre environment and the friendliness of people – was particularly salient to most groups of place consumers.

Non-representational Tourism Research

Recent studies which emphasise the embodiment of tourism and tourist encounters, rather than representations *per se*, are encouraging due to their much greater emphasis on experience, knowledge and values. While these studies are essentially a development within cultural studies, they also represent a renaissance of more humanistic approaches to research. The urban tourist, and other place consumers such as residents, can therefore be conceptualised as active, moving around the city, and grasping encounters in a multi-sensual way. As Haraway (1988) argues, the body is located and situated in space, and the researcher should aim for situated knowledges. As Crouch

(2000a:96) explains, the individual 'imagines, plays with places, and their content, subjectively, on their own terms, refiguring them'. Fullagar (2001) engages with both the travel writing of Alphonso Lingis and the 'phenomenology of the flesh' developed by Merleau-Ponty (1968) to discuss the embodied encounters characteristic of tourism. She emphasises the liminal, or in-between, nature of travel, where conventional oppositions of self and otherness, mind and body, are unsettled. Merleau-Ponty's later work (1968) is influential in understanding how the tourist body is intertwined with the physical world, and is neither a subject nor an object. An obvious aspect of urban tourist experience is the presence of other bodies, yet these possess an uncertain status in their encounters with the destination.

Although the concept of embodiment is used by some researchers merely as another metaphor, replacing or complementing the tourist gaze, the concept has underpinned some recent humanistic research. Crouch (2000a) demonstrates the potential of the approach in a project to write an alternative heritage trail in northeast England. He engages with the 'content and felt value of places in peoples lives through enquiry into what they do, feel, grasp, by making long, deep interviews in empathy with the subjects' (ibid.:97). It is significant that Crouch comments on the often surprising nature of ordinary experiences, far removed from academic or technical language. This strength of humanistic research helps to reveal the 'complex experience...a feel for the area' (ibid.:99).

Recent attempts at understanding the performative nature of tourism are exemplified by researchers such as Kirshenblatt-Gimbett (1998). In *Destination Culture*, the performances inherent in an exhibition of Jewish life, world fairs and 'Plimoth Plantation' are examined. In each study she manages to demonstrate what is hidden and unsaid, uncovering the things which can't easily be presented in the official tourist version. Bauman (1994) has been influential to researchers concerned with the embodiment of tourism, stating that 'the purpose is new experience; the tourist is a conscious and systematic seeker of experience, of a new and different experience' (Bauman 1994:29). As Crouch (2000a:96) describes, the world is grasped in a kaleidoscope, and as the kaleidoscope changes, memory is drawn upon as different events occur and are sensed. This 'making sense' of the city involves a feeling of doing (ibid.:96), and contributes to people's practical knowledge of the city. The embodying process is affected by the landscapes and representations encountered, and by cultural contexts such as gender and ethnicity.

As discussed in previous chapters, authors such as Mellor (1991), Kershaw (1993) and Bagnall (2003) have highlighted the performativity of heritage and urban tourism. Rojek and Urry (1997:14) describe the characteristics of reminiscence in the context of heritage. Reminiscence involves a concentrated rather than distracted viewing of objects and performances. Visitors clearly understand the 'staged' nature of the experience – that actors are performing, and that objects are copies or have been placed in a simulated environment. An effect of reminiscing is the reawakening of dreams, whether personal, focused around a certain neighbourhood or locality, or of broader collective interest relating to class, gender or ethnic grouping. According to Rojek and Urry (1997:14), this may be to 'reawaken repressed desires and thereby to connect past and present'. Tourism reflexivity – the way tourists and residents make sense of their lives through tourism – challenges universal or fundamental concept-ualisations of tourist experience.

Recent work in the social sciences focusing on the embodied nature of space and place has led in several directions. As discussed in the last chapter, extreme psycho-analytical approaches do not bring us much nearer to understanding urban tourism experience, as the emphasis on the non-verbal prohibits even ethnographic research with urban tourists. In the context of urban tourism it is argued here that a more pro-mising direction is the re-engagement with phenomenology (e.g. Werlen, 1993; Crang 1997; Strohmayer 1996). Various types of phenomenology are critically examined later in this chapter, and approaches useful for understanding urban tourism are presented in more detail.

Heritage Experience

An innovative approach is taken by Prentice et al. (1998) in one of the rare experi-ential studies of heritage. The study, focusing on the Rhondda Heritage Park in south Wales, is concerned both with experiences and benefits gained by visitors. Inductive qualitative techniques are used initially, followed by a structured survey, and cluster analysis to identify salient experiences and benefits gained by visitors. The study enabled five distinct clusters or market segments to be identified on the basis of both experiences at the attraction, and benefits gained by visitors (Prentice et al. 1998:7). Herbert (2001) uses an experiential approach to examine 'literary places' which have acquired meaning from their links with writers and novels. Qualitative research is used to evaluate the kinds of satisfaction that 'literature tourists' gain from their experience, and how significant issues of authenticity and conservation are to the experience.

An important conclusion from such studies is that the same product can be expe-rienced in very different ways, demonstrating the need to consider the experiential dimensions of tourism. It is interesting that Prentice et al. (1998) found that the socio-demographic attributes of visitors, so often the focus of researchers and marketers, appeared to be largely independent of both experiences and benefits gained. The authors conclude that 'investigations of tourist experience need to be grounded in the realities tourists themselves describe', and that inductive approaches to research are essential (ibid.:2). The focus of studies should therefore be 'the social and personal constructions, as part of the life-worlds of individuals' (ibid.:2).

Also in the context of heritage, Bagnall (1998, 2003) demonstrates the signifi-cance of emotion and memory in consuming tourism. Bagnall draws upon the work of researchers such as Campbell (1987), who argues that in the context of consumption, emotion acts as a crucial link between mental images and physical stimuli. Bagnall's study (1998) of two heritage sites in northwest England demonstrates how urban tourism 'consumption is as much a matter of feeling and emotion as rational behaviour'

(Bagnall 1998:68). The qualitative study, focusing on Wigan Pier (see case study 3.1) and the Museum of Science and Industry (Manchester), demonstrates how heritage consumption is an active process, in which visitors uses their memories and life histories to enable and enhance the experience. It was found that the sites were able to engage visitors on emotional and imaginary levels, and provoke feelings which were considered both meaningful and authentic (Bagnall 2003). Authenticity was found to be related as much to the everyday lives and life histories of visitors as to factual certitude.

The active nature of tourism consumption revealed by Bagnall (1998, 2002) highlights the neglect of tourist experience in both materialist and behaviouralist accounts. Visitors were found to construct, and use as a resource, imagined worlds. These were based on their past experiences in the context of work, family and various social relationships. This seems to be an active process, which involves not only viewing but also the physical embodiment of consumption. Visitors acted out their emotions, and used their memory and imagination to experience a whole range of physical sensations. Many visitors found that the heritage sites provoked an emotional response through which they felt in touch with their past and their own sense of place. The majority of visitors identified with the version of the past that was offered, using their experience and memories to confirm the story presented. Illustrating the active nature of the process, however, a minority of visitors employed their personal experiences to dispute the interpretations offered by the site. These visitors told an amended story, using phrases such as 'I know the way people lived' and 'I did that' (Bagnall 1998:365).

Personal Constructs

For several decades, researchers in the field of environmental perception have drawn upon personal construct theory through an interest in understanding human environmental behaviour (see case study 6.1). Personal construct theory, and the related research method known as repertory grid analysis, was inspired by the work of George Kelly (1955). It is concerned with capturing the language (constructs) which people use to understand events, and is particularly applicable to tourist decision-making. Originally developed in the context of psychoanalysis, personal construct theory sought to uncover the positive and negative constructs by which individuals make sense of their world. Coining the phrase 'man as scientist' (1969:97), Kelly was interested in the framework into which an individual places their experiences. In repertory grid analysis, constructs are bi-polar adjectives which denote the similarities and differences between the objects being construed. Elements are the objects which are construed, and in repertory grid analysis they are normally compared and contrasted in groups of three.

Constructs are essentially 'working hypotheses', as they are revised as part of a progressive evolution. Rather than events themselves representing experience, it is the successive construing and reconstruing which is significant. Although personal construct theory has been accused of being too 'mentalistic' in some quarters, it actually avoids many of the established dichotomies within psychology, such as the cognition-emotion division. Through the technique of repertory grid analysis, it also represents a powerful research tool.

Stringer (1976) comprehensively reviews a range of applications of personal construct theory to environmental studies, and describes his own research in the context of town planning. Harrison and Sarre used personal construct theory to analyse retail images, and to study the perceptions of the city of Bath amongst middle-class women (Harrison and Sarre 1975). In Stringer's study of perceptions of planning proposals in south London (Stringer 1976), six alternative proposals were presented to 197 female residents, each relating to the redevelopment of a Victorian shopping centre.

One application specifically addressing tourist decision-making is Riley and Palmer's study of perceptions and experiences of seaside resorts (1976). Repertory grid analysis was seen as offering a solution to the qualitative–quantitative dichotomy prevalent in market research. Riley and Palmer argue that repertory grid analysis offers a valuable alternative to either full-scale quantitative studies, or 'impression-istic reports on attitudes' (Riley and Palmer 1976:154). Using seaside resorts and a representative sample of 60 respondents from six major cities the researchers produced a grid containing 672 constructs or attributes. This was subjected to principal components analysis, indicating groups of respondents with different attitudes towards the seaside resorts. In Gyte's 1988 examination of images of Mallorca, it is noted that repertory grid analysis can be used to identify recurrent images. Using a seven-point scale and a sample of 17, Gyte aimed to measure the various dimensions of image and evaluate how images changed, including 'the dimensions of image that are most relevant at the group level' (Gyte 1988:1). Gyte's study is notable for the formation of a 'consensus repertory grid', representing shared (intersubjective) images amongst respondents.

Tourist experience has been explored through repertory grid analysis by Botterill (Botterill and Crompton 1987, 1996). As the authors argue (1996), amongst the few experiential studies of tourism, most tend to adopt a fairly mechanistic view of human experience. In contrast, Botterill and Crompton (1996) present the experiences of two tourists visiting Britain from the US. Each subject selected six photographs from brochure images, and two of their own. Using these as elements, constructs were then elicited at various stages in the cycle of the trip. An 'anticipations grid' was formed before the trip was made, and this was subjected to cluster analysis using specialised software to reveal distinctive themes in the way the photographs were construed. 'Return grids' were completed after the trip, instructing the respondents to re-evaluate the photographs. The study also enabled the tourists to discuss changes to their constructs, and culminated in the respondents selecting six of their own photographs which best represented their experience.

The results of the study revealed that for one of the respondents, perceptions of the role of history and culture in Britain had changed. A walking tour of Rochester, an informal meeting with a resident of Canterbury and a meeting with an ex-schoolmistress who lived in a disused school building, all made an impression on him. In particular, he re-evaluated his perception of the extent to which history plays a role in the contemporary lives of British people. His repertory grids also reflected his specialist knowledge of agriculture. The other tourist appeared to construe English landscapes in a different way following the trip, although she found it more difficult to account for the changes. In an earlier report, Botterill and Crompton (1987) present the personal constructions of a visitor to Mexico using the same technique. Six months after the trip, a repertory grid was developed and subjected to analysis. For this visitor, there was a clear distinction between positive and negative aspects of the trip. While unpleasant experiences were related to the both the city and rural poverty, pleasant experiences were related to peaceful and sacred places, rituals and culture. Botterill and Crompton (1996) argue that repertory grid analysis can reveal the idiosyncratic experiences so important to tourism, and demonstrate the significance of tourism to everyday life beyond the trip itself.

CASE STUDY 6.1 REPERTORY GRID ANALYSIS OF URBAN TOURIST EXPERIENCE

In addition to analysing the personal constructions of individuals, personal construct theory can also be used to focus on a particular social group or market segment. This case study shows how a consensus repertory grid can enable urban tourism researchers to elicit the intersubjective language used by the group in their decision-making. This was the aim of an urban tourism study which focused on the decision-making of the urban tourism market of Cardiff, Wales (Selby 2000). As it was also intended to include 'non-visitors' who only had naive images of Cardiff, the research was also conducted in two of the destination's competitors – Edinburgh and Bristol.

In the initial piloting stage, a data-recording sheet was produced, with space to record both elements and constructs elicited. Consistent with the aim of maximising the salience of responses, it was decided that both the elements and the constructs would be freely elicited. Consequently, the respondent was required to supply the elements, which were arranged into triads, before supplying constructs based on the similarities and differences perceived in relation to these elements. If the elements are to be elicited, the choice of role group becomes crucial. The role group provides the orientation for the construing of events, so it was decided to link the role groups as closely as possible to decision-making action, whilst keeping the classifications as broad as possible. The role groups devised with the use of the pilot study were as follows:

i) 'Cities that you have visited and would like to visit again in the future.'

ii) 'Cities that you have visited in the past, and would not like to visit again in the future.'

iii) 'Cities that you have not visited, but would like to visit in the future.'

iv) 'Cities that you have not visited, and would not like to visit in the future.'

It was decided to use a convenience sample of independent English-speaking leisure visitors at tourist information centres and attractions. Following permission from the relevant authorities, three sites in Cardiff were chosen: Cardiff Castle, the Civic Centre and Cardiff Bay Visitor Centre. Drawing upon the Cardiff Strategic Tourism Plan (L&R Leisure 1995:2), the sample included visitors to the comparable cities of Bristol and Edinburgh in order to elicit 'naive images' of Cardiff amongst consumers with no first-hand experience of the destination. Edinburgh is obviously a capital city, and in many ways represents a best-case UK example of urban tourism development. Bristol is Cardiff's closest English competitor, with a comparable population and volume of visitors.

Over an eight-month period a total sample of 60 was recruited, divided equally between the three cities. The conversational style of the interviews proved to be a great strength. This was exemplified by a couple from the US visiting Edinburgh. Following an hour-long interview, they were still eager to offer their thoughts during a chance meeting in a bar later in the evening. On average, the interviews lasted 40 minutes, which surprisingly seemed to pass fairly quickly for both researcher and interviewees.

Among the 60 interviews, the number of constructs elicited varied from 5 to 28, but averaged 11. Although socio-demographic data was collected, and a considerable number of elements elicited, the consensus repertory grid is concerned with only the most commonly occurring constructs. Once the researcher was satisfied that the sample generating the 669 constructs was representative, a consensus repertory grid consisting of the most commonly occurring (inter-subjective) constructs was formed. The data was input into a database so that it could be examined in terms of the most commonly used phrases. A series of searches were then made in order to establish the most commonly occurring for both construct and contrast poles.

From the 669 constructs elicited, a consensus repertory grid of 11 of the most commonly reoccurring constructs emerged. The greatest consensus amongst the respondents, concerned the distinction between destinations considered 'old/historical', and those considered 'modern/lacking history'. This construct appeared to be particularly closely related to decision-making action in this particular market. Some of the constructs which emerged were rather predictable in terms of their importance in drawing visitors. These included 'unique/ interesting' as opposed to 'uninteresting', 'arts and culture' as opposed to 'lacks arts and culture', and 'impressive buildings', as opposed to 'unimpressive buildings'. A slightly more holistic construct to emerge was 'good atmosphere' versus 'lacks atmosphere'.

Other constructs seemed to be elicited out of characteristics which detract from the visitor experience in urban destinations. These included 'unsafe/high crime' as opposed to 'safe/low crime', 'congested/crowded' with the contrast 'open', 'dirty' versus 'clean', and 'accessible' versus 'inaccessible'. Surprisingly, despite the significance of industrial heritage in urban tourism, 'industrial' emerged as a term with negative connotations, contrasted with the positive connotation of 'countryside/parks'.

Although some of the constructs are already well used by urban tourism researchers, and are perhaps unsurprising, other aspects of the decision-making language of these tourists are less predictable. For example, rather paradoxically, urban destinations which offer an 'open environment', with access to 'countryside/parks' seem to be perceived particularly positively. The data from the study is of interest *per se*, but also significant is the potential of the technique in underpinning and informing larger-scale quantitative studies. As discussed in chapter four, the lack of salience of many place image studies to consumer decision-making detracts from their validity and potential for policy analysis.

Humanistic Geography

The most notable application of phenomenology to geographical studies occurred during the 1970s, motivated by the dominance of the 'peopleless' spatial science. The conceptualisation of geography as spatial science employed a reductionist view of humans which was 'overly objective, mechanistic and deterministic' (Entrikin 1976:616). Under the assumption of perfect knowledge, the meanings, values and emotions of humans were completely omitted. Spatial science was criticised for its insistence on the use of law-like statements and certainty in referring to human decision-making (see Olsson 1980; Philo 1984), and conceptualising the decision-maker as 'rational economic man' (see Wallace 1978). Dissatisfaction with attempts to provide a cognitive-behavioural alternative (see Harvey 1969) increased the need to truly capture the human perspective and 'people' human geography.

Increasingly, human geographers began to draw upon phenomenology in an attempt at 'understanding meaning, value, and human significance of life events' (Buttimer 1979:7), seeking 'an expansive view of what the human person is and can do' (Tuan 1976:34). For phenomenologists, knowledge of places does not exist independently of the knower. Knowledge is produced through experiencing the world, and can only be analysed on that basis. Rather than seeking explanations, the researcher should be interested in a sensitive appreciation of experiences of places. Lowenthal (1961:257) argues for 'personal geographies ... inspired, edited, and distorted by feeling', thereby placing a much greater emphasis on the interpretation of environments. An innovative application of phenomenology is Seamon's exploration of daily lifeworlds (1979). Three main themes are used: movement, rest and encounter. Movement denotes everyday environmental transactions, rest represents person-to-place attachments and encounter is interaction and observation of the world. Using 'environmental experience groups', Seamon (1979:17) develops the concept of 'place ballets – an interaction of many time-space routines' (Seamon 1979:56). This approach emphasises everyday experience, and also addresses the spatial dialogues of different groups. An example of such dialogues is the way planners' notions of place are contested by various groups of place consumers.

Tuan's influential book *Topophilia* is devoted to 'all the human beings' active ties with the material environment' (Tuan, 1974:93). Tuan puts an explicit emphasis on phenomenology, advocating that humanistic geography fosters 'an understanding of the human world by studying people's relations with nature, their geographical behaviour, as well as their feelings and ideas in regard to space and place' (Tuan 1976:266). Tuan (1974) uses the term 'existential response' to reject spatial science in preference for the meaning of space, as 'it is a sign of something beyond itself, to its own past and future, and to other objects' (Tuan 1971:184). Tuan goes on to state that 'under "existentialism" he seeks meaning in the landscape, as he would in literature, because it is a repository of human striving' (ibid.:184). Using examples such as the front-back symmetry of the human body and the social proximity of Greenland Eskimos, Tuan shows an unusual sensitivity to place.

Another geographer who draws upon phenomenology is Relph, who is perhaps more loyal to the ethos of existentialism in his 'phenomenology of geography'. He argues that human geography exists precisely to codify the everyday experiences of people: 'the experience of places, spaces and landscapes in which academic geography originates are a fundamental part of everyone's experience, and geography has no exclusive claim to them' (Relph 1985:16). One of Relph's worthwhile aims is to recover the true character of everyday experiences, and to prevent a situation where 'abstract technical thinking has begun to submerge geographical experiences' (ibid.:28). Through examining four basic concepts – region, landscape, space and place – he seeks to build an interest in 'sense of place'. Relph also contributes to an impressive collection of humanistic writing contained in *Dwelling, Place and Environment* (Seamon and Mugeraurer, 1985). 'Sense of place' has also been taken up by authors such as Samuels, an existential geography which aims to 'reconstruct a landscape in the eyes of its occupants, users, explorers, and students' (Samuels 1981:129). Recognising the potential of existential geography in examining social knowledge and meaning, Jackson (1981:303) claims that 'it allows an analysis of the spatial structure of social relations'.

Limitations of Experiential Approaches
Individualistic Studies

Any renaissance of humanistic approaches raises familiar questions about the limitations of phenomenology. Although some recent experiential studies refer only implicitly to phenomenology, it is worth revisiting some of the past debates concerning the use of humanist approaches. An element of this critique which is relevant to contemporary applications, relates to the tendency of studies to focus upon individuals and essences, rather than social groups and variety. The former can be seen as relegating the social nature of phenomena such as urban tourism, and denying the structure which defines the limits of action. This debate is also relevant to the challenges of combining non-representational geography with cultural analysis.

Perhaps one of the clearest calls for the use of a pure Husserlian phenomenology comes from Pickles (1985), one of the least accommodating humanistic geographers, finding serious problems in any movement away from a rigorous and pure phenomenological geography. He is absolutely opposed to any form of 'geographical phenomenology...concerned with lifeworld as object of study and as everyday mundane experience' (Pickles 1985:45). Pickles would therefore consider anything other than a pure application of phenomenology to human geography invalid. It is interesting, therefore, that contemporary humanistic researchers (e.g. Strohmayer 1996; Ryan 2000) cite Husserl as an important influence.

Edmond Husserl is considered to be the founder of phenomenology, and he advocated a rather strict and pure search for 'essences' (1965). Essences refer to the essential characteristics of phenomena, beyond the surface manifestations. As Spiegelburg states:

> The phenomenological approach...confines itself to the direct evidence of intuitive seeing...it constitutes a determined attempt to enrich our experience by bringing out hitherto neglected aspects of experience...an unusually obstinate attempt to look at the phenomena and to remain faithful to them before even thinking about them [Spiegelburg 1971:700].

Husserl's motto 'to the things themselves' implied that the researcher must focus on the meaning given to the items in an individual's world. In the context of urban tourism, this approach might focus attention on the fundamental motivations to travel to a city, and the fundamental meaning of the experiences to individual tourists. This involves a study of the 'natural attitude' in which individuals live their lives. Husserl's 'pure science of the mind', however, was more concerned with stripping away meanings deposited by scientific and everyday understandings of the world, attempting to 'bracket' them out through phenomenological reduction in order to discover the deepest relationships that humans have with the world.

The main attraction to social researchers was the powerful critique of the way in which scientific and positivist researchers ignored their own role in the research process, a mistake he termed the 'sickness of European society' (1965). This 'universal and pure science of the spirit' (ibid.:154) was particularly influential in considering how the humanity of the researcher should be incorporated into the research process. He believed, however, in a transcendal subjectivity, a search for fundamental truths. This obviously sits very uneasily with contemporary 'postmodern' society and contemporary social science.

Accessibility and Terminology

Relph (1981:102) points out that the language of phenomenology is 'exceedingly difficult to penetrate'. Billinge (1977:64) is pessimistic about any adoption of 'pure' phenomenology, writing of the disturbing tendency to adopt terminology the exact meaning of which is manifestly misunderstood. There is little doubt that Seamon's concepts such as 'place ballets' (1979) also fall foul of Relph's concern about the lack of accessibility of humanistic terminology (Relph 1981). It is ironic that the language of humanistic concepts can seem alien and even intimidating, detracting from their potential for understanding how ordinary people interact with their surroundings. The effectiveness of applying phenomenology within Tuan's renowned work (1971, 1974) is also difficult to assess. Tuan is primarily concerned with teasing out universal essences of people–place relations, uncovering the essential ways in which meaning exists *a priori* in the world. This is not dissimilar to the tendency within the tourism literature to seek universal explanations of tourist motivations, ignoring the wide variety of contexts in which tourism exists. Furthermore, it could be argued that Tuan's work exemplifies another flaw of humanistic geography – romanticism. As Relph argues in a retrospective review, it is actually the contemporary importance of place marketing and urban tourism which makes aspects of Tuan's work problematic:

> *Topophilia* seems almost too positive in its account of environmental experiences and it is tempting to see it almost as a work of nostalgia…environmental attitudes and values, even in former nonliterate cultures, are now profoundly influenced by everyday processes of imposition and distortion, such as those of television, advertising, heritage invention and the deliberate exploitation of place identities by entrepreneurs seeking attractive locations for flexible capital. How can these be ignored? (Relph 1994:359)

Contemporary Issues

Some of these limitations can be recognised in contemporary humanistic tourism research. Ryan (2000:122) states that phenomenographers 'trace its antecedents to the conceptualisation of intentionality by Husserl (1970)'. The limitations of Husserl's strict approach to experience are again relevant. In Ryan's discussion, however, a contradiction emerges. Dall'Alba (cited in Ryan 2000:122) states that 'understanding or perceiving cannot be separated from what is understood or perceived'. Earlier, however, Ryan confidently asserts that 'phenomenography is…not to be confused with phenomenology. Phenomenology is a study of what people perceive in the world; phenomenography is a study of the way they perceive the world' (ibid.:122). Ryan also states that 'phenomenology creates constructs of the researcher, whilst phenomenography elicits the individual's construction' (ibid.:123). Ryan later cites Marton (ibid.:124), who notes that 'as phenomenological research is empirical research, the researcher (interviewer) is not studying his or her own awareness and reflection, but that of their subjects'. These contradictory statements demonstrate the sort of misunderstanding of terminology which was of concern to Billinge (1977).

Not only is phenomenology misrepresented by Ryan as only consisting of the Husserlian variety, but there is also an absence of the spirit of humanistic research. Given the strong aversion amongst phenomenologists to both positivism and behaviourism, it is curious that Ryan (ibid.:124) cites Skinner in a discussion of learning. Despite citing Husserl, the most extreme phenomenologist of all, he states that 'phenomographic research shares more with post-positivistic research methodologies than with the (de)constructionist theories normally associated with Urry, Rojek, Lash, Dann and Hollinshead in their commentaries on tourism' (ibid.:125). Having presented an impressive experiential study Li (2000) reverts to a discussion of 'cognition' using behaviouralist, rather than humanistic, terminology. Despite the richness of the data produced by the study, Li (2000:878) ultimately presents a rather simplistic and mechanistic model representing stages of tourist behaviour, and associated experiences which are either 'positive' or 'negative'. If, as post-positivism asserts, there is an objective reality but it can only be imperfectly understood, what authors such as Ryan (2000) is advocating is little different from the cognitive-behaviouralist studies which complemented (rather than challenged) 'spatial science' in the 1960s. What appears to be an innovation within tourism studies appears rather less revolutionary on closer inspection.

We have examined how MacCannell calls for an appreciation of tourist agency, stating that he wants to 'move very quickly to dispel any sense that this formulation of the second gaze is merely theoretical' (2001:31). It is ironic, however, that in order to challenge the 'tourist gaze', particularly the overemphasis on tourism texts, he chooses a text written in 1836. Although *Memoires of a Tourist* (Stendhal cited in MacCannell 2001:31–35) does enable the existential characteristics of tourism to be discussed, the 'second gaze' is intended to conceptualise the contemporary experience of tourists. The argument would be much more convincing, therefore, if it was demonstrated through examples of the experiences of actual tourists. Likewise, Crang's (1997) study of 'Research Through the Tourist Gaze' suggests 'strategies for academic research' rather than engaging with actual tourists. For an alternative conceptualisation of tourist agency, it is surprising that MacCannell treats 'tourists' in a universal and unproblematic way. Amongst the few references to research with tourists, MacCannell states:

> I could summarize the central finding of all the research I have done on tourists as follows: the act of sightseeing is itself organised around a kernel of resistance to the limitations of the tourist gaze. The strongest indication of this resistance is the desire to get beyond touristic representation. This is a desire which almost all tourists will express if given an opportunity [MacCannell 2001:31].

The only other reference to research with actual tourists is MacCannell (1976). MacCannell (2001) provides a welcome discussion of tourist experience, and presents a useful alternative to Urry's 'deterministic' and 'narcissistic' tourist gaze. However, despite emphasising variations in tourist experience and discussing the unexpected and existential characteristics of tourism, it is unfortunate that the universal tourist is still presented. Just as not all tourists fall into Urry's model of searching for a contrast with the everyday, not all tourists resist touristic representation. From visitors to theme parks to clubbers on Ibiza, resistance is minimal. It may be that the 'second gaze' is particularly important to urban tourists, but any references to the universal tourist somewhat devalue the argument.

Despite some useful applications of phenomenology, it would seem that the humanistic genre has been rather fragmented. A tendency towards a Husserlian search for essences, or individualistic forms of existentialism, has made much humanistic research rather inaccessible. In relation to the early phenomenological studies, Mercer and Powell stated that 'it is not possible to prove anything by the phenomenological method, and ... argument is impossible' (Mercer and Powell 1972:14). Gould was particularly scathing, asking 'how much further do we push back – to psychoanalytic studies that tell us that some "lolits" (Little Old ladies in Tennis Shoes) avoid certain stores because they have red shutters ...' (Gould 1976:87). Given the interest in inter-subjectivity by authors such as Samuels (1981), however, it is surprising that so few authors have drawn upon the work of writers such as Schutz (e.g. 1962, 1972).

Ley was perhaps one the first geographers to recognise the significance of the intersubjective and taken-for-granted meanings of different groups in their experience of place. Long arguing for the sensitive incorporation of place into geographical research (Ley 1980a, 1981a, 1981b, 1982), he made considerable progress in his study of inner-city Philadelphia (Ley 1974). Both explicitly (Ley 1977, 1981a), and implicitly, Ley recognised the fundamental (yet largely unrealised) contribution of Alfred Schutz to human geography. In particular, a Schutzian framework allows geographers to escape from restrictive Husserlian traditions of phenomenology. Instead, the geographer can gain an understanding of the shared meanings and everyday 'common sense' knowledge of groups of people. Rather than encouraging individualistic or subjective studies, this provides a means of exploring the consumption of cultural texts.

Existential Perspectives
Being-in-the-world

A form of phenomenology, of inspiration to humanistic geographers past and present, is existentialism. Existentialist philosophers, such as Sartre (1948) and Merleau-Ponty (1962), although differing in their emphases, sought to escape from the obsession with essences. They focused instead on existence, conceptualising reality as that which is created by actors themselves. Human beings are seen as possessing will and consciousness, creating meaning through their actions. Sartre, for example, insisted that 'man (sic) is nothing more than that which he makes of himself' (Sartre 1948:28). Merleau-Ponty also emphasised the way understanding is embedded in the actions of people, 'according to the way we settle ourselves in the world and the position our bodies assume in it' (Merleau-Ponty cited in M. Crang 1997:371). This conceptualisation is implicit in recent studies emphasising the embodied nature of tourism, in which the tourist is conceptualised as active, alert and seeking experience through their movement and interaction with the physical environment and other people.

To existentialists, therefore, humans are not initially in possession of meaning, but create it through decisions. The notion of 'alienation' in existentialism stems from the need to constantly strive to create meaning in the world, and fill the 'existential void'. This latter concept was attractive to Marxists, as the capitalist mode of production was believed to alienate humanity from nature, and encourage people to fill the void with ever-increasing amounts of material possessions. To humanistic geographers, however, the emphasis on experience, meaning and identity is particularly attractive when related to localities and the 'sense of place' of people. Researchers such as Albers and James (1988) have identified a form of alienation caused by tourism. Within representations of tourism, from tourist brochures to postcards, the signs that mark out what should be seen can become more important than the sites themselves. Any authentic engagement with the landscapes of tourist cities is therefore lost.

Fiction has often been used by existentialists (and 'closet existentialists' such as Camus) to emphasise the absurd and tragic aspects of the search for an authentic self. Merleau-Ponty (1963) was particularly notable for his emphasis on perception, particularly the way in which the various projects of different individuals influences their gaze. Significantly for urban tourism, any movement towards an understanding of society would start from the perceptions of individuals. Heidegger (1967) became renowned for his conceptualisation of 'Dasein' or 'Being-in the-world'. This is a state dominated by the spatial and temporal relationships between humans and objects in the world. While perhaps a little more concerned with essences than other existentialists, it is worth noting that Heidegger's notion of Dasein remains attractive to contemporary social and cultural geographers.

Existential phenomenology is concerned with the notion of *Gestalt*, meaning form or structure. There is a belief that neither behaviour nor experience is reducible to the sum of the parts but displays a primordial structure (Merleau-Ponty 1963:125–28). This holistic conceptualisation of the city is not consistent with positivist or rationalist approaches, which are concerned with (possibly irrelevant) causal relationships between separate components. Although such contributions were made some years ago, it is significant that the well-documented complexity, ambiguity and blurring of the constituent parts of the postmodern city would seem to add credence to holistic conceptualisations.

According to existentialists, the individual is neither completely knowledgeable of their surroundings (objective) nor psychologically constituting their environment (subjective). Merleau-Ponty writes of 'a certain consistency in our "world", relatively independent of stimuli...' and '...a certain energy in the pulsation of existence, relatively independent of our voluntary thoughts' (Merleau-Ponty 1962:xviii). It is necessary, therefore, to look at the 'the whole mode of existence of the subject(s) in question, on the way he (sic) projects an environment around himself, on the way he is in the world' (Spurling 1977:15). It is this intentional arc, as it 'projects round us our past, our future, our human setting, our physical, ideological and moral situation', which sets the scene for intentional behaviour (Merleau-Ponty 1962:xviii).

Consistent with a holistic approach to the city, it is argued that there are 'lived' impressions of the city which are not immediately open to logical deductions by individuals. Both Husserl (1969) and Merleau-Ponty (1962) differentiate 'operative intentionality', from the more conscious and voluntary judgments involved in the 'intentionality of acts'. Crucial to phenomenology, the former is a common (if neglected) aspect 'of the world and of our life, being apparent in our desires, our evaluations and in the landscape we see, more clearly than in objective knowledge' (Merleau-Ponty 1962:xviii). It is, then, by striving to closely examine the foundations of pre-reflective experience in specific contexts, that social scientists can understand, and eventually begin to predict, intentional acts such as travelling.

For phenomenologists, perception is 'the always presupposed foundation of all rationality, all value, and all existence' (Merleau-Ponty 1963:7). In many epistemologies, including both materialism and behaviouralism, there is a basic dichotomy between subject and object, inside and outside, the physical world and the psychological world (see Luckmann 1973). The objective world is conceptualised as given, data passes into sense organs, data is deciphered and the picture reassembled. This approach is common in the urban tourism literature, exemplified by Page (1995) in chapter two. Images become distortions of the objective world, inadequacies of the reassembling process. Schutz (1962:128) describes this as a 'dualistic cleavage', influenced by the 'unclarified rationalism of the mathematical sciences'.

It is possible, however, to break away from this 'dualism of being and appearance' (Sartre 1969) and the search for a hidden reality, replacing them with the 'monism of phenomenon'. Perceptions are posited by existentialists to be patterned into fields. Significantly, the contents of these fields, particularly the patterning of perceived objects, depends on how individuals focus their gaze. This depends on their interests at hand, as much as on the nature of the object itself (Spurling 1977). Each individual's unique perspective, therefore, causes perception to be embodied. As M.Crang (1997:365) argues, in the context of tourism, 'images, sights, activities are all linked through the embodied motion of the observer...'. Individuals, in their everyday 'natural attitude', live through perception, with each perceptual subject charged with different emotions and motivations, and each perceptual object viewed from a particular perspective.

Existing in the City

If 'perception is the background from which all acts stand out' (Merleau-Ponty 1962:x–xi), the significance of the perceived city becomes apparent. Furthermore, the perspectival nature of perception, allied with individuals' general lack of awareness of that perspective, implies that intentional acts are based on only profiles of objects, parts of conversations and chance encounters with representations and landscapes.

Different groups of urban tourists, therefore, will base their intentional acts on their own unique foundations. These foundations are built from fragments of experience, imperfect knowledge from a plethora of sources.

Where existential phenomenology goes further than most epistemologies, is its transcendence of the subject–object dichotomy. If there are 'no things, only physiognomies' (Merleau-Ponty 1963:168), objects are not determinate and external to the perceiver, but the embodiment of perceptual intentions. This is obviously very different from Foucault's 'panoptic gaze' (Foucault 1977) on which Urry (1990a) bases his conceptualisation. The openness of a city, its atmosphere, its people, and its style, will influence the visitor's experience of individual objects (see Canter 1979, 1988). An individual's positioning within, gaze upon and openness to the city, creates its form. As MacCannell (2001:34) argues, tourists rearrange what they are seeing to make them more interesting, or more consistent with their version of history. Objects are not, however, inert and passive receptacles of this process; instead they form systems of interlocking objects, some emphasising other objects, some obscuring them. In vision, it is the visual field as a whole which directs one's gaze, assigning value and significance to each part. As M.Crang (1997) points out, although sight-seeing is an important part of the practice of tourism, Merleau-Ponty does not believe the world is merely a series of images. Instead, the embodied movement of the tourist structures how the world is grasped, and sight is one of the ways of obtaining this embodied knowledge of the tourist destination.

Perception 'arranges around the subject a world which speaks to him of himself (see Canter 1979), and gives his own thoughts their place in the world' (Merleau-Ponty 1962:132). Despite the gender-specific language of Merleau-Ponty in this case, feminist writers (see Nash 1996) have also demonstrated how ways of seeing the world are always closely related to the subject who is doing the observing and 'knowing'. As Jamal and Hollinshead (2001:69) explain in the context of tourism, the self is intimately related to the other, requiring an interpretive relationship between the seer and that which is seen, for example the tourist gaze and the experience of the tourist. Furthermore, ways of seeing tourist destinations can reshape the physical world. Stallabrass (cited in M.Crang 1997:361) argues that tourist photographs have this effect, and 'we might consider the estimated sixty billion photographs taken each year as points of light on the globe, densely clustered around iconic sights and trailing off into a darkened periphery'.

The fragmented and schizophrenic nature of the postmodern city has received considerable attention (e.g. Harvey 1989a; Jameson 1984). It has been suggested that this is primarily due to a breakdown of traditional signifying chains, producing 'a rubble of distinct and unrelated signifiers' (Jameson 1984). A consequence of this plethora of messages is an increase in the instances of dissonance between different signifiers. From the perspective of urban tourists, it is also clear that these messages influence expectations of geographical experience. The perceived absence of things which were expected, therefore, can be particularly significant to experiences of the city, resulting in a feeling of 'non-being' (Sartre 1969:11). This sense of 'non-being' in cities, when people's expectations of what they will find in a place are jolted by what they actually find, is explored by Canter (1979) in the context of environmental psychology.

Existential approaches conceptualise meaning as that which makes a difference, whether directly intended or not, 'as reliefs and configurations ... in the landscape of praxis' (Merleau-Ponty 1963). Humans create meaning in the world, even when they do not intend to signify anything, as every gesture, or even the lack of a gesture, signifies something. Interrelated and interlocking layers of significance are produced, and these are always open to different interpretations. Of relevance to the contemporary city, this is 'enough to question the cleavage between the real and the imaginary' (Merleau-Ponty 1970).

The transcendence of the subject–object dichotomy is particularly relevant to urban tourism. The city is increasingly a stage for media-led participation, spectacle and images (Ley and Olds 1988). The urban tourist is an object of economic development, the recipient of promotional messages and 'staged authenticity', yet also an agent of capital, consuming commodified culture and objectifying people and places. M.Crang (1997:366) argues that in holiday photographs the tourist may be the object of a photograph, but is simultaneously involved in an act of self-expression. It is quite possible that ambivalent attitudes towards the tourism industry and the polarised academic perspectives discussed in chapter three stem from the challenging ontological status of the tourist.

Urban Tourist Knowledge
The Tourism Lifeworld

Whilst it is apparent that existential phenomenology can provide insights into urban tourism, it would seem that an emphasis on intersubjectivity and action (Schutz and Luckmann 1974; Schutz 1972) has more potential. Schutz grounds his work with the belief that 'everyday life is ... fundamental and paramount reality' (Schutz and Luckmann 1974:3). As MacCannell (2001:25) argues, 'everyday life is where character is gained and lost; it is the original locus of psychological and other kinds of drama'. As Bhabha (1994) argues, small events and everyday actions are crucial in forming the identity of people and places. While many tourism theorists dichotomise everyday life and tourism, authors such as Schutz show how the experience of tourism as a whole is finely integrated into everyday life. The individual takes experiences for granted as common sense, whilst also sharing experiences with others in an intersubjective world. The tourist destination, therefore, is nether material nor imaginary, but 'a reality which we modify through our acts and which, on the other hand, modifies our actions' (Schutz and Luckmann 1974:6). As Entrikin (1991:6) argues, 'place is both a center of meaning, and the external context of our actions'.

The understanding of tourists and hosts draws upon a great variety of both immediate and mediated experiences, termed the 'stock of knowledge' by Schutz (1972). An individual understands experiences of places on the basis of similar previous experiences. Furthermore, individuals only become aware of the gaps in their knowledge if an experience does not fit into what had previously been taken for granted. This incongruency, when 'the taken for granted experience explodes' (Schutz and Luckmann 1974:11), demands a re-explanation of experience. The stock of knowledge of tourists and hosts develops with new experiences. In familiar situations, however, they can rely on previously proven 'recipes' for acting, and these are likely to have been socially transmitted. Such recipes include the acting out of tourist rituals, such as taking photographs at famous landmarks or following guided tours of attractions which 'can't be missed'. The tourism industry, with the collaboration of travel writers, provides these recipes particularly through their use of promotional cliches (see Voase 2000), inviting tourists to 'step back in time', 'rediscover' or 'trace the steps'. The hosts of urban tourist destinations also practice 'recipes' for acting. In destinations such as London, for example, residents may avoid certain areas of the city regularly congested with crowds of tourists, yet join the tourists for particular events such as a carnival or film premiere. These acts are based on both previous experience, and 'local knowledge' acquired socially.

Cultural meaning, therefore, exists in linguistic typifications, yet in the 'natural attitude', 'everyone' in the same social group experiences and takes for granted these meanings. In this way, every individual belongs to a social system divided by familial relationships, age groups, generations, divisions of labour and occupations – all of which affect the distribution of typical experiences. Both tourists and hosts partly experience tourism individually, and partly through positions and perspectives forced upon him or her through an intersubjective 'natural world view'. In every situation, an urban tourist will find elements of their surroundings which are unalterable, and elements which can be modified. Tourists are in a 'spatiotemporal and social situation…in a naturally and socially articulated surrounding world' (Schutz and Luckmann 1974:19). Tourists understand the typical consequences of acts, and they have, therefore, 'a system of motivations for practicable goals' (ibid.:20).

The Stock of Tourist Knowledge

Because language has such an influence, it is possible to 'grasp the knowledge based on it as the core area of the lifewordly stock of knowledge' (Schutz and Luckmann 1974:123). Experiences may bring nothing new to the stock of knowledge, and are merely fitted into existing types. Alternatively, they may be regarded as worthy of forming new types. The knowledge of urban tourists and hosts is obviously acquired in different 'provinces of reality', whether they be first-hand experience at the destination, tourism promotion, education, the mass media or various social contexts. The style of lived experience determines what is taken for granted, and what is problematic amongst the knowledge acquired. MacCannell (2001) argues that the tourist is increasingly aware of the institutionalised tourist gaze, and may seek out what is missing from the tourism 'product'. It is not argued, therefore, that each province of reality is accorded an equal level of priority by the tourist or resident, as previous meanings are often left behind with the arrival of more credible provinces of reality.

Kelly's concept of 'constructive alternativism' is useful in understanding environmental experience (1955). This concept asserts that reality cannot reveal itself to us, instead it is subject to as many ways of construing it as we can invent. In order to understand and anticipate experience, each individual develops a system of constructions which can be imposed upon the events encountered. Since it is the meaning contained within these constructions that is argued to be central to anticipating, this meaning is vital in any attempt at predicting action. His 'fundamental postulate' is that 'a person's processes are psychologically chanelised by the ways in which he [sic] anticipates events' (Kelly 1955:46). Kelly argues that a construct is both an integrating and differentiating process, whereby at least two events are perceived as similar to one another and different from at least one other event. The tourist destination is therefore 'grasped not only as that which is, but rather also that which it is not' (Schutz and Luckmann 1974:173). The stock of knowledge therefore contains 'not only … "positive" aspects of knowledge, but also … "negative" determinations' (ibid.:167). As Ryan (2000:120) argues, tourists are actors in 'self-selected sets of action' and 'affective assessments of difference'. In this way, the system of constructs which a person establishes for themselves represents the network of pathways along which they are free to move (Bannister and Mair 1968:27).

Following Schutz and Luckmann (1974), it is only when an individual is faced with contradictory information about a tourist destination that an active attempt to confirm or reject knowledge is sought through the accumulation of further information. Of interest to image marketers, it would seem that contradictions are less likely if knowledge is gained in different provinces of reality. It would seem, therefore, that the 'image reconstruction' engaged in by place marketers may be considerably more complex than commonly thought. It is common for destination marketers to conceptualise the 'information search' stage in consumer decision-making models. According to Schutz and Luckmann, however, it would seem more important to consider contradictions between promotional messages in different 'provinces of reality' or discourses. The montage of representations encountered by consumers results in a vast stock of knowledge to be drawn upon. Schutz and Luckmann maintain that additional information is only sought when there is contradictory or insufficient knowledge gathered as part of everyday life.

Immediate and Mediated Experience

Tourists' memories of places play an important role in the experience of tourism, and some 'become more and more vivid through typifications embedded in contexts' (Schutz and Luckmann 1974:38). As M.Crang (1997) argues, the destination is captured in photographs, which are then presented to friends and relatives as evidence of 'being there'. Analysing the memories of tourists is a useful avenue of humanistic tourism research, exemplified by Botterill's (1989) study using photographs to elicit the memories and experiences of a visitor to Mexico. Experiences are said to be in 'restorable reach' (Schutz and Luckmann 1974:38) when they are stored in the stock of knowledge and can be re-experienced. The spatial zone of the future is termed 'the world within attainable reach' (ibid.:39). Schutz and Luckmann recognise that 'attainable reach' depends on the level of development and technology in a society. This also influences the extent to which individuals are already familiar with the world in attainable reach. Schutz and Luckmann, writing some years ago, recognised that technology has 'enormously extended our possibilities of action in respect to distance, quantity, and results' (ibid.:44), and that: 'through technological development there has entered here a qualitative leap in the range of experience and an enlargement of the zone of operation … In the end, this concerns the questions of the nonmediated and mediated character of action and experience in general' (ibid.:44). The transition between immediate and mediated experience is rarely problematic, and eased through the use of 'ideal types' (ibid.:57). Contemporary tourism is characterised by a blurring and overlapping of what is primary and what is secondary knowledge, and therefore a seemingly endless extension of what is within attainable reach. Endless representations of tourist destinations via television, the Internet and printed media continuously raise awareness and expectations about the possibilities of travel, and expand the 'pleasure periphery'. As M.Crang (1997) argues, the representations and experience of tourism are closely interrelated, and should not be artificially separated. Fullager (2001) also argues that tourism demonstrates how the spatial present is never free of the past. Because past lives are inscribed on the tourist destination, the present is 'haunted by the possibility of involuntary memories and stories' (Game cited in Fullager 2001).

Some typifications, however, have been handed down to individuals, through sign systems and language. Also significant are the 'legitimatizations of social institutions, laws, and recipes for acts' (Schutz and Luckmann 1974:95). A person's role within society is also influential in forming the 'possibilities, impossibilities, and taken-for-grantedness for his (sic) course of life' (ibid.:95). Factors such as a person's social class, ethnic group, age, occupation, lifestyle and personality, and way that people define themselves, determine the 'degree of freedom in the choice of various courses of life' (ibid.:95). It is argued that geographical knowledge is first formed through the influence of significant others, particularly parents and teachers. Subsequently, throughout an individual's life, their role within society continues to have a strong influence on the stock of knowledge.

The level of mediacy or immediacy influences the character of the everyday world, although this does not imply that some sources are more significant than others. Indeed, in the case of tourism, a much larger proportion of knowledge will be acquired through mediated sources. The review in the last chapter demonstrates how cultural researchers have analysed various representations of urban tourist destinations. However, it is surprising that so few have sought to either identify or analyse representations typically experienced by place consumers. Only in immediate situations at the tourist destination

6.3: Rome: past lives inscribed on the tourist destination. Courtesy of Department of Geography, Liverpool John Moores University.

can actors share the same spatial and temporal sectors, and, therefore, similar 'thematic relevances' (ibid.:254). Although immediate experiences of a tourist destination will be more intersubjective than mediated experiences, individuals will obviously differ in both their specific encounters and their interpretation.

Intersubjective Tourist Experience

Society influences urban tourist knowledge in two ways. Firstly, society determines the experiences which are considered relevant and communicable. Secondly, the majority of an individual's knowledge itself is gained within social groups rather than individually. Most of the stock of knowledge is mediated, therefore, rather than immediately acquired. Of particular significance, then, is the fact that the place consumer, whilst having subjective experiences, also learns through intersubjective events. Social relations are imposed upon the child, particularly by parents and teachers. These authority figures, although influential, are in turn influenced by social institutions and society's norms and values. From early childhood, even experiences acquired first hand are 'embedded in intersubjectively relevant, socially determined, and predelineated contexts' (ibid.:246–47). Ringer (1998:6) argues that it is vital for tourism researchers to understand the multiple realities of social groups within tourism destinations, and the different ways in which they experience, interpret and articulate the values and meanings of their destination.

6.4: Hong Kong: now within the attainable reach of Western European tourists. Courtesy of Department of Geography, Liverpool John Moores University.

Language plays a fundamental role in intersubjective knowledge, particularly as individuals are born into a situation where language is already given as 'a component of the historical social world' (Schutz and Luckmann 1974:233). Language, therefore, contains ready-made categories or types, built up from experience over generations. While the individual is free to form their own types, society removes the burden of so doing, and also indirectly influences type construction through imposing language which reflects society's priorities. Language, therefore, acts as a framework for everyone's subjective experiences.

The subjective experiences of members of a society are, in effect, stabilised around median values for typical experiences. In this way, 'subjective experiences become comparable to each other' (ibid.:250) within the flow of experience. If the knowledge of tourists is partly socially distributed, analysing the factors which influence this distribution of this knowledge becomes a fundamental activity for urban tourism researchers. It is argued here that contrary to psychoanalytical cultural studies, which are concerned only with the pre-linguistic, language plays a major role in both structuring and understanding tourist experience.

Experiencing Representations

Schutz and Luckmann (1974) discuss the 'reality' of representations. In particular, it is stressed that reality is created through the meaning of our experience. Citing the Greek sceptic Carneades, Schutz emphasises that representations cannot be either true or false; instead, more or less plausible truths exist for different individuals. A tourism representation's plausibility depends on the state of the individual at the time, and whether or not it contradicts other representations. The tourist, therefore, acts on the basis of more or less probable representations. This implies that tourism and cultural researchers should avoid privileging particular landscapes or representations, without establishing which are salient to place consumers. As M.Crang (1997:364) argues in the context of tourism, it is important 'to avoid dichotomising the world of represent-ations and experience'.

Schutz's conceptualisation of representations is not unlike the process of 'indexing, dragging, and social construction' discussed by Rojek (1997). Rojek describes an index of representations (ibid.:53) consisting of signs, images and symbols which make a tourist site familiar in everyday life. The process of indexing involves a 'file of representation', containing the media and conventions associated with signifying a particular tourist site. This might include novels, poems and television drama, which are just as important as, if not more important than, factual information about the tourist destination. These diverse elements are dragged from separate files of repre-sentation to create a new value for the site or destination. It is significant that this process occurs as part of the everyday life of the tourist, and visiting the actual destination may result in a feeling of disappointment when it fails to live up to expectations. The process itself is argued to reduce the aura of tourist destinations.

The Production and Consumption of Representations

Of relevance to the images projected by tourism organisations, the term 'objectivation' is used to denote the 'embodiment of subjective processes in the objects of the everyday life-world' (Schutz and Luckmann 1974:264). It refers to the use of a sign system, and the possibility of interpreting the 'results of acts' (ibid.:271). Certain activities, such as tourism promotion, or heritage interpretation, 'leave behind traces in lifewordly objects' (ibid.:272). These traces may vary in terms of how intentional they were, but they refer back to the activities of those producing both the landscapes and representations of urban tourism.

In the case of second-hand (mediated) knowledge of a tourist destination, the interpretation of this knowledge is detached from the original spatial, temporal and social contexts. It depends, therefore, on the familiarity between the interpreter and the creator of the signs. The interpreter must be familiar with the system of signs for the signs to be translated back to subjective knowledge. Conversely, the better the user of signs '... knows the Other, the better he can anticipate the Other's "retranslations"' (ibid.:282). As M.Crang (1997) demonstrates, in the case of tourist photography, the destination is captured through typical signs, and these are chosen on the basis that they will be understood by friends and family as proof of having been there.

It is significant that 'the interpretation of signs in terms of what they signify is based on previous experience and is therefore itself a function of the scheme' (Schutz and Luckmann, 1974:119). The sign is also an indication of an event in the mind of the sign-user. This, termed the 'expressive function' (ibid.:119) should be distinguished from the 'interpretative function' (ibid.:120) which depends on the past experience of the interpreter. In studies of urban tourism, it is often assumed that the two coincide and are not problematic. This leads to an emphasis on the 'expressive function' of signs within the landscape or representations, with little emphasis on the interpretation of signs by place consumers. Whilst this may be acceptable (and necessary) in retrospective studies, place-consumption research should surely be concerned with both expressive and interpretive functions.

It is when knowledge can be objectivated by the tourism industry, while also being embodied by consumers, that it can be transmitted easily to others. Knowledge in signs, therefore, has some rather contradictory qualities: it can have an overwhelming and taken-for-granted independence, yet the meaning is also dependent on the experience of individuals underpinning their interpretation. It follows therefore, that new knowledge can only be transmitted if the categories of meaning in the sign system are familiar. While categories of meaning constantly evolve, in the fragmented and fluid social structures of postmodern society there seems to be some risk in assuming that the producers and consumers of cultural texts use the same categories of meaning.

Social Knowledge

It is important to note that only a fraction of experience is objectivated, and only a fraction of objectivated knowledge enters the social stock of knowledge. The social structure plays a major role in determining which knowledge is objectivated. The contemporary significance of institutions such as the mass media, however, makes for complex power–knowledge relations which influence the process. Even in primitive societies there is a differentiation of knowledge according to typical problems and typical members of society. 'Inherent in this is the tendency for the association of provinces of knowledge in social roles' (Schutz and Luckmann 1974:292). Although in principle such knowledge could be comprehended by everyone, there are typical recipients of certain knowledge.

Certain types of knowledge are considered relevant for certain social roles, and the transmission of this knowledge is conditioned by these roles. The social stock of knowledge, therefore, contains a system of hypothetical solutions related to the problem at hand. Thus both the knowledge and the transmission of knowledge is conditioned by social roles. This process begins with the family – particularly through 'imposed' roles associated with gender – continues through education and progresses to a complex amalgam of occupational and social roles. This transmission of knowledge is also affected in the roles of knowledge transferrers, whether they be parents, teachers, multinational companies, newspaper editors, politicians or tourism organisations.

The individual, through the solutions provided by the social stock of knowledge, is relieved of the need to find their own solutions. The maintenance of such knowledge, therefore, can be interrupted by changes in social structure, or by the discovery of alternative knowledge, including promotional messages. The latter, however, will not be taken for granted in the same way as social knowledge. Of interest to debates concerning the use of mythology and heritage in place marketing, it would seem that 'non-everyday knowledge' is likely to be both resilient and influential to consumers. Such knowledge also occupies an important place in the hierarchy of knowledge, as it can overshadow stereotypes. It is no coincidence that destination marketers often decide not to tackle negative images directly, but to concentrate on place myths and unique destination imagery. From a humanistic perspective, therefore, the reimaging process discussed in chapter two is only likely to be successful when promotional messages are credible and resilient enough to replace the existing social stock of knowledge held by potential visitors. It follows that:

> One of the most important tasks of empirical sociology of knowledge is the examination of structural factors (e.g., the density of communication) and the dimensions of the relative natural world view (e.g., the religiously strengthened 'fixity' of some traditions) which play a decisive role in the historical processes of the accumulation of knowledge [ibid.:299].

Therefore, it is important to understand both the distribution of knowledge amongst different social groups, particularly the distribution of 'higher knowledge' legitimised by institutions and associated representations. Any assumption of a homogeneous distribution of knowledge is flawed. According to Schutz and Luckmann (1974: 330–31), the unequal distribution of knowledge creates configurations of the 'lack of knowledge, half-knowledge, and knowledge of "power" and dependence'.

Tourist Action
Action or Behaviour?

One of Schutz's fundamental contributions, with the potential to inform urban tourism studies, is his theory of action. As Anderson and Gale (1992:4) argue, 'in the course of generating new meanings and decoding existing ones, people construct places, spaces, landscapes, regions, and environments...they fashion certain types of landscapes, townscape, and streetscape'. Tourist destinations are constantly being invented and transformed by people's actions, yet the actions themselves are influenced by geographic arrangements.

With behavioural models of decision-making, there is a lack of attention paid to the distinction between behaviour and action. As Werlen (1993:9) argues, behaviour is correctly used to describe observable responses to stimuli, even if these stimuli are filtered by a cognitive component. By contrast, action is reflexive and intentional, involving goal-orientated human activity. Furthermore, while action refers to 'effecting or preventing a change in the world' (Wright 1971:83 cited in Werlen 1993:11), an 'act' is 'the outcome of this ongoing process, that is, the accomplished action' (Schutz 1962:67). Whilst there are undoubtedly activities which lack conscious attention and therefore 'action' (termed 'conduct' by Schutz), there are persuasive arguments for focusing on action, rather than behaviour, in relation to urban tourist experience and decision-making.

It is argued that by taking socio-cultural factors as given, and by concentrating on the psychological, behaviouralist researchers are unable to capture social context. Social relations, institutions, rules and class structures become mere responses to past stimuli, and are conceptualised as external to behaviour (Werlen 1993:16). Schutz, however, shows how the intersubjective stock of knowledge forms the basis for all action. It is by ignoring the context of action that behavioural approaches fail to fully explain social phenomena, including consumer decision-making. As Schutz puts it:

> Of what use is it to talk about the intended meaning of an action if one ignores that phase which is relevant to the actor and substitutes for it as the interpretation an arbitrarily chosen segment of the observed performance – 'the facts'? When one is watching a woodcutter it will make a great deal of difference whether we try to analyse 'objectively' the individual blows of the ax or whether we simply ask the man what he is doing and find that he is working for a lumber company [Schutz 1972:63].

It is common, therefore, for researchers to assume that the decision-making of consumers can be defined in terms of a unity as designated by the researcher. This often leads to a dissonance between research observations and motivation theory, as the researcher 'defines the concrete action arbitrarily, without reference to the intended meaning of the actor' (Schutz 1972:62). The total act tends to be divided into separate components, and the 'objective' researcher is in no position to know whether each separate goal has been reached, or whether there is more to observe. Significantly, it becomes clear that an act is 'meaningless as action apart from the project which defines it' (ibid.:62).

Projecting Acts of Tourism

The action of tourists is embedded in the everyday and 'home' culture of tourism:

> As winter draws in, millions of us begin wondering, dreaming and possibly planning. Most of us will talk with friends and family, will hear of their past experiences, chat about our hopes and so forth. We read novels, guidebooks, watch programmes of

greater or lesser solemnity, all of which produce for us a phantom landscape which guides our understanding of the one we eventually see [Franklin and Crang 2001:16].

Central to Schutz's action theory is the projecting of action into the future. Significant in any action is a form of 'map-consulting' (Schutz 1970:129). Whilst 'retention' is defined as 'holding the picture before our inner eye' (ibid.:129), 'reproduction' relates to memories of past experiences which are called to mind. Conscious actions, therefore, have been previously mapped out in the future perfect tense in terms of the completed act. As Urry (1990a:3) argues, 'places are chosen to be gazed upon because there is an anticipation, especially through daydreaming and fantasy'. Underlying this process of projection is the belief that one can bring about a similar state of affairs as resulted from a previous similar action: 'these anticipations and expectations follow the typical structures that have held good so far for our past experiences and are incorporated into our knowledge at hand' (Schutz 1970:137).

Of significance for urban tourism, it is the structure of our stock of knowledge at hand that forms the basis for these projections, and these are only filled in by the event itself to 'make it a unique individual occurrence' (ibid.:138). A further justification for monitoring intersubjective stocks of knowledge of tourists stems from their dynamic nature, as 'not only the range but also the structurization of our stock of knowledge changes continually' (ibid.:138). Expectations of a tourist destination are met, therefore, if the occurring event corresponds with the stock of knowledge at the time of anticipating. Through viewing the action in hindsight, satisfaction or dissatisfaction can arise.

In contrast to most theories of tourist decision-making, Schutz argues that decision-makers place themselves 'at a future time when this action will already have been accomplished, when the resulting act will already have materialised' (Schutz 1972:69). Once the act is projected in the future perfect tense, the 'actor becomes self-consciously aware of his phantasying' (ibid.:68). The next act is projected, and this then becomes the focus of the actor's reflective attention. These are then 'retained, reproduced, and compared' (ibid.:68) – evaluated according to the prevailing frame of reference.

When there are overlapping or conflicting interests, the actor is not sure which parts of the stock of knowledge are relevant. This doubt necessitates deliberation, and each act 'takes its turn in projecting itself upon the screen of the imagination. It unrolls a pictures of its future history...' (cited in Schutz 1970:153). Contradictory 'propulsive tendencies' (ibid.:153) also allow habit a role in choice. The decision is reached in a process of clarification of the contesting tendencies by which either the weakness of the counterpossibilities become more and more visible or by which new motives arise which reinforce the prevailing weight of the first (ibid.:155).

A distinction of relevance to urban tourism should be recognised, relating to the status of localities. Whilst most products are objects, and 'the problematic possibilities are, so to speak, ready made and well circumscribed' (ibid.:159), choosing between places involves the rehearsal of future courses of action in the actor's imagination. The true alternatives have to be produced through the process of projecting. The mind successively creates the various projects in 'inner time'. One is dropped in favour of another, and then a previous act is returned to, or recreated (ibid.:159). Because time has elapsed between the two, and the individual's experience has been enlarged, the original project has been modified since the original projecting. This last point, in particular, highlights the danger of approaching tourist decision-making though experimental methodologies which ignore the context of this process. Experiential research (see case study 6.1) suggests that urban tourists do indeed rehearse the typical experiences of destinations that they haven't visited, according to their previous experiences of destinations that they consider 'similar'.

Conclusion

A detailed examination of experiential approaches suggests that studies of the experience of urban tourism should start not from the position of either universal theories, or pure subjectivity. Instead, it is vital to focus on tourists' entire mode of existence in relation to the city – an existential dialectic (Canter 1988). The substantive contribution of phenomenology to urban tourism, however, is found in the work of Alfred Schutz. The intersubjective nature of knowledge and its influence on action is invaluable in understanding urban tourist experience.

It has been seen how the re-enforcement and structuring of the 'natural attitude…of common-sense consciousness' (Berger and Luckmann 1966:23), creates intersubjective knowledge. In addition to immediate experience, the transformation of intersubjective experience into language and tradition plays a crucial role. The representations produced by various institutions, therefore, shape the expectations of urban tourists. Whether knowledge is constituted and transmitted linguistically or visually, it leads to accepted, taken for granted beliefs, and social realities. It is through understanding intersubjective experience, therefore, that researchers can begin to understand the action of place consumers.

The perceived subjectivism and inaccessibility of humanistic geography may have limited the contemporary influence of phenomenology. The conceptualisation of intersubjective knowledge and action proposed by Schutz (1970; Schutz and Luckmann 1974), however, is invaluable in conceptualising and researching tourist experience. It is difficult to dismiss Schutzian phenomenology as 'subjective' or 'individualistic'. His detailed and rigorous theories of intersubjectivity, stock of knowledge and action offer considerable hope in capturing both the immediate and mediated knowledge which is fundamental to understanding urban tourist experience.

Chapter summary:

- There have been some useful humanistic studies of urban tourism, although such studies are few in number.
- Humanistic geographical studies draws upon phenomenology to understand the meanings, knowledge and emotions of people as they experience different places.
- Existential approaches particularly emphasise perception, and are useful in understanding embodied relationships between people and places.
- Common limitations of humanistic approaches include an overemphasis on individuals, a search for universal 'essences' and confusion over terminology.
- The 'social phenomenology' of Schutz overcomes many of the limitations of humanistic approaches, and focuses on social groups rather than individuals.
- Social phenomenology is a powerful (and undervalued) approach to understanding the knowledge, images, experiences and decisions of urban tourists.

Further Reading

Botterill, T.D. and J.L. Crompton (1987) 'Personal Constructions of Holiday Snapshots', *Annals of Tourism Research* 14 (1), 152–56.

— (1996) 'Two Case Studies Exploring the Nature of Tourist's Experience', *Journal of Leisure Research* 28 (1), 57–82.

Bramwell, B. (1998) 'User Satisfaction and Product Development in Urban Tourism', *Tourism Management* 18 (1), 35–47.

Crang, M. (1997) 'Picturing Practices: research through the tourist gaze', *Progress in Human Geography* 21 (3), 359–73.

Crouch, D. (2000) 'Places around us: embodied lay geographies in Leisure and Tourism', *Leisure Studies* 19, 63–76.

Harrison, J. and P. Sarre (1973) 'Personal Construct Theory in the Measurement of Environmental Images', *Environment and Behaviour*, March, 3–38.

Jacobs, J. (1993) 'The City Unbound: Qualitative Approaches to the City', *Urban Studies* 30 (4/4), 827–48.

Jamal, T. and K. Hollinshead (2001) 'Tourism and the forbidden zone: the underserved power of qualitative inquiry', *Tourism Management* 22, 63–82.

Prentice, R.C., S.F. Witt and C. Hamer (1998) 'Tourism as Experience: the case of heritage Parks', *Annals of Tourism Research* 25 (1), 1–24.

Riley, S. and J. Palmer (1976) 'Of Attitudes and Latitudes: a repertory grid study of seaside resorts', in P. Slater (ed.) *Explorations in Interpersonal Space. Vol. 1*, John Wiley and Sons, London.

Chapter 7

Understanding Urban Tourism: A Synthesis

> *The following topics are covered in this chapter:*
>
> - A review of the contributions of the different theoretical perspectives.
> - The development of a conceptual model, termed the 'Culture and Experience of Urban Tourism'.
> - A research agenda for urban tourism, drawing upon the conceptual framework.

Introduction

In an endeavour to consider urban tourism from different perspectives, the discussion has drawn upon the literature focusing on urban tourism, specifically postmodernity, place image, the culture of consumption and the urban tourist experience. One recurring theme is that, despite the proliferation of contemporary references to the images and experiences of urban tourism, there are actually very few integrated frameworks useful for conceptualising and researching the phenomenon. It has also become apparent that experiential and cultural perspectives are relatively rare.

This chapter identifies salient concepts and principles, including them within a framework for conceptualising the images, culture and experience of urban tourism. Attention subsequently turns towards research, and an attempt is made to provide a research agenda for urban tourism. The aim is certainly not to prescribe specific methods or to operationalise the framework, but to synthesise both the conceptual and methodological contributions from the various perspectives. There is an attempt to address limitations of urban tourism research identified throughout the book, suggesting how the various perspectives might contribute to urban tourism research.

The detailed examination of various theoretical perspectives has demonstrated how no single epistemology is capable of conceptualising the phenomenon of urban tourism. It has become clear, however, that the literature on postmodernity, the place image literature, cultural studies and phenomenology all have important contributions to make. In order to construct a framework or conceptual model of urban tourism, it is necessary both to identify the particular concepts which each epistemology has contributed, and decide how these concepts may be related to each other.

Towards a Synthesis
Urban Tourism Literature

Despite the theoretical weaknesses of urban tourism research, there are several promising contributions. The case study featuring Mersey Tourism's benchmarking research indicates that destination-marketing organisations are beginning to conduct useful research into the quality of the urban tourism experience. This helps to identify both the strengths and the weaknesses of the place product. Researchers such as Evans et al. (1995) have drawn attention to the need for strategic approaches to developing urban tourism, and researchers such as Ram et al. (2000) and Paddison (1993) demonstrate the complexity and inflexibility of the city as a tourism product. Authors such as Ashworth (1989), Shaw and Williams (1994), Page (1995) and Bramwell (1998) have all emphasised the need to focus on the experience of consumers of urban tourist destinations.

Authors such as Postina and Jenkins (1997) and Gilbert and Joshi (1992) contribute to an understanding of urban tourism quality through their application of the service quality model to urban tourism. This analysis of urban tourism in terms of both expectations and perceptions taps into the potential of research instruments such as SERVQUAL. Despite some doubts concerning the salience of constructs to consumers, the approach at least acknowledges the contemporary significance of urban tourist expectations. Page also stresses the need 'to constantly evaluate to establish if the actual experience met the tourist's expectations' (1995:24). Page is drawn more towards the mental-map research pioneered by researchers such as Lynch (1960), and applied by tourism researchers such as Walmsley and Jenkins (1992). Such studies introduce a subjective perspective to complement the ubiquitous quantitative visitor survey. It is argued, however, that the uncritical adoption of the behavioural epistemology can be problematic, as it can sit uncomfortably with contemporary conceptualisations of culture and experience.

Postmodernity

Materialist studies, almost by definition, tend to focus on the macro-level and the economic. Characterised by the work of authors such as Harvey (1989), materialists identify the process by which localities attempt to differentiate themselves in global markets for inward investment and tourism. Authors such as Hewison (1987) are also interested in the use of urban tourism and heritage as a form of economic development. The use of urban tourism in economic development has come to be discussed in the context of the entrepreneurial approach to government developed by the 'new right'. The majority of direct references to urban tourism tend to invoke a critique of place marketing and heritage, based on the commodification of culture in a vain attempt to resist flows of capital. This is useful in drawing attention to the contested identities of tourist destinations, the images, schizophrenia and superficiality of contemporary culture, and the politics and ideologies underlying both the representations and landscapes of urban tourism. In short, materialist writers also draw attention to the role of urban tourism in the local–global nexus, and the danger of losing sight of the material world in urban tourism research.

The debate on postmodernity has inspired alternative perspectives, arguably with greater contributions to the field of urban tourism. By developing meta-narratives, and by seeking to develop theories of the general process of capital accumulation, materialists leave no place for the actors within particular contexts. As Harvey himself concedes in the introduction to *Consciousness and the Urban Experience* (1989b:1), materialists usually prefer a vantage point on a hill, far above particular towns and cities, rather than within the everyday life on the streets. Feminist writers (e.g. Deutsche 1991) have articulated their objections to materialists, and deny the existence of human agency and actors who make conscious decisions. Writers characterising the 'postmodern attitude' are more likely to engage with the everyday experience, culture and sense of place of localities, drawing upon authors such as Lefebvre (1970) and Lyotard (1984). Although extenuated and well documented, the postmodernity debate inspires researchers with a greater affinity to culture, local knowledge, everyday life and specific contexts.

Place Image Research

It has been argued that the most significant contributions of place image studies are centred around research that differentiates between different types of images of a destination held by urban tourists. Several researchers (e.g. Madsen 1992; Selby 1995; Selby and Morgan 1996; Bramwell and Rawding 1996) have developed methodologies to measure, analyse and compare different types of images amongst urban tourists. Whilst there are important differences between a range of organic and induced images, it is considered that the most fundamental discrepancies exist between the naive image of a destination amongst potential visitors who do not have first-hand experience, and actual visitors who have experienced the destination first hand.

Comparing different types of images can help to identify discrepancies between the two, and such discrepancies can have important policy implications. Discrepancies may be used to identify and rectify sources of dissatisfaction with the urban tourism product, or they may be used to identify negative images which can be addressed through promotion. In short, place image research can act as an invaluable tool in the crucial process of positioning the destination. This is also consistent with service-quality models as applied to urban tourism (e.g. Gilbert and Joshi 1992), as the most important gap is between the expectations and perceptions of the destination amongst consumers. One of the most useful concepts within place image literature, therefore, would appear to be the concept of *naive image*, representing expectations of the destination by potential visitors without first-hand experience of the destination. This can be distinguished from the experiences of the destination, which include first-hand (immediate) experience (Gunn 1972).

The limitations of place image studies are also significant in attempting to understand urban tourism. It is clear that behaviouralist approaches do not adequately incorporate social relations or culture into research. The context in which decisions are made is neglected, as are social relations and variations in the decision-making process. Behaviouralist studies of place image assume that there is an objective reality of a destination, and that images are distortions of that objective reality. The contrast with the contested realities of cultural studies is striking, and cannot be ignored.

Cultural Studies

The growth of cultural studies has fundamental implications for social science research in general, far beyond the provision of *ad hoc* concepts. The crisis of representation questions the validity of all knowledge, including that of academics. The application to tourism of research techniques such as semiotics, however, demonstrates that the textual approach is also capable of less dramatic conceptual and methodological contributions. Although it has been extensively demonstrated that cultural texts come in diverse forms, it is useful to distinguish between landscapes and representations. Landscape, in the context of urban tourism, can be understood as a cultural text consisting of aspects of the physical environment which can be experienced first hand by place consumers. Although landscapes have a physical 'reality', their meaning is always contested between different textual communities. Representations, in the context of tourism, can be understood as visual images, text, conversations or any sign system conveying meaning in relation to particular localities. In this project, representations are understood to refer to mediated knowledge of localities.

Cultural geography asserts that the meanings and realities of both landscapes and representations are always subjective, unstable, and contested. Tourism represents an important cultural phenomenon, bound up in the ways that humans 'assess their world, defining their own sense of identity in the process' (Jackle 1985:xi). Textual analysis is particularly concerned with the codes through which meaning is constructed. A crucial aspect of the contemporary cultural approach is 'the landscape as text' model, through which cultural researchers assert that it is possible, indeed essential, to read landscapes as if they were documents. As Duncan and Duncan (1988: 117) argue, literary theory provides a means of examining the text-like qualities of landscapes. In this conceptualisation, texts may also be in the form of maps, paintings, photographs and even social and political institutions. In a crucial and refreshing difference from behavioural approaches, these forms are seen as representing reality, rather than mimicking it.

It is possible to conceptualise a discourse within urban tourism which represents a collection of narratives, concepts, signs and ideologies developed by a particular group. As meaning is only created when texts are interpreted by readers, it is also significant that different groups of readers fall into different textual communities, each gaining different sets of meanings from their readings. As contemporary societies increasingly 'turn their citizens into image junkies' (Sontag 1978:24), the significance of representations increases. As Shields argues, 'a shroud of representations stand between us and even the concrete objects in the city' (Shields 1996:229). In the context of urban tourism, therefore, research should concentrate on reading the urban environments consumed by tourists, and the numerous representations encountered.

As authors such as Gregson (1995) have argued, however, there is a tendency to read representations and landscapes on behalf of the consumers of localities, rather than seeking any insight into their experiences. The dominance of the visual metaphors such as the 'tourist gaze' have also been criticised. The limitations of textual studies are serious enough for some to question the value of analysing texts *per se*, encouraging 'non-representational' approaches emphasising the performativity of tourism. However, a variation on the textual model with particular relevance to tourism and place marketing is the circuit of culture framework developed by Johnson (1986). This model, rather than concentrating merely on the text itself, focuses on the dynamic process by which representations are both produced and consumed. Cultural communication is conceptualised as a process of rendering a cultural text public through production, and subsequently private again on consumption. A crucial consequence of this private consumption is the way in which cultural texts are read differently by consumers. Johnson's model (1986) is invaluable, therefore, in focusing attention on the consumption of cultural texts and variations in experience between groups of place consumers.

Experiential Studies

The limitations of the purely ocular textual model of cultural analysis in the context of tourism are increasingly being recognised. While some researchers are looking to psychoanalytical approaches for inspiration, we are also seeing a renaissance of phenomenology. Existential phenomenology conceptualises perception as embodied and influenced by the environment that an individual casts around themselves in an 'intentional arc' (Merleau-Ponty 1962:xviii). Rather than examining individual components of a locality and casual relationships, it is necessary both to take a holistic view of a place and to analyse the whole mode of existence of subjects within that place. Rather than dichotomising subjects and objects, existentialists would conceptualise the urban tourist landscape as the 'embodiment of perceptual intentions' (ibid.). Experiences are created through the embodied motion of the place consumer, and meaning is that which makes a difference, whether intentional or not.

Whilst existential contributions are important, it is argued in chapter six that the work of Schutz is also undervalued (e.g. Schutz and Luckmann 1974). The concept of intersubjectivity is particularly important, as not only do groups of people have similar experiences of cities, but these experiences also reproduce social relations. The possibility of identifying and analysing groups of urban tourists, as defined by their first-hand or mediated knowledge of a destination, has considerable potential. It is argued here that intersubjectivity is a concept which runs through the veins of consti- tutive phenomenology, rather than being an organ which can be isolated and detached.

An obvious contribution of the humanistic approach is the (intersubjective) stock of knowledge. In the context of urban tourism, the stock of knowledge can be under- stood as the collection of sedimented knowledge of a destination, including both mediated and immediate experiences. Whether knowledge of a particular destination consists of mass-media representations or first-hand experience of the tourist landscape of the destination, it will enter the stock of knowledge. The stock of knowledge, there- fore, is an archive of official and unofficial images and experiences of a destination, formed since childhood, and exerting a vital influence on tourist decision-making. It has become apparent that Schutz also makes a vital contribution to conceptualising the tourist decision-making process. In contrast to the behavioural approach, which emphasises distinct and universal stages of decision-making, Schutzian action theory is closely linked to the stock of knowledge. In the context of urban tourism, the process of projecting the likely consequences of a visit in order to form expectations, is extremely useful. The Schutzian concept of action, therefore, is vital to an experi- ential understanding of urban tourism.

Culture and Experience of Urban Tourism
Introducing the Model

It is now possible to conceptualise a framework which has been termed 'culture and experience of urban tourism' (figure 7.1). The model represents both the mediated and immediate experiences of a particular urban tourist destination. It is necessary to distinguish between a mediated circuit, whereby people are not present at the desti- nation and acquire only mediated knowledge, and an immediate circuit whereby people are present and experience a locality first hand. It is important to acknowledge the influence of Johnson (1986) on both the structure and the emphasis on the consumption of cultural texts. It is hoped, however, that the framework benefits from the inclusion of important concepts from phenomenology and place image theory, in addition to insights from cultural studies.

It should be noted that the term 'place consumer' is used in the context of consuming or reading cultural texts, including both landscapes and representations of tourist destinations. It does not, therefore, denote the 'consumer' as understood by marketers. The term 'place consumer' is preferred to 'visitors' and 'non-visitors', as resi- dents also consume the representations and landscapes of urban tourist destinations.

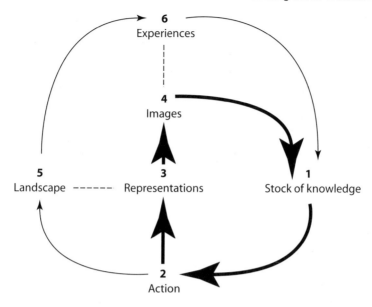

Figure 7.1: Culture and experience of urban tourism.

It should be noted that the place consumer will at times be involved in producing as well as consuming. The place consumer, for example, may simultaneously consume the tourist landscape while producing representations in the form of photographs. Place consumers also produce images, develop knowledge and produce action. As cultural studies assert, neither landscapes nor representations are conceptualised as having meaning beyond that which is created when they are interpreted as cultural texts. Although visually reading landscapes and representations is important to urban tourism, it is assumed that senses other than vision will be significant in tourist experience. Landscape, therefore, should also be understood as 'soundscape', smellscape', 'taste-scape' and 'touchscape'. It is argued that senses other than sight can be incorporated into the textual model when applied to urban tourism culture.

Stock of Knowledge

In the model, whether people are represented by the mediated or immediate circuit, the stock of knowledge (1) plays a crucial role. The total stock of knowledge will consist of a vast array of information collected over a considerable number of years. Place consumers may have come into contact with information through their education, through literature, through politics, through the mass media or through word of mouth; alternatively, they may have first-hand experience of a destination. Whatever the source (or the senses used), knowledge relating to the particular destination becomes sedimented in the stock of knowledge. This information, which for the majority of place consumers is based on secondary sources rather than first-hand experience, has been sorted and classified into 'types'. People use these typifications in order to better predict the outcome of their course of action in the future.

It follows that there will be intersubjective groups with similar stocks of knowledge of a particular destination. Furthermore, such groups will differ in their propensity to visit the destination and engage in either the mediated or immediate circuit. As Schutz and Luckmann (1974) argue, part of the stock of knowledge of place consumers is acquired socially, in the form of recipes for action provided by institutions, social groups, families etc. While the stock of knowledge of individual place consumers will always vary, there will also be areas of intersubjectivity due to the social nature of the acquisition of knowledge.

Action

As discussed in chapter six, the act of deciding to consume a place first hand involves people projecting the likely outcome of their decision into the future (Schutz 1970). The process of projecting action (2) into the future draws upon the stock of knowledge. The accumulated information from a wide range of sources is used to predict the likely outcome of a decision to visit. Although it is possible that much of the information within the stock of knowledge has been collected subconsciously, the action stage is a deliberate process.

Only a very small minority of all potential visitors to a destination will project the act of visiting into the future and believe that their goals will be achieved – the destination will satisfy their needs. For this group, the stock of knowledge is favourable enough to justify positive action. These place consumers, having considered a range of positive and negative attributes of the destination, will decide to visit the destination in question, and thereby enter the immediate circuit. It should be added that although the role of intermediaries is not explicitly addressed, organisations such as tour operators may play a significant role in the stock of knowledge of place consumers, thereby influencing action. In addition, some place consumers will make a positive decision to travel to a destination, and later encounter constraints which prevent them from so doing. *Ceteris paribus*, however, a positive outcome in the act of projecting will result in the consumer entering the immediate circuit.

The vast majority of potential place consumers of a particular destination, however, will continue in the mediated circuit. The act of projecting action into the future will only occur if there is sufficient awareness of the particular destination within the stock of knowledge. It is also necessary for the destination to appear as a credible candidate capable of satisfying consumers' needs. For the majority of place consumers, a low level of awareness of the destination will mean that it will not even be considered as a contender. Such place consumers will continue to engage in the mediated circuit for that particular destination.

Even if place consumers are aware of the destination, it is common for it to not be chosen, as the information at hand is not sufficiently favourable. In this case, the sedimented information comprising the stock of knowledge results in the destination being dropped as a possibility for immediate consumption. Projecting a visit to the destination produces an imaginary preview which is not sufficiently enticing. Such place consumers will therefore continue around the mediated circuit, and this cycle will continue indefinitely. They will only enter the immediate circuit if they subsequently encounter information which is sufficiently favourable to justify a positive decision.

Representations

For every place consumer apart from those actually visiting the destination, the mediated circuit of tourist experience will apply. These people will not gain first-hand experience of the destination, but they will experience representations (3). As Johnson (1986) demonstrates, these representations could be through the press, television, radio, education, politics or the promotional activity of destination marketers. Representations are 'read' by place consumers, and interpretations will vary. People will also differ in the representations they encounter, depending on factors such as their lifestyle, interests, age etc. Although cultural studies demonstrate that the meaning of representations is always contested and unstable, there will also be some intersubjectivity in the interpretation of representations by place consumers. In considering the representations of an urban tourist destination, both discourses and textual communities are important. There may be a consistent collection of narratives, signs and ideologies that represent a discourse of an urban tourist destination. We have seen, for example, how place marketing creates a discourse for a locality signifying its attractiveness, uniqueness and high quality of life. There will also be textual communities which interpret representations in similar ways.

It is important to acknowledge the interrelationship between representations and landscapes, indicated by the broken line in the model. The distinction is blurred in the case of tourist photographs of a destination, for example, whereby consumers both experience the destination immediately, and also produce representations to be consumed when they return home. Representations in the destination, such as heritage interpretation, also blur the distinction. The representations of tourist information will be significant, including guide-books, tourist maps and promotional leaflets. The framework does not, therefore, present a deterministic and unidirectional relationship between either representations and images, representations and landscapes, or production and consumption. Representations may be both produced and consumed by place consumers, and representations may play a crucial role in the tourist landscape. The significance of representations inherent in the Las Vegas landscape, for example, is discussed in chapter five.

Images

Consumers develop an overall image (4) of a destination through consuming and interpreting representations (Gunn 1988). Although people will differ both in terms of the representations encountered and their own interpretations, it is assumed that some intersubjective images will develop. Place consumers who encounter similar represent-ations of a destination and interpret these representations in a similar way, will hold similar images of the destination. Conversely, variations in either the representations encountered or the ways in which representations are interpreted, will lead to different images. It has been argued, in the context of the performance of tourism, that cognitive approaches tend to artificially separate thinking from acting. It is not intended to argue here, therefore, that the meaning of representations exists independently from the contents of images; place consumers encounter a combination of representations, the 'reading' of which contributes to an overall impression of the destination.

As suggested above, it should be noted that there may be some blurring of the distinction between images and experiences of the urban tourist destination. Word-of-mouth information from friends and family who do have immediate experience seems particularly credible to place consumers, almost elevated to the status of immediate 'experience'. More significantly, even at the destination the place consumer reads further representations, whether they be tourist maps, guide-books or other tourist information. In all cases, however, the images formed will enter the stock of knowledge, where they will be arranged according to existing knowledge of the destination. Only when the newly formed images contradict the typologies already existing will they significantly change the stock of knowledge of the place consumer. If there is no discrepancy between new and existing images, the newly formed images will merely add depth to the stock of knowledge relating to the particular destination.

Landscape

Only when place consumers make a positive decision to gain first-hand experience of a destination will they enter the immediate circuit. It is only by participating in immediate place consumption that they will have the opportunity to 'read' the landscape (5) of the destination. By experiencing the destination first hand, the place consumer will not merely encounter representations of the locality, but they will experience the attractions, accommodation, catering, transport network and a range of ancillary services. As place consumers, it is likely that they will evaluate the urban tourist landscape and reflect upon their experiences, not unlike a cultural researcher. However, the meaning ascribed to tourist landscapes – the way that the locality is interpreted – may differ significantly from an academic reading.

A brief reflection on what constitutes the tourist landscape indicates why it is essential for senses other than vision to be incorporated into the textual model of culture. The same parts of the tourism landscape will be simultaneously 'read' through a combination of senses. A visit to a restaurant, for example, will certainly be read in the visual sense by place consumers, who may interpret the architecture, the decor, the colours, the branding, the amount of space, the amount of light etc. The visit will obviously be read by the taste of the food and drink, including the texture, the sweetness, the spiciness, strength of flavour and combination of flavours. Simultaneously, the visual appearance of the food, smell and the temperature as it touches the mouth are experienced. Likewise, the atmosphere of the restaurant, the service and even the presence of fellow diners is simultaneously read though a number of senses, including hearing, sight and possibly touch. As Merleau-Ponty (1962) demonstrates, all of these experiences are also flavoured by the individual's personality, previous experience and expectations. A change of physical perspective – the position of the body – will change what is sensed, and experiences which do not conform to expectations in some way can make a particularly significant impression.

It should be noted that the model contains a broken line between landscape and representations. As discussed earlier, this is because the place consumer, whilst encountering the landscape of the destination, will continue to read representations. Material published by tourist boards and attractions, such as guide-books and maps, are likely to be particularly influential. In recent years, considerably more attention has been paid to interpretation at attractions, heritage sites, monuments and art galleries. A range of representations, often underpinned by commercial and political imperatives, will therefore complement first-hand tourist experience.

Experiences

Consistent with the conceptualisation of experience developed in chapter six, experience is here conceptualised as knowledge resulting from 'reading' the tourist landscape (and representations) of a particular destination. The process of 'reading' may sometimes add relatively little in terms of new experience, ultimately consolidating the existing typifications within the stock of knowledge. It is possible, however, for the process of reading a particular tourist landscape to add something significant to the stock of knowledge (Schutz and Luckmann 1974). It is probable, for example, that the stock of knowledge of first-time visitors to a destination will be changed by the process of reading landscapes first hand. The place consumer may not reflect upon and analyse every aspect of the landscape encountered, yet some features of the landscape may make a significant impression. The experience component of the model therefore comprises a holistic impression of the locality, provided by knowledge gained by the process of reading and interpreting the landscape.

The interpretation of a destination will differ due to consumers experiencing different aspects of the urban environment. It is virtually impossible for two consumers visiting the destination to have an identical set of experiences during their visit. It is also likely that each consumer will interpret the same object in a slightly different way. As Merleau-Ponty (1962) argues, the individual place consumer projects

vironment around themselves, in the form of an 'international arc'. This pre-
atic ground is often concealed behind the objective world, making it necessary
to establish which elements of experience 'make a difference'. As perception depends
on the interests of the place consumer as much as objects themselves, experience
is embodied by place consumers. The place consumer's positioning within the city
will create its form, and objects in the city will direct the movement and senses of
the place consumer. This not only questions the cleavage between the real and the
imaginary, but asserts that experience is meaning which makes a difference to the
knowledge of the place consumer.

The credibility of knowledge may vary between different consumers. It is quite
possible for images to persist, even if experiences contradict such images upon visiting.
Place consumers may, for example, still believe that a city is 'unsafe', even, if they
do not have any first-hand experience to support that image. For this reason, there
is a broken line in the model between images and experiences. Although the tourist
landscape and representations will always be read and interpreted differently by
different place consumers, there will be a degree of consensus amongst groups, or
intersubjectivity. As with images, experiences will enter the stock of knowledge, where
they will be added to existing knowledge. Whether or not the typifications within the
stock of knowledge have been substantially changed by either a consumptive or non-
consumptive circuit, as the building blocks of the knowledge of place consumers,
images and experiences deserve considerable attention from urban tourism researchers.

A Research Agenda for Urban Tourism
Social Science Perspectives

It is clear from the previous section that the conceptual framework represents different
components of the culture and experience of urban tourism. The research agenda,
summarised in figure 7.2, encourages the urban tourism researcher to draw upon the
social science perspectives and concepts considered to advance the understanding of
urban tourism. These include urban tourist knowledge, urban tourist experience,
place image, and the landscapes and representations of urban tourism. Both the focus
of research and specific methodologies will obviously depend upon the objectives of
the particular study, and cannot be prescribed *a priori*. Few of the research strategies
discussed are exclusive to individual fields of research or concepts identified in figure
7.2. The research agenda, however, is intended to summarise the potential of the
various perspectives to future research in the field of urban tourism. It is also
intended to address some of the limitations of urban tourism research identified in
chapter two.

Urban Tourist Knowledge

Some studies of urban tourism would benefit from focusing on urban tourist knowledge. It is apparent from the humanistic literature, that the stock of knowledge is closely related to decision-making action. By focusing on the knowledge of urban tourists, it might be possible to understand the typical structure and content of place consumers' knowledge of a particular destination. It is particularly useful to identify 'types' or constructs into which different destinations are classified, as these appear to be closely linked to decision-making action. It has been argued that tourist knowledge includes both first-hand experiences and mediated images, yet the important task for the researcher is uncovering the knowledge that is salient to particular respondents within specific contexts. Methodologies addressing urban tourist knowledge, therefore, might aim to establish a language which is salient to consumers, whether they have first-hand or mediated experience of a destination. This implies the use of interpretive research which elicits the term of reference used by place consumers themselves.

It would seem very doubtful that tourist knowledge can be studied through positivistic research, using methods inherited from the natural sciences. As Bowen (2001 citing Agar) argues, in discussions about social research, from professionals to laypersons, 'you hear the old bells tolling – "what's your hypothesis?"… "What's the independent variable?"… "How can you generalise with such a small sample?"… "Who did you use for a control group?"'

While this book advocates methodological pluralism, and there is a need for quantitative urban tourism research, studying tourist knowledge seems very difficult without the use of inductive approaches. As Ryan (1995b) suggests, 'research which

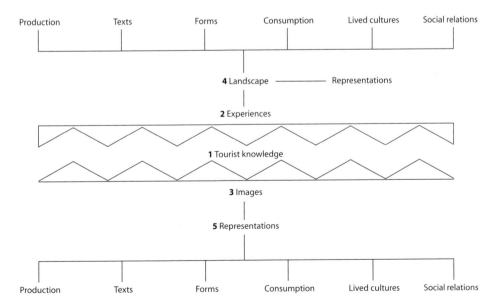

Figure 7.2: **Social and cultural urban tourism research.**

denies the opportunity for holiday-makers to speak about their own experiences in their own words' is common but flawed. Just as Ryan (1995a) argues that an understanding of tourist satisfaction is severely limited by positivist approaches, urban tourist knowledge appears to be even more within the realms of qualitative research. Researchers such as Ryan (1995a, 2000) advocate the use of conversations with tourists as a research tool. As tourist knowledge may have been developed over a long period of time from both immediate and mediated sources, researching conversations seems to have particular potential. As Ryan (1995a) points out, the use of conversation as a research method has a long and honourable tradition in social research. Although the researcher becomes a confidant, the conversation is rarely unstructured. Themes and agendas have to be prepared, and clear objectives are necessary. The sampling of respondents has to be appropriate, and data needs to be recorded accurately. As tourism is a popular conversation topic in everyday life, conversation seems particularly suited to eliciting urban tourist knowledge.

As Jamal and Hollinshead (2001:71) argue, the qualitative-research scenarios in which conversation might be a valid research tool tend to be 'messy'. It tends to be difficult to grasp holistically the population in question. It may be difficult to know whether one is analysing one distinct population or several subsets. It is also difficult to know when the research is finished, as the phenomenon is continuously evolving. The problems are not insurmountable, however, as they encourage the qualitative researcher 'to develop a "third ear" to apprehend the essence of communication and non-communication involved in the delivery of an incomplete/ellipsian/fractured vocabulary' (Wichroski cited in Jamal and Hollinshead 2001:71). As Ryan (1995a) argues in the context of conversations, the researcher must also accept the negative as a valid strategy by the respondent. Botterill (1989:289), citing Thomas and Harri-Augstein, points out that:

> Conversation is not chit-chat, not is it pre-planned formal exchange totally determined by the intervention of one participant. Conversation, in this technical sense, implies some degree of creative encounter, which neither participant could have predicted. People do not emerge from this type of conversation feeling manipulated, but they do feel as if hard collaborative work has been done.

Jamal and Hollinshead (2001:72) make a valuable contribution to qualitative tourism research, in presenting a list of the properties of a social text or conversation which the researcher should be vigilant towards. The list includes properties which help to create the identity of social groups, such as 'traits' and 'norms'. Also included in this group are 'life-space goals', which refer to the important goals of social groups which orientate their action. A second group of properties are concerned mainly with the style of talking. These include 'semantic moves', 'storytelling models' and 'augmentation structures'. Augmentation structures are defined as a particular subset of beliefs or incidental lines of thought of a population. The third group of properties are more specific to the actual language of respondents, including 'lexical styles', 'rhetorical figures', 'silences' and 'concealments'. Conversational research, therefore, may be particularly suited to eliciting urban tourist knowledge, but it is certainly not casual or unplanned. Furthermore, the greater the awareness of the subtleties of conversation by the researcher, the more they will be concerned about their own role in the production of knowledge. As all texts are shaped by the writer's traditions and prejudices, ensuring 'engaged interestedness' is a major challenge (ibid.:74). This implies ensuring that the author's voice is decentred, while acknowledging the researcher's influence on the conversation.

Both phenomenography and repertory grid analysis focus on conversations, and both have been successfully applied to studies of tourism. Repertory grid analysis has been termed a 'conversational science'. As demonstrated in case study 6.1, and discussed in chapter six, Kelly's personal construct theory (1955) is consistent with Schutz's emphasis on the formation of 'types' within the stock of knowledge. Through repertory grid analysis, the researcher may uncover constructs which seem rather obscure or illogical to the researcher, but which are salient to the respondent. As discussed in chapter six, repertory grid analysis usually presents triads of elements, using them to elicit bi-polar constructs on the perceived similarities and differences between elements. Personal construct theory also enables the formation of a consensus repertory grid, reflecting intersubjectivity amongst a group of respondents. Grids of constructs are formed, and these are designed to be amenable to statistical analysis of the associations between constructs.

Although early repertory grid analysis was concerned with individuals, a consensus repertory grid consists of the most commonly recurring constructs amongst a group of respondents. As individuals tend to produce approximately eight constructs before repeating themselves, it is possible to establish a consensus of knowledge of an urban tourist destination by combining the repertory grids of a group of place consumers. Repertory grids are amenable to statistical analysis such as factor analysis and cluster analysis. The ethos of the research, however, is supposed to be inductive, in that the constructs elicited reflect the frames of reference of place consumers themselves, rather than the researcher.

Phenomenography also has potential in the context of urban tourist knowledge. The researcher is likely to have no more than five questions, and is concerned with helping the respondent to clarify their thinking. Ryan (2000) reports that the most common questions in phenomenographic studies tend to be 'can you give me an example?', 'what do you mean by that?' and 'could you explain that a little more?'. Interviewing is thus non-directive, and does not draw upon *a priori* classifications or constructs. Phenomenography is therefore intended to be 'an exploration of respondents' processes of clarification of their concepts' (Ryan 2000:125). Significantly, details provided by place consumers cannot be dismissed as disorderly, accidental or irrelevant. This requires keen listening skills on the part of the researcher, and also a respect and empathy for the silences within the conversation. They may be both expressive in themselves and an invitation for further theme development by the researcher.

The analysis of phenomenographic transcripts is also fairly challenging. As Ryan (2000) points out, data may be considered to be both ideographic and nomothetic.

Most phenomenographic analysis is fairly holistic in the early stages, with transcripts read as a whole, and then re-read in an attempt to identify themes. A second researcher may be used to achieve a consensus on the categories and structures within the data. Again, the researchers' role in reinterpreting data is contentious and needs to be acknowledged in studies. Ryan (2000) notes that similar to repertory grid analysis, phenomenography tends to produce a small number of dimensions underlying knowledge of an issue. Qualitative software packages such as NUDIST may be useful in producing hierarchical tree diagrams, which show classifications and relationships within tourist knowledge. Artificial neural software might have potential for evaluating transcripts, analysing both the frequency of words and the words associated with them. As Ryan and Sterling (1997) demonstrate, the data can be expressed in the form of perceptual maps or dendograms, or by using cluster analysis. As Ryan (2000) points out, it is important that such techniques merely aid the process of understanding tourist knowledge and experience. They should foster a closer relationship between the transcripts and the researcher.

The Experience of Urban Tourism

As figure 7.2 suggests, urban tourism researchers need to understand tourist experiences. It should be noted that research strategies aiming to evaluate urban tourist experiences are not necessarily distinct from those focusing on knowledge. The experience of tourists, however, is likely to be more contextually and spatially specific, focusing on particular events and landscapes rather than the more abstract and superordinate realms of knowledge. First-hand experiences are therefore conceptualised as comprising the overall impression of the landscape on place consumers. Although the experience of place consumers will differ, it is again possible to identify intersubjective groups. Drawing upon the urban tourism and place image literature, it is argued that there is a need for researchers to identify intersubjective experiences, whether they be positive or negative. It is particularly when there appears to be a discrepancy between the expectations and experiences of place consumers – or dissatisfaction – that specific experiences are of interest. It would seem, therefore, that an experiential methodology should be capable of identifying particularly positive or negative experiences of a destination, enabling further analysis of both the aspects of the tourist landscape and the composition of groups of consumers with such experiences.

Experience of a tourist destination, however, also consists of more subtle and complex encounters. Researchers of urban tourist experience should also be concerned with the embodied perception of the destination landscape and the ways in which place consumers position themselves within the destination. This implies an interest in all of the senses, and the ways in which place consumers project an environment around themselves. Research into urban tourism experience should therefore be concerned with the 'operative intentionality' of place consumers in particular environments, as this imbues localities and objects with properties. The emphasis of research might therefore be on the different perspectives of the city experienced by place consumers, and the ways in which perspective is created by the embodied movement of the place consumer.

Urban tourist experience, as well as tourist knowledge, could be evaluated through the use of conversational techniques. More structured interviews, however, are also useful in researching tourist experience. While interviews may have limited potential in the context of the embodied experience of urban tourism, the technique has been used successfully to evaluate tourist satisfaction. As Ryan (1995a) notes, the unstructured interview is akin to a planned conversation, but differs in the sense that both parties are aware of the agenda. The in-depth interview allows the researcher to probe deeply into the experiences of urban tourists, allowing respondents to explain and qualify their answers. Interviews are particularly suited to researching tourist experience, as they tend to take on a life of their own depending on the terms of reference of the interviewee. The challenge for the researcher is to ensure that their checklist of questions are covered, whilst encouraging respondents to provide rich data in language they are familiar with.

In order to elicit experiences salient to place consumers, the interviewer should avoid leading respondents through agreeing or disagreeing with responses. Veal (1997) cites Whyte's hierarchy of 'interviewing interventions'. Varying from non-verbal responses, to directing the respondent to a new topic, the interventions are ordered in terms of their intrusiveness. As with conversations, the researcher should not feel uncomfortable about silences, as respondents should be allowed the time to express experiences in their own terms. As with conversations, Jamal and Hollinshead's (2001:72) guide to the deconstruction of 'messy' social texts may be useful in appreciating the subtleties of experience. In analysing in-depth interview transcripts, the coding or 'flagging' of topics is particularly important, allowing relevant topics to be arranged into themes which cut across questions and individual respondents. Computer packages such as NUDIST may be useful in manipulating the data, although simple techniques using word-processing packages may be sufficient.

Although the less abstract nature of urban tourist experience makes interviews more viable than in the case of tourist knowledge, conversational techniques should not be discounted. Repertory grid analysis, for example, has proven to be an effective technique for eliciting the language of tourist experience and decision-making (see case study 6.1). Conversational research and interviews also have the potential of underpinning more quantitative research into urban tourist experience, such as structured interviews or questionnaires. As pluralistic methodologies have been demonstrated in place image studies, they will be discussed in the next section in the context of 'images of urban tourism'. It is worth noting, however, that combinations of methods have been successfully used to research urban tourist experience, exemplified by Li's study of Canadian tourists on trips to China (Li 2000). Li's study combines questionnaire surveys, unstructured long interviews and participant observation to reveal some rich and existential insights into the tourist experience of Chinese cities. In pluralistic studies of tourist experience, the validity can be increased through the cross-referencing of data elicited from the different techniques.

Since Cohen's influential studies (e.g. 1982), the approach has proved to be invaluable in understanding the multi-sensual encounters of tourist and residents. As Bowen (2001) argues, although often overlooked, such data may also be particularly valuable to tourism practitioners, as the more accurately the data predicts the decisions made by tourists, the more useful the study to marketers and managers. Despite the appetite of business and government for a mass of quantitative data, qualitative research such as participant observation provides an understanding rather than a description of tourism. As Bowen (ibid. citing Jorgenson) argues, participant observation is exceptional for studying processes, relationships among people and events, continuities over time and the socio-cultural contexts of existence. Participant observation is concerned with human meanings and interactions viewed from the insider's perspective. This access to the context in which tourist experience takes place enables the rich and multi-sensual nature of experience to be understood, allowing direct involvement with the multiple realities of place consumers.

As Ryan (1995a) points out, the participant observer might play one of four roles. The researcher may be a complete participant, or they fulfil the role of 'participant as observer'. With lesser degrees of immersion within the situation, the researcher may act as the 'observer as participant', or with less interaction still, the 'complete observer'. The specific methodology will obviously depend on the objectives of the study, but there is little doubt that all of these strategies have the potential to provide rich insights into urban tourist experience. A notable variation on participant observation is 'service blueprinting', which has been successfully applied to heritage attractions. As Laws (1999) shows in his study of Leeds Castle in Kent, southern England, it is important to establish the critical incidents which are salient to place consumers. As with all participant observation, it is important that the researcher avoids being influenced by their 'expert' knowledge to the extent that they project meanings and motives upon the tourists, residents or industry being observed. Whatever the form of participant observation, it would seem that local knowledge will be important. This does not simply imply *locals'* knowledge, but contextual, intersubjective experiences of the tourism landscape. In urban tourism research there seems to an urgent need for research which begins at the level of the experiences of ordinary people and works towards establishing areas of consensus and intersubjectivity.

Images of Urban Tourism

Images (3) of the destination that are particularly positive or negative should be of interest to urban tourism researchers. Urban tourism images may be positive or negative, and they will vary in terms of both the degree of consensus (intersubjectivity), and the strength of place consumers' attitudes. It may also be useful to examine images which contrast with first-hand experiences of a destination. Particularly salient images of the destination may be subjected to further analysis, evaluating the content of images in detail, the characteristics of the groups with particular images and the representations that consumers have encountered. It is useful, for example, to establish whether images are formed from organic or induced sources, and the kinds of representations of the destination which are commonly 'read' by place consumers.

Drawing on the place image literature, there may be particular value in comparing the images of potential tourists of a destination with the experiences of actual visitors. The gaps between destination images and experiences are particularly significant in the context of urban tourism policy analysis. By examining the discrepancies between the two, the researcher is in effect examining the discrepancies between expectations and perceptions of the place product. It has been argued that any comparison of the images of different groups of place consumers should be based upon language salient to place consumers. Provided that the language of research is salient to place consumers and not just the researcher, there are potential benefits in quantitative analysis of both urban tourism images and experiences.

Although service-quality models have had a relatively minor influence on conceptualising urban tourism, it is interesting that figure 7.2 is consistent with researchers such as Gilbert and Joshi (1992) and Postina and Jenkins (1997) who apply service-quality models to tourism. It is also noteworthy that the validity of both service-quality research and place image studies is greatly increased by using constructs which are salient to specific groups of consumers (see Williams 1998). Repertory grid interviews, in-depth interviews or focus groups might be used to elicit constructs which are salient to consumers, incorporating them into survey research. Focusing on gaps between images and first-hand experiences can therefore enable the researcher to identify both the personal characteristics of consumers predisposed to have positive or negative images or experiences and the particular representations and landscapes 'read' by these groups. It would seem, therefore, that there are potential benefits in splitting the samples used in studies between different groups of place consumers. Residents' images and experiences may be important to some studies. However, a comparison of the experiences of actual visitors who have encountered the destination's landscape with the images of potential visitors who have only encountered representations appears to be particularly informative.

Provided that questions are salient to place consumers, survey research has an important role to play in researching urban tourism images. Semantic differential and Likert scales have been used to gauge the strength of images and experiences of destinations, whether in the form of face-to-face surveys or self-completion questionnaires. Structured questionnaires can be supplemented with open-ended questions, particularly in order to elicit specific examples. The use of semantic differential or Likert scales enables statistical analysis. Both cluster analysis (see Prentice et al. 1998) and factor analysis (see case study 4.1), have been used to evaluate the composition of groups of place consumers with particular images or experiences. Indeed, it would appear that rather than merely obtaining socio-demographic data about respondents, researchers should also pay attention to associations between particular images and experiences, and lifestyle and psychographic variables. As factor analysis evaluates the multiple correlations between variables, it is particularly suited to examining the profiles of intersubjective groups of place consumers. A group of variables that correlate with one another form a factor, and, depending on the focus of the study, a factor may contain particular images and experiences, demographic and psychographic variables, and variables relating to representations encountered by respondents. It is thus possible to identify groups of place consumers with a propensity to have particular images or experiences or the destination.

More qualitative research strategies for researching urban tourism images include some of the techniques relevant to knowledge and experiences such as conversational techniques and in-depth interviews. One technique that has not been discussed, but which is capable of providing insights into both tourism images and experiences, is the use of focus groups. As Veal (1997) notes, the researcher takes on the role of the facilitator of a discussion, rather than an interviewer. Focus groups, consisting of eight to ten people, may be particularly useful to research into urban tourism images. This is due to both the intersubjective nature of images, and the role of groups in tourist decision-making. It has already been noted that images of a tourist destination tend to be expressed in a small number of constructs. The interaction of groups – whether they be urban tourists, residents or tourism practitioners – is also consistent with the contested nature of tourism representations and landscapes. It is common for commercial market researchers to use focus groups to assess promotional campaigns, facilitating, for example, a discussion focusing on a proposed advertising campaign.

A focus group might be presented with tourism representations in order to facilitate a discussion of a destination's image. Also relevant to research strategies for 'urban tourism representations', this use of focus groups might foster an understanding of how place consumers read and interpret representations, and form an overall composite image of a tourist destination. The focus group may therefore confer a number of benefits relative to techniques such as in-depth interviews (Veal 1997: 118). The group may display synergies, whereby the cumulative effect produces more ideas than individual interviews. The group may encourage spontaneity amongst participants. Finally, snowballing may occur, whereby a single comment acts as a catalyst for a range of confirmatory or modifying statements. Focus groups may be used to evaluate specific urban tourism representations, in terms of the connotations of particular signs, the layout and the content of text. Consistent with the concept of urban tourism images, the emphasis may also be on a more holistic understanding of images and experiences amongst place consumers.

Urban Tourism Landscapes

The engagement with cultural studies enables the vital link to be made between images/experiences and cultural texts. One conclusion from the discussion of cultural studies is that the identification and analysis of contemporary representations and landscapes should be based on a prior understanding of which texts are salient to place consumers in their everyday experience. It follows that images of the destination elicited by primary research will have representations of the city as their source. Likewise, experiences can be linked to a locality's landscape. Even if a detailed analysis of specific representations and landscapes is beyond the scope of some urban tourism studies, it should at least be possible to suggest the type of 'texts' which have been read by place consumers.

As shown in figure 7.2, a wide range of landscape components underpin the experiences of a destination. Landscape (4), in this model, incorporates all of Johnson's 'moments', and what might be termed 'sub-moments' (Johnson 1986). The researcher may be interested in the production of the urban tourism landscape. For example, this might include the processes of tourism planning and development. Research into the urban tourist landscape might focus on the texts themselves, analysing, for example, the styles and cultural references embedded within the landscape. Cultural researchers would also have at their disposal techniques for analysing the form of the texts, including their structure and signs.

As cultural texts are read by consumers as well as cultural researchers, these readings may differ significantly between different groups of readers. To understand texts as transformations of meaning, the 'miss-readings' may be particularly signifi- cant. It follows that it is important for researchers to gain a knowledge of the cultural elements already encountered by the reader. The act of reading a cultural text makes an impression on lived cultures, defined as 'reservoirs of discourses and meanings' (ibid.:285). The researcher may also be interested in the social relations that underpin lived cultures, and the way in which they shape the environment in which new land- scapes are produced. Consistent with Johnson's framework, however, preoccupation with any one moment prevents the others from being recognised. If the researcher is interested in the text alone, he or she will not be able to understand either the complex acts of production, or the consumption of the landscape by readers.

In a physical sense, the urban tourism landscape consists of the physical built environment of the destination such as its architecture, monuments, roads, parks and open spaces. The tourist landscape includes the attractions in the destination, the people of the destination, whether workers, residents, or visitors, the augmented tourism product and tourist facilities, the transport network and a range of ancillary services targeting both consumers themselves and commercial organisations in the tourism sector. Landscape, in effect, is everything in a destination which can be read as a cultural text by visitors, contributing to their immediate experience of the destination.

It is beyond the scope of this discussion to explain in detail research procedures for analysing landscape as text. However, there is little doubt that semiotics – the analysis of signs and meaning – plays a major part. The application of semiotics to urban tourism research is discussed in the next section under 'representations of urban tourism'. Although contemporary semiotics is concerned with multiple and contested readings of landscapes and representations, it should be clear from the previous discussion of Johnson's circuit of culture framework (1986) that in the context of urban tourism, the consumption of cultural texts deserves particular attention. Far too often, researchers have focused on cultural texts *per se*, working back to the production of the texts. While this is perhaps easier to justify in retrospective studies, in the context of urban tourism place consumers read the texts themselves in a process which is fundamental to the experience of tourism. As urban tourists constitute an army of semioticians (Culler 1981:127), it is essential to understand their readings of the landscape and representations.

In addition to the methods of semiotics discussed in the next section, there would seem to be an urgent need for interpretive urban tourism research aiming to evaluate the consumption of landscapes. Such research is likely to use methods already familiar to researchers, such as in-depth interviews and focus groups. In the case of both landscapes and representations, it is important to evaluate how tourists, residents and practitioners read cultural texts. The everyday readings, as people go about their shopping, work, sight-seeing or dining, may differ significantly from academic readings. There will also be variations between different textual communities, groups who interpret texts in similar ways. These groups may also be much more salient to tourism practitioners than traditional market segments. The use of in-depth interviews, focus groups or even conversational techniques may enable the identification of groups of place consumers based on their readings of landscape and representations.

In the case of landscapes, it may also be possible to gain a more naturalistic understanding of the consumption of cultural texts. Participant observation, for example can reveal both which landscapes are salient to place consumers and how they are interpreted. Edensor (2000), for example, uses observation to reveal the unexpected ways in which tourists read the Taj Mahal. In Bowen's study (2001), participant observation provided an insight into both the performativity and the surprising readings of tourist activities such as dining in a Malaysian pontoon restaurant. Most attempts to understand the consumption of cultural texts reveal readings which contradict both academic readings and the assumptions of tourism practitioners. As Bowen (2001) reveals, rather surprisingly, the chaotic and poor-quality meal discussed earlier was read by tourists as an entertaining performance.

Likewise, the researcher should not assume that the focus of the tourist gaze – the selection of landscapes read by consumers – is unproblematic. As authors such as MacCannell (2001) argue, tourists often seek out the hidden and the unexpected, resisting the institutionalised tourist gaze. Without knowing what exactly is gazed upon by urban tourists, it is difficult to know how landscapes are consumed as cultural texts. Again, participant or non-participant observation may be useful in directing the researcher to the texts which are read. In Li's study (2000), in-depth interviews reveal the more private moments of tourism consumption, particularly the sensitive and subtle encounters with the residents of the destination as they go about their everyday lives. M.Crang (1997) uses photographs taken by tourists to conduct 'research through the tourist gaze'.

Surprisingly, quantitative methods also have potential in directing researchers to the landscapes and representations which are read by place consumers. As case study 4.1 demonstrates, survey research into the images and experiences of tourists might also obtain data on the representations and landscapes encountered. The associations between particular perceptions and the landscapes and representations consumed may be useful in identifying texts which are salient to place consumers. Even geographical information systems can also help to orientate cultural researchers towards the landscapes which are actually consumed. Middleton (forthcoming), for example, creates a spatial database of the city of Manchester. The digital representation of the city includes 'spatial entities', which constitute the landscape, including tourist attractions. Used in conjunction with surveys and interviews, the technique allows the mapping of tourist routes onto the landscape, by both use and preference. Whatever the specific methodology, there is little doubt that a knowledge of the texts actually consumed is a prerequisite for research into the reading of urban tourism texts. Only then can cultural research inform our understanding of the lived cultures and social relations of tourists, hosts or practitioners.

Urban Tourism Representations

The urban tourist may encounter a wide range of representations (5) of a destination (see figure 7.2). Consistent with landscapes, the analysis of representations may focus on any of Johnson's (1986) moments in the circuit of culture. Researchers may focus on the production of representations. Analysis may focus, for example, on the processes underlying the creation of promotional messages about the urban destination. The texts themselves might be of interest, and particularly their form: for example, studies might analyse the semiotics of brochure images projected by a tourist board. As consumers differ in their readings of representations, studies may focus on the meanings given to representations by different groups of urban tourists (or textual communities). For example, this approach has potential in the context of heritage interpretation, identifying differences in the ways in which interpretation at attractions is read. The ways in which lived cultures are related to such readings is also important. It may be particularly useful, for example, to identify the characteristics of urban tourists belonging to particular textual communities. The wider relationships between social relations and the reading of urban tourist representations may also be analysed. As with landscapes, however, it is important to recognise the dangers of focusing exclusively on one particular moment of culture.

For those consumers who have purchased a tourism package, the representations created by intermediaries will be important. Promotional activity by destination marketers may also be influential in creating representations consumed by potential visitors. Advertising, sales promotion, public relations and media relations may all play a role in forming the representations of a destination encountered by the potential consumer. It is considerably more likely, however, that consumers will have encountered unofficial representations such as those in the mass media, travel writing, literature, education, politics and the advice of family and friends. The latter type of representation is likely to have been encountered over a considerable number of years. It is also likely that the official representations of promotional activity are perceived as considerably less credible by potential consumers than organic representations. Consistent with the conceptual model in figure 7.2, representations (4) are linked to landscape by a line. This is to acknowledge the significance of representations on the first-hand experience of tourists, through phenomena such as interpretation at heritage attractions, and the influence of maps, guide-books and other promotional material.

The potential of semiotic analysis in understanding tourism representations is illustrated by Echtner (1999). Echtner also provides a clear and concise guide to researchers applying semiotics to tourism. It is necessary to initially choose a representative body of data for analysis. Echtner (1999:50) cites de Saussure in arguing that the sample of representations should be synchronic – a distinct and self-sufficient system. It is argued here that the representations should also be salient to particular groups of place consumers, rather than selected arbitrarily by the researcher. The researcher should then break the representations into constituent parts, informed by the theoretical underpinning of the particular study. Once the elements to be analysed have been identified, the researcher analyses their usage. This initial stage is therefore fairly quantitative, concerned with content. The researcher will then be interested in the structured relationships between constituent parts. As Echtner (1999:51) explains, the syntagmatic structure refers to the creation of meaning through combinations of signs. The paradigmatic structure is concerned with the creation of meaning through the selection of particular signs.

While the initial stages of semiotic analysis are concerned with creating an inventory of signs, the subsequent analysis is concerned with creating a taxonomy (Echtner 1999:51). This is concerned both with combinations of elements and similarities between different representations. The latter is particularly important in identifying the existence of a discourse. These processes help to reveal the underlying structure and 'rules' of the system of meaning. Only at this stage can the researcher focus on the connotations of signs. The analysis thus becomes more interpretive, and the connotations of signs will vary between different readers. Meaning is far from absolute, hence the importance of understanding how different place consumers read representations. As ideology plays a large part in the connotations produced, it is also useful for the researcher to be open about any ideological framework guiding their interpretation.

Echtner (1999:53) suggests that in the context of tourism, the various sides of the semiotic triangle have not been given equal attention. Although the relationship between designatum and the producer has received attention (e.g. Dann 1996a), there is still potential for research which analyses a much wider range of representations than merely those within tourist brochures. There is also potential for more research relating to the symbolic nature of tourist experience, including how urban tourism symbolically expresses self-identity, status and social roles (Echtner 1999:54). Most significantly, however, there is an urgent need for more research into the interpretation of signs by potential tourists. As Echtner (1999:54) points out, this should focus on both the holistic impression of representations, and meanings conveyed by particular signs.

Figure 7.2 also implies that it is essential for researchers to evaluate the consumption of representations and landscapes. As chapters five and six argue, a plethora of urban tourism representations are consumed as part of everyday life. Initially, it is important to gain an understanding of which representations are encountered by different groups of place consumers. As discussed above, research into urban tourist images may provide researchers with an insight into which representations have been read. Many of the techniques discussed above, such as focus groups and in-depth interviews, are then useful in evaluating how consumers read representations of urban tourist destinations. It is unlikely that consumers will read representations in the same ways as academic researchers, and place consumers will also differ greatly in their interpretations.

Although it is not uncommon to use techniques such as focus groups to evaluate how consumers interpret promotional material, there is a an urgent need to analyse consumers' readings of a much wider range of representations. The media of representations might include films, novels, poetry, television programmes or paintings. Whatever the genre of representation, it is no longer acceptable to ignore the readings of ordinary people. Not only do these readings underpin tourist decision-making, but they also have a profound and complex relationship with social relations. The reading of representations by urban tourists has an influence on lived cultures in the context of tourism itself. The formation of place images by consumers, and any decision-making action based upon that knowledge, is an important part of tourists' lives, helping to define their lifestyle and identity. The reading of representations also contributes to the success or failure of tourist destinations in attracting visitors, and the associated economic, social and cultural impacts upon the locality. Perhaps most significantly of all, the ways in which representations are read by place consumers has a profound effect on the identity of host populations. The development of a discourse – whether in literature, place marketing, television or the press – moulds the identity of the host population according to the imperatives of the producers of representations. In some cases, the representations themselves are insidious in their use of references, exemplified by the feminine, childlike, exotic and servile 'Far East' (see Morgan and Pritchard 1998). In all cases, the reading of representations by place consumers feeds back into the material realities of the people and places represented.

Conclusion

This chapter has attempted to draw together the concepts developed in the previous chapters into both a conceptual framework and an agenda for social and cultural urban tourism research. Having revisited the most significant contributions of each perspective, an attempt has been made to identify concepts which can combined into an integrated framework. While there will always be a risk of oversimplifying complex theoretical ideas, and worse still, linking together inconsistent concepts, it is hoped that this has been avoided. Hopefully, the detailed review and discussion of each theoretical perspective has provided an insight into the spirit of each, and not merely the semantics. Although it has been necessary to be selective, the framework is under-pinned by at least four different theoretical perspectives examined in various chapters of this book. While these perspectives have contributed towards a conceptualisation of urban tourism which is fairly inductive and interpretive in nature, it is argued that this is justified considering the relative neglect of culture and experience within the urban tourism literature.

Having also turned towards methodological considerations, it would appear that methodological pluralism has an important role to play in urban tourism research. There would certainly appear to be a strong case for incorporating more interpretive approaches into studies, particularly in order to analyse experiential and cultural aspects of urban tourism. The complex nature of urban tourism, however, is likely to necessitate methodologies which combine different methods and theoretical perspectives. The images and experiences of consumers may form the focus of some urban tourism studies. Other studies might address specific landscapes and repre-sentations, with variations in the relative emphases on the different moments of culture. While the perspectives themselves are not new, it is intended that the discussion and the subsequent synthesis at least makes some valuable concepts and methods from the social sciences accessible to students of urban tourism. It is hoped that this contributes to understanding the phenomenon of urban tourism.

Chapter summary:

- Theoretical perspectives contributing directly towards an understanding of urban tourism include the place image literature, cultural studies and humanistic geography.
- It has been possible to highlight certain concepts that have been provided by the different perspectives, and these have been synthesised into a conceptual framework.
- The conceptual framework, named the 'The Culture and Experience of Urban Tourism', incorporates the stock of knowledge, images, experiences, action, representations and landscapes.
- This chapter has also developed a research agenda, discussing strategies for researching urban tourism from social science perspectives.

Further Reading

Crang, M. (1997) 'Picturing practices: research through the tourist gaze', *Progress in Human Geography* 21, 3, 359–73.

Echtner, C.M. (1999) 'The semiotic paradigm: implications for tourism research', *Tourism Management* 20, 47–57.

Edensor, T. (2000)' Staging Tourism: Tourists as Performers', *Annals of Tourism Research* 27 (2), 322–44.

Jamal, T. and J. Hollinshead (2001) 'Tourism and the forbidden zone: the underserved power of qualitative inquiry', *Tourism Management* 22, 63–82.

Li, Y. (2000) 'Geographical Consciousness and Tourism Experience', *Annals of Tourism Research* 27 (4), 863–83.

Ryan, C. (1995) *Researching Tourist Satisfaction: issues, concepts, problems*, Routledge, London.

Veal, A.J. (1997) *Research Methods for Leisure and Tourism: A Practical Guide*, Second Edition, Financial Times/Pitman, London.

Chapter 8
Conclusion

The following topics are covered in this chapter:

- Conclusions relating to conceptualising urban tourism.
- Conclusions relating to researching urban tourism.
- A reflection on the practice and praxis of urban tourism research.

Conceptualising Urban Tourism

It has been necessary, in order to capitalise fully on the contribution of each theoretical perspective, to draw out the weaknesses as much as the strengths. Despite the relative neglect of urban tourism within many epistemologies, its significance to contemporary theoretical debates has become apparent. Whilst each area of the literature has made important contributions, it can be concluded that the most significant progress towards conceptualising urban tourist experience has occurred on the fissures and fault lines of hegemonic epistemologies.

It has been apparent throughout the project, that the phenomenon of urban tourism has a tendency to disclose such weaknesses. Chapters two and three demonstrate the centrality of the images and experiences of place consumers to the contemporary city. Through a discussion of the postmodern city, the aim has been to uncover the polarisation of the postmodernism debate, between the universal meta-theories of materialism and studies which can be characterised as acknowledging culture. This acknowledgement, implying an orientation towards everyday contexts and local knowledge, has a subtle but important influence on subsequent discussions, emphasising the everyday experience and culture of urban tourism.

The process of evaluating the limitations of place image theory have highlighted a lack of theoretical debate within much urban tourism research, and a lack of epistemological diversity within the tourism marketing literature. In addition to building on the strengths of place image research in terms of conceptualising different types of images, an exploration of weaknesses has enabled slightly more profound conclusions to be reached. These relate particularly to the importance of theoretical debate amongst tourism researchers, the necessity of appreciating and engaging with past and present theoretical debates within the social sciences, the perils of unquestioningly relying on just one epistemology, and the dangers of an apparent obsession with statistical analysis at the expense of validity in research design.

Although cultural studies make an invaluable contribution to conceptualising urban tourism, the phenomenon of urban tourist experience also reveals interesting fault lines within the cultural approach. The surprisingly problematic inclusion of place consumers in studies concerned with reading landscapes and representations raises fundamental questions. Particularly significant are the problems associated with reading representations and landscapes on behalf of groups of people who regularly experience them in their everyday lives. In the quest to demonstrate that knowledge is subjective, unstable and relative, crucial contradictions are apparent. While such contradictions have been articulated by feminist researchers, it is ironic that people in general are overlooked in many cultural studies of consumption. It is argued, therefore, that the emphasis on the consumption of cultural texts provided by Johnson's circuit of culture framework (1986) is invaluable to cultural studies of consumption. The increasing attention devoted to performativity and embodiment also contributes towards a multi-sensual understanding of the culture of urban tourism.

The contribution of the humanistic approach, in many ways, is also born out of a critique of previous humanistic studies. It is apparent that individualistic studies that search for the universal essences of place experience have little to contribute to understanding urban tourism. It is also clear, however, that cultural studies brings us only part of the way towards an understanding of place consumers, not unlike the place image literature. As there is a tendency in humanistic studies to overstate the case in order to make an impression, it is considered necessary to re-examine the foundations. As humanistic geography is largely underpinned by phenomenology, chapter six revisits the epistemology, exploring contributions that focus on society, rather than individuals. Hopefully it is apparent that this endeavour is not concerned with self-indulgence and reminiscing, but with finding inspiration. Existential work by authors such as Merleau-Ponty (1962) provides a sophisticated explanation of the embodied ways in which people experience places. The work of Schutz (1972; Schutz and Luckmann 1974) is considered inspirational because it unites the concerns of cultural studies with theories of action and decision-making. Through focusing on the intersubjective, therefore, Schutz provides a sophisticated link between the representations and landscapes encountered by groups of people and the action of urban tourists.

One objective of this book has been to develop both a conceptual framework of urban tourism and an agenda for social scientific urban tourism research. This has evolved with each theoretical contribution, enabling a more explicit discussion in chapter seven. It was intended to engage with each epistemology in sufficient depth to understand both the ethos and the underlying assumptions. Whilst purists may feel some unease at a framework which cuts across established fields of enquiry, it is hoped that the concepts within the framework are consistent and compatible. It is envisaged, for example, that researching the consumption of urban tourism texts will increasingly be viewed as part of the cultural studies agenda. Researchers such as Burgess (1990), Gregson (1995) and Jackson and Taylor (1996) have shown an empathy with the circular model of culture for some time. It is also hoped that concepts such as stock of knowledge and action sit comfortably with place image and marketing theory, despite the very different philosophical assumptions.

Although a theoretically and methodologically pluralistic approach is being advocated by the synthesis, it is argued that this is necessary and appropriate in a multi-disciplinary field such as tourism. There is, after all, an extraordinary failure of individual epistemologies to address the all-pervading, everyday phenomenon of urban tourism. It is hoped that the implications are not limited to directly researching this phenomenon, and that such multi-disciplinary work does indeed have the potential to contribute to the separate disciplines with which the book has engaged.

Urban Tourism Research

It hoped that the different theoretical perspectives and the synthesis also have concrete research implications. In terms of academic communities, it would seem that the study has implications for place image researchers. It is argued, for example, that a more critical approach to place image studies would increase both their potential in tourism policy analysis and their validity. There would appear to be a strong case for arguing the need for place image researchers to pay considerably more attention to the frames of reference of respondents themselves. Too many studies use language which is not salient to respondents, and develop overly deterministic methodologies. The discussion of place image research emphasises the benefits of conducting comprehensive qualitative research with consumers before developing more quantitative research instruments. Repertory grid analysis is one way of proceeding, although in-depth interviews or focus groups may also have potential. Whatever the precise methods used, it is considered essential to establish an intersubjective language that is salient to the decision-making of consumers in the particular context.

In addition to ensuring that context and social relations are included in place image studies, an obvious contribution of the theoretical discussion to place image research relates to optimising the contribution of place image theory. A lengthy discussion has been based on the potential of focusing on different images of destination. This particularly draws upon the conceptualisation of different images according to stages in the consumer decision-making cycle. Relatively few place image researchers have taken advantage of this contribution to place image theory. Only a handful of academic studies engage with both actual and potential visitors to a destination, or with groups of consumers at different stages of decision-making. There are strong indications, however, that comparing and contrasting images relating to different stages of decision-making has great potential in terms of policy analysis and strategic planning.

It would seem that the theoretical discussion might have a contribution to make to cultural research. The evaluation of cultural studies highlighted a number of contradictions inherent in the cultural turn within human geography. The phenomenon of urban tourism, involving consumers as well as representations and landscapes, provides a significant challenge to cultural researchers. It is hoped that, rather than being drawn further into a self-destructive and rather self-indulgent relativism, cultural researchers will begin to address the experience of consumers. While reading texts on behalf of groups of people is necessary in retrospective studies, it is difficult to justify the same approach in studies of consumption. Studies concerned with embodiment and multi-sensual experience are promising, and also go a long way to addressing the preoccupation with cultural texts *per se*. In the context of urban tourism, however, it is important that representational studies are rejuvenated rather than reaching the end of their life-cycle. The representations of urban tourism continue to be intimately bound up with the culture and experience of the phenomenon. The discussion has emphasised at various points the significance of mediated urban tourist knowledge, encountered as part of everyday life.

Likewise, it is hoped that humanistic researchers will fight the currents taking them towards individualistic studies and a search for essences. Humanistic geography has at times displayed a self-destructive streak. In order to be heard over the din of quantitative approaches, humanistic researchers have often been attracted to the confines of an individual's mind. A thorough appreciation of phenomenology, however, is invaluable in reorientating humanistic approaches. If one leaves behind the debris of humanistic geographical studies influenced by 'pure' forms of Husserlian phenomenology and engages with the work of Schutz (e.g. 1972) and Merleau-Ponty (1962), the implications are very different. Phenomenology, then, is about the everyday experiences of groups of people. It is about recognising that the same environment can be interpreted very differently by various groups of people. It is also about understanding how action is based upon past experiences and how these past experiences can be used to predict decision-making. Both practitioners and social scientists can benefit enormously from such an insight. It is necessary to look beyond the misconceptions regarding this neglected body of literature, and benefit from concepts such as stock of knowledge, intersubjectivity and action.

Urban Tourism Practice

In the realm of practice, the examples and case studies throughout the book suggest some of the potential of the different perspectives for informing tourism and place-marketing policy. Potential contributions to tourism and place-marketing practitioners, for example, are the evaluation of negative images of the destination and the identification of sources of salient representations. Destination marketers around the world are placing a greater emphasis on media relations, and targeting key opinion-formers. Given the apparent impact of negative naive images, however, it would seem that more attention should be paid to the sources of unfavourable representations of a destination. Rather than merely targeting quality newspapers and upmarket magazines, it is necessary to identify more accurately the journalists, editors, publications and television programmes contributing to negative images of a city.

Another possible contribution of this book to the practice of destination marketing relates to the tourism product of urban destinations. Despite the widespread and regular visitor surveys undertaken by destination marketers, there would appear to be a relative lack of understanding of the visitor experience. It is hoped that more destination-marketing organisations will conduct interpretive studies of both first-hand experience of the destination and the images formed though mediated information. Many destination-marketing organisations have developed fora for the exchange of ideas and information, often in the form of meetings for the members of the tourist board or bureau. Destination-marketing organisations have the potential – indeed a duty – to provide their subscribers with qualitative data which helps to improve satisfaction with the individual components of the urban tourism product. For understandable reasons, the vast majority of research studies conducted by destination-marketing organisations consist of large-scale quantitative visitor surveys. The imperative of justifying the existence and value of destination-marketing organisations sacrifices an understanding of the output of urban tourism – the consumer experience. The latter has considerable potential for improving weaknesses of the place product through *ad hoc*, common-sense measures, and it is hoped that recent trends towards more commercial interpretive research will continue.

Evaluating different theoretical perspectives may also contribute towards the practice of positioning urban destinations. Chapter four and the research agenda encourages the evaluation of both the visitor experience and the images of place consumers who have not experienced a particular destination first hand. It is important to build upon both positive images and positive experiences in order to position a city within domestic and international tourism markets. Considering that authors such as Harvey (1989a) dismiss place marketing as a 'zero-sum game', it is absolutely vital for place marketers to capture the unique and salient attributes of their particular destination. It is only by evaluating and identifying these attributes, that destination marketers can communicate and satisfy all of the key benefits sought by target market segments. To be successful in this process, a city's tourism and marketing organisations need to be absolutely clear about both the strengths and weakness of their product relative to competitors and the precise benefits sought by each market segment. Not surprisingly, it is argued in this book that the starting point for this process is an appreciation of the knowledge of groups of place consumers.

Urban Tourism Praxis

Within the academic community of urban tourism research, it is important to ask why there is so little engagement with alternative epistemologies and social theory. There is convincing evidence that urban tourism studies are at best theoretically impoverished, and in some cases flawed by a theoretical naivety. It is possible that part of the explanation lies with the need to address both the theory and practice of urban tourism. Some tourism researchers may be reluctant to dwell on theory for fear of alienating practitioners. It is also possible that the ambivalent treatment of tourism research by governments, and particularly bodies awarding research funding, leads to an overly fragmented, pragmatic and applied field of study. Whatever the contributory factors, it would seem that there is an overemphasis on developing deductive research methodologies, and a lack of theoretical discussion underpinning urban tourism research. This lack of epistemological diversity perhaps contributes towards the emphasis on the statistical reliability of research rather than validity and the existence of some studies which are seemingly conducted in a theoretical vacuum. Whatever the explanation, it is important for urban tourism researchers to acknowledge the theoretical debates raging in the social sciences, even if life becomes more messy than that within the confines of the tourism academy.

Another important conclusion relating to urban tourism research concerns disciplinary boundaries. There seems to be a growing unease about the disciplinary boundaries erected around tourism research in general (see Franklin and Crang 2001; Tribe 1997). Not only is there a serious lack of dialogue between tourism and social science disciplines, but there are rather artificial sub-fields within tourism research. If tourism is an interdisciplinary field, it is difficult to understand why it has been delimited so rigidly. There are at least signs that the tourism–leisure border is being breached (e.g. Williams and Chaplin 1998), and it is envisaged that the further dissolution of artificial boundaries will bear more fruit in terms of theoretically informed research.

It is also of some concern that a phenomenon so significant in economic, cultural, methodological and epistemological terms has remained so neglected by social scientists. It has been apparent that the major encounters with urban tourism from outside the tourism and marketing literature have been either to provide a universal critique, or to read tourism landscapes and representations on behalf of consumers. It is possible that the dialogue between tourism researchers and those working in disciplines such as human geography and sociology can be improved through greater collaboration in research projects. There can be little doubt that research on the interfaces of disciplines can inspire greater contributions to knowledge than theoretically purer projects conforming to the epistemological hegemony.

In many ways, the reticence of social scientists on the phenomenon of urban tourism is an indication of its worth as a field of enquiry. Forcing the researcher to engage with dichotomous concepts – production and consumption, images and experiences, representations and landscapes – is a challenge with which many researchers are unwilling to grapple. Some writers prefer to stare across the landscape, searching for suitable metaphors; others become rather insensitive and heavy-handed in the manner in which they brandish research instruments; there are also those who would rather climb to the top of a hill and look down on the locality. However, there is a place between deterministic approaches and a self-destructive relativism. It is not a utopia, it is not a panacea, it is merely a place where groups of people can be heard.

Chapter summary:

- Although contemporary social-science perspectives are neglected in the field of urban tourism, they enable us to understand the images, experiences, action and culture of urban tourism.
- These perspectives have important implications for researching urban tourism, necessitating a much broader range of methods than is currently used.
- The issues discussed in this book raise important questions about both the practice of urban tourism and the academic environment in which research takes place.
- There is an urgent need to incorporate culture and experience into urban tourism theory and research, using both inductive and deductive approaches.

References

Adler, J. (1989) 'Origins of Sightseeing', *Annals of Tourism Research* 16, 7–29.

Adorno, T. and M. Horkheimer (1972) 'The Culture Industry: enlightenment and mass deception', in J. Cumming (trans.) *Dialectics of Enlightenment*, Seabury Press, New York.

Ahmed, S. (2000) *Strange Encounters*, Routledge, London.

Ahmed, Z. U. (1991) 'The Influence of the Components of a State's Tourist Images on Product Positioning Strategy', *Tourism Management* 12 (4), 331–40.

— (1996) 'The Need for the Identification of the Constituents of a Destination's Tourist Image. A Promotion Segmentation Perspective', *Journal of Professional Services Marketing* 14 (1), 37–60.

Aitcheson, C. (1999) 'New Cultural Geographies: the spatiality of leisure, gender, and sexuality', *Leisure Studies* 18, 19–39.

Ajzen, I. (1991) 'Benefits of Leisure: A Social Psychological Perspective', in B.L. Driver, P.J. Brown, G.L. Peterson (eds) *Benefits of Leisure*, Venture Publishing, Pennsylvania State College, PA, 411–17.

Albers, P.C. and W.R. James (1988) 'Travel Photography: a methodological approach', *Annals of Tourism Research* 15 (1), 134–58.

Alford, P. (1998) 'Positioning the Destination Product: Can Regional Tourist Boards Learn from Private Sectors Practice?' *Journal of Travel and Tourism Marketing* 7 (2), 53–68.

Althuser, L. (1969) *For Marx*, Penguin Books, Harmondsworth.

Anderson, K. and F. Gale (eds) (1992) *Inventing Places: studies in Cultural Geography*, Longman Cheshire, Melbourne.

Ang, I. (1996) *Living Room Wars*, Routledge, London.

Ankomah, P.K. and J.L. Crompton (1992) 'Influence of Cognitive Distance on Vacation Choice', *Annals of Tourism Research* 23 (1), 138–50.

Ascherson, N. (1995) 'Down Memory Lane', interview with B. Butler, *Museums Journal* April, 15–17.

Ashworth, G.J. (1987) 'Geografische Marketing, een brunik bare invalshoek voor onderzoek en planning', *Stedebouwn and Volkhuisvestig* 3, 85–90.

— (1988) 'Marketing the City: concepts, processes and Dutch applications', *Town Planning Review* 59 (1), 65–80.

— (1989) 'Urban Tourism: an imbalance in attention', in C.P. Cooper (ed.) *Progress in Tourism, Recreation and Hospitality Management* vol. 1, Belhaven, London, 33–54.

— (1992) 'Is there Urban Tourism?' *Tourism and Recreation Research*, 17 (2), 3–8.

Ashworth, G.J. and T.J. De Haan (1987) 'Modelling the Resort Region: the Languedoc Coast', *Field Studies* 11, GIRUG.

Ashworth, G.J. and B. Goodall (1988) 'Tourist Images: marketing considerations', in B. Goodall and G.J. Ashworth (eds) *Marketing in the Tourism Industry*, Croom Helm, Beckenham, 215–38.

Ashworth, G.J. and J.E. Tunbridge (1990) *The Tourist-Historic City*, Belhaven, London.

Ashworth, G.J. and H. Voogd (1988) 'Marketing the City: concepts, processes and Dutch applications', *Town Planning Review* 59 (1), 65–80.

— (1990) *Selling the City: Marketing Approaches in Public Sector Urban Planning*. Belhaven, London.

Asseal, H. (1987) *Consumer Behaviour and Marketing Action*, PWS Kent, Boston MA.

Babalikis, S. (1998) 'A Critical Review of the Urban Regeneration Process In Britain Within the New-Right Influence in Policy-Making Since 1979 and with Particular Reference to Cardiff Bay Regeneration', *Concord* 8 (2), Special Issue, Postgraduate Research Conference, UWIC, July.

Bachalard, G. (1964) *The Poetics of Space*, Orion Press, New York.

Backes, R. (1997) 'Reading the Shopping Mall City', *Journal of Popular Culture* 31 (3), 1–18.

Bagnall, G. (1996) 'Consuming the Past', in S. Edgell, K. Heterington and A. Warde (eds) *Consumption Matters*, Blackwell/The Sociological Review, Oxford.

— (1998) 'Mapping the Museum: The Cultural Consumption of Two North West Heritage Sites', unpublished PhD thesis, University of Salford.

— (2003) 'Performance and Performativity at Heritage Sites', *Museum and Society*, vol. 1 no 3, July, 1–33.

Bailey, J.T. (1989) *Marketing Cities in the 1980s and Beyond*, American Economic Development Council, Cleveland OH.

Baloglu, S. and D. Brinberg (1997) 'Affective Images of Tourism Destinations', *Journal of Travel Research* 35 (4), 11–15.

Baloglu, S. and K.W. McCleary (1999) 'A Model of Destination Image Formation', *Annals of Tourism Research* 26, 808–99.

Banerjee, T. (ed.) (1990) *City Sense and City Design: Writings and Projects of Kevin Lynch*, MIT Press, Cambridge MA.

Bannister, D. and F. Fransella (1974) *Inquiring Man: The Theory of Personal Constructs*, Penguin, Harmondsworth.

Bannister, D. and J.M.M. Mair (1968) *The Evaluation of Personal Constructs*, Academic Press, London.

Barke, M. and K. Harrop (1994) 'Selling the Industrial Town: Identity, Image, and Illusion', in J.R Gold and S.V. Ward (1994) *Place Promotion: The Use of Publicity and Marketing to Sell Towns and Regions*, John Wiley and Sons, Chichester.

Barnes, T.J. and J.S. Duncan (1992) *Writing Worlds: Discourse, Text, and Metaphor in the Representation of Landscape*, Routledge, London.

Barrett, G., T. Jones and D. McEvoy (1996) 'Ethnic Minority Business: Theoretical Discourse in Britain and North America, *Urban Studies*, 33, 4–5, 783–809.

Bartels, C. and M. Timmer (1987) *City Marketing: Instruments and Effects*, Regional Science Association, Athens.

Barthes, R. (1972) *Mythologies*, trans. A. Lavers, Hill and Wang, New York.

— (1984) 'The Eiffel Tower', in R. Howard (trans.) *The Eiffel Tower and Other Mythologies*, Hill and Wang, New York.

— (1986) 'The Blue Guide', in A. Lavers (trans.) *Mythologies*, Hall and Wang, New York, 74–77.

— (1987) *Empire of Signs*, trans. R. Howard, Hill and Wang, New York.

Bartlett, F.C. (1932) *Remembering*, Cambridge University Press, Cambridge.

Baudrillard, J. (1983) *Simulations*, Semiotext(e), New York.

Bauman, Z. (1993) *Postmodern Ethics*, Blackwell, Oxford.

— (1994) 'Fran Pilgrim till turist', *Moderna Tider*, September, 20–34.

Begg, I., M. Moore and J. Rhodes (1986) 'Economic and Social Change in the Inner Cities', in V.A. Hausner (ed.) *Critical Issues in Urban Economic Development* vol. 1, Clarendon Press, Oxford.

Belanger, M. and G. Gendreau (1979) 'Le reamenagment du vieux Quebec et l'analyse de al perception de l'environnement', *Espece Geographique* 72 (2).

Bell, D. (1973) *The Coming of the Post-industrial Society*, Basic Books, New York.

Bengston, D.N. and Z. Xu (1993) 'The Impact of Research and Technical Change In Wild Land Recreation: Evaluation Issues and Approaches', *Leisure Sciences* 15, 251–72.

Benjamin, W. (1979) *One Way Street*, New Left Books, London.

— (1983) *Charles Baudelaire: A Lyric Poet in the Era of High Capitalism*, trans. H. Zohn, Verso, London.

— (1986) *Gesammelte Schriften IV*, Suhrkamp, Frankfurt.

— (1989) *Paris, Capital du XIXe Siècle: Le Livre des Passages*, ed. R. Tiedman, trans. R. Lacoste, CERF, Paris.

Bennett, T. (1983) 'A Thousand and One Troubles: Blackpool Pleasure Beach', in *Formations of Pleasure*, Routledge, London.

— (1986) 'Hegemony, Ideology, Pleasure: Blackpool', in T. Bennett, C. Mercer, and J. Woollacott (eds) *Popular Culture and Social Relations*, Open University Press, Milton Keynes.

Berger, P.L. (1970) 'The Problem of Multiple Realities: Alfred Schutz and Robert Musil', in M. Natanson, *Phenomenology and Social Reality, Essays in Memory of Alfred Schutz*, Northwestern University Press, Evanston IL, 213–33.

Berger, P.L. and T. Luckmann (1966) *The Social Construction of Reality: A Treatise in the Sociology of Knowledge*, Allen Lane, Penguin Press, London.

Bhabha, H. (1994) *The Location of Culture*, Routledge, London.

Bianchini, F. and M. Parkinson (1993) *Cultural Policy and Urban Regeneration: The West European Experience*, Manchester University, Manchester.

Billinge, M. (1977) 'In Search of Negativism: Phenomenology and Historical Geography', *Journal of Historical Geography* 3, 55–68.

Birmingham City Council, (1987) *Action Programme for Tourism in Birmingham*, Birmingham City Council, Birmingham.

Bishop, P. (1992) 'Rhetoric, Memory, and Power: depth psychology and postmodern geography', *Environment and Planning D: Society and Space* 10, 5–22.

Blunt, A. (1994) *Travel, Gender, and Imperialism: Mary Kingsley and West Africa*, Guildford, New York.

Boiven, Y. (1986) 'A free response approach to the measurement of brand perceptions', *International Journal of Research in Marketing* 3, 11–17.

Boniface, P. and P.J. Fowler (1993) *Heritage and Tourism in the Global Village*, Routledge, London.

Boorstin, D. (1964) *The Image: A Guide to Pseudo-Events in American Society*, Atheneum, New York.

Bordieu, P. (1984) *Distinction*, Routledge, London.

Borges, J.L. (1988) *Other Inquisitions*, Texas University Press, Austin TX, cited in B. Genocchio (1995) 'Discourse, Discontinuity and Difference', in S. Watson and K. Gibson (1995) *Postmodern Cities and Spaces*, Blackwell, Oxford.

Botterill, T.D. (1989) 'Humanistic Tourism? Personal constructions of a tourist: Sam visits Japan', *Leisure Studies* 8, 281–93.

Botterill, T.D. and J.L. Crompton (1987) 'Personal Constructions of Holiday Snapshots', *Annals of Tourism Research* 14 (1), 152–56.

— (1996) 'Two Case Studies Exploring the Nature of Tourists' Experience', *Journal of Leisure Research* 28 (1), 57–82.

Boudieu, P. (1984) *Distinction: a social critique of judgement of taste*, Routledge, London.

Bowen, D. (2001) 'Research on Tourist Satisfaction and Dissatisfaction: overcoming the limitations of a positivism and quantitative approach', *Journal of Vacation Marketing* 7 (1), 31–40.

Bramwell, B. (1998) 'User Satisfaction and Product Development in Urban Tourism', *Tourism Management* 18 (1), 35–47.

Bramwell, B. and L. Rawding, (1994) 'Tourism Marketing Organisations in Industrial Cities', *Tourism Management* 15, 425–34.

— (1996) 'Tourism Marketing Images of Industrial Cities', *Annals of Tourism Research* 23, 201–21.

Briggs, S. (2000) 'Destinations with a Difference - attracting visitors to areas with cultural diversity', *Insights*, English Tourism Council.

Bristol City Planning Department (1990) *Proposed Tourism Strategy for Bristol* (Draft), Bristol City Planning Department.

Britton, S. (1979) 'The Image of Third World Tourism in Marketing', *Annals of Tourism Research* 6, 318–29.

Brooker-Gross, S.R. (1985) 'The Changing Concept of Place in the News', in J. Burgess and J.R. Gold (eds) *Geography, The Media, and Popular Culture*, Croom Helm, Beckenham, 63–85.

Bruner, E.M. (1995) 'The Ethnographer/tourist in Indonesia', in M.F. Lafont, J.B. Allcock and E.M. Bruner, *International Tourism: Identity and Change*, Sage Studies in International Sociology, vol. 47, Sage, London.

— (1996) 'Tourism in Ghana: the representation of slavery and the return of the black diaspora', *American Anthropologist* 98 (2), 290–304.

Bryman, A. and D. Cramer (1990) *Quantitative Methods for Social Scientists*, Routledge, London.

— (1994) (2nd ed.) *Quantitative Data Analysis for Social Scientists*, Routledge, London.

Buck, R.C. (1977) 'The Ubiquitus Tourist Brochure', *Annals of Tourism Research* 4, 195–207.

Buckley, P.J. and S. Witt (1985) 'Tourism in Difficult areas: case studies of Bradford, Bristol, Glasgow, and Hamn', *Tourism Management* 6, 205–13.

— (1989) 'Tourism in Difficult Areas II: case studies of Calderdale, Leeds, Manchester, and Scunthorpe', *Tourism Management* 10 (2) June, 138–52.

Buck-Morss, S. (1989) *The Dialectics of Seeing: Walter Benjamin and the Arcades Project*, MIT Press, Cambridge MA.

Burgess, J. (1982) 'Selling Places: Environmental Images for the Executive', *Regional Studies* 16, 1, 1–17.

— (1990) 'The Production and Consumption of Environmental Meanings in the Mass Media: a research agenda for the 1990s', *Transactions of Institute of British Geographers* (NS) 15, 139–61.

Burgess, J. and J.R. Gold (1995) *Geography, the Media, and Popular Culture*, Croom Helm, Beckenham.

Burgess, J. and P. Wood (1988) 'Decoding Docklands: place advertising and the decision-making strategies of the small firm', in J.D. Eyles and D.M. Smith (eds) *Qualitative Methods in Human Geography*, Polity Press, Cambridge.

Butler, J. (1993) *Bodies that Matter: On the Discursive Limits of Sex*, Routledge, London.

Butler, R. (1991) 'West Edmonton Mall as a Tourist Attraction', *Canadian Geographer* 35, 287–95.

Butler, R. and D. Pearce (eds) (1995) *Change in Tourism: People, Places, Processes*, Chapman and Hall, London.

Buttimer, A. (1979) 'Reason, Rationality, and Human Creativity', *Geografiska Annaler* 61b, 43–49.

Calantone, R.J., C.A. Di Benedetto, A. Hakam and D.C. Bojanic (1989) 'Multiple Multinational Tourism Positioning Using Correspondence Analysis', *Journal of Travel Research* 28 (2), 25–32.

Campbell, C. (1987) *The Romantic Ethic and the Spirit of Modern Consumerism*, Basil Blackwell, Oxford.

Camus, A. (1952) *L'Etranger*, trans. Stuart Gilbert, Penguin, London.

Canter, D. (1979) 'Y a-t-il des Lois d'Interaction Environmentale?' in J.G. Simon (ed.) *Experiences Conflictuelles de L'Espaces*, Universite Catholique, Louvain-La-Neuve, 391–98.

— (1988) 'Action and Place: An Existential Dialectic', in D. Canter, M. Krampen and D. Stea, *Environmental Perspectives*, Gower Publishing, Aldershot.

Cardiff County Council (1997) *City Centre Strategy, 1997–2001*, Planning Department, Cardiff County Council, Cardiff.

— (1998) *Croeso*, Economic Development Department, Tourism Development Group, Spring.

— (1999) *Croeso*, Economic Development Department, Tourism Development Group, Winter.

Cardiff Marketing Ltd (1988) *Business Plan, 1999–2001*, CML, Cardiff.

Cardiff Research Centre (1995) Cardiff Visitor Study, Tourism Development Group, Economic Development Department, Cardiff County Council.

— (1999) Cardiff Visitor Study, Tourism Development Group, Economic Development Department, Cardiff County Council.

Castells, M. (1977) *The Urban Question*, Edward Arnold, London.

— (1983) *The City and the Grassroots: a cross-cultural theory of urban social movements*, Arnold, London.

— (1985) *High Technology, Space, and Society*, Sage, London.

Cater, E. (2001) 'The Space of the Dream: a case of mistaken identity', *Area* 33 (1), 47–54.

Cattell, R.B. (1966) 'The Meaning and Strategic Use of Factor Analysis', in R.B. Cattell (ed.) *Handbook of Multivariate Experimental Psychology*, Rand McNally, Chicago IL.

CBDC (1997) *Cardiff Bay Visitor Guide*, Cardiff Bay Development Corporation, Cardiff.

Chang, T.C. (1997) 'From "Instant Asia" to "Multi-faceted Jewel": Urban Imagery Strategies and Tourism Development in Singapore', *Urban Geography* 18, 542–62.

Chang, T.C., S. Milne, D. Fallon and C. Pohlmann (1996) 'Urban Heritage Tourism: the Global nexus', *Annals of Tourism Research* 23, 1–19.

Chon, K.S. (1990) 'The Role of Destination Image in Tourism: A Review and Discussion', *Tourist Review* 45 (2), 2–9.

Clarke, D.B. (1991) 'Towards a Geography of the Consumer Society', Working Paper 91/2, Leeds School of Geography, University of Leeds, Leeds.

Clarke, D.B. and M. Bradford (1989) 'The Uses of Space by Advertising Agencies in the United Kingdom', *Geografiska Annaler* 77 (8), 139–51.

Clarke, J.S., S. Hall, T. Jefferson and B. Roberts (1976) 'Subcultures, Cultures and Class: a theoretical overview', in S. Hall and J. Henderson (eds) *Resistance through Rituals*, Hutchinson, London/Centre of Contemporary Cultural Studies, 9–94.

Clarke, D.B. and M. Purvis (1994) 'Dialectics, Difference and the Geographies of Consumption: Environment and Planning', *Society and Space* 29 (7), 109–31.

Clewer, A., A. Pack and M.T. Sinclair (1992) 'Price Competitiveness and inclusive tour holidays', in P. Johnson and B. Thomas (eds) *Choice and Demand in Tourism*, Mansell, London.

Clifford, J. (1986) 'Introduction: partial truths', in J. Clifford and G.E. Marcus (eds) *Writing Worlds*, University of California Press, Berkeley CA.

Clifford, S and A. King (eds) (1993) *Local Distinctiveness: Place, Particularity and Identity*, Common Ground, London.

Cloke, P., C. Philo and D. Sadler (1991) *Appoaching Human Geography: An Introduction to Contemporary Theoretical Debates*, Paul Chapman, London.

Cohen, E. (1972) 'Towards a Sociology of International Tourism', *Social Research* 39, 164–82.

— (1979) 'A Phenomenology of Tourist Experiences', *Sociology* 13, 179–201.

— (1982) 'Thai Girls and Farang Men: the edge of ambiguity', *Annals of Tourism Research* 6, 18–35.

— (1989) 'Primitive and Remote: hill tribe trekking in Thailand', *Annals of Tourism Research* 16, 30–61.

— (1993) '"Unspoilt and Enchanting": Island Tourism in Southern Thailand', *Paper at 13th Annual Congress of Anthropology and Ethnological Sciences*, Mexico City.

— (1995) 'Contemporary Tourism - trends and challenges: sustainable authenticity or contrived post-modernity?' in R. Butler and D. Pearce (eds) *Change in Tourism. People, Places, Processes*, Routledge, London and New York.

Collinge, M. (1989) *Tourism and Urban Regeneration*, Vision for Cities Conference Paper, ETB, London.

Conforti, J. (1996) 'Ghettos as Tourism Attractions', *Annals of Tourism Research* 23, 830–42.

Cooke, P. (1989) *The Changing Face of Urban Britain*, Unwin Hyman, London.

— (1990) 'Modern Urban Theory in Question', *Transactions of Institute of British Geographers* 15 (3), 331–43.

Cooper, A. (1994) 'Negotiated Dilemmas of Landscape, Place, and Christian Commitment in a Suffolk Parish', *Transactions of Institute of British Geographers* (NS) 19, 202–12.

Cooper, C., J. Fletcher, D. Gilbert, R. Shepherd and S. Wanhill (1998) *Tourism Principles and Practice*, Longman, Essex.

Corner, J. (1986) 'Meaning, Genre, and Text', in J. Curran and M. Gereritch (eds) *Mass Media and Society*, Edward Arnold, London.

Corner, J. and S. Harvey (1991) *Enterprise and Heritage: Cross-currents of National Culture*, Routledge, London.

Cosgrove, D. (1984) 'The Idea of Landscape', in D. Cosgrove, *Social Formations and Symbolic Landscape*, Croom Helm, London, 13–38.

— (1985) 'Prospect, perspective, and the evolution of the landscape idea', *Transactions of the Institute of British Geographers* (NS) 10, 43–62.

Cosgrove, D. and P. Jackson (1987) 'New Directions in Cultural Geography', *Area* 19, 95–101.

Cosgrove, D.E. and S.J. Daniels (eds) (1987) *The Iconography of Landscape*, Cambridge University Press, Cambridge.

Coste, G. and B. Toulier (1984) 'La Demeur Urbain: Experimentation et Methode: l'example de tours', *Revue de l'art* 65, 88–92.

Cox, N.J. (1989) 'Levels of Abstraction in Locality Studies', *Antipode* 21, 121–32.

Craik, J. (1997) 'The Culture of Tourism', in C. Rojek and J. Urry (1997) *Touring Cultures: Transformations of Travel Theory*, Routledge, London.

Crang, M. (1994) 'On the Heritage Trail: maps of and journeys to Olde Englande', *Environment and Planning D, Society and Space* 12, 341–55.

— (1997) 'Picturing Practices: research through the tourist gaze', *Progress in Human Geography* 21 (3), 359–73.

Crang, P. (1994) '"It's Showtime": on the workplace geographies of display in a restaurant in Southeast England', *Environment and Planning D: Society and Space* 12, 675–704.

Crawshaw, C. and J. Urry (1997) 'Tourism and the Photographic Eye', in C. Rojek and J. Urry (1997) *Touring Cultures: Transformations of Travel Theory*, Routledge, London.

Crewe, L. (2000) 'Geographies of Retailing and Consumption', *Progress in Human Geography* 24, 27–90.

Crompton, J.L. (1977) 'Recreation System Model', *Leisure Sciences* 1 (1), 53–65.

—— (1979) 'An Assessment of the Image of Mexico as a vacation destination and the influence of geographical location on that image', *Journal of Travel Research* 18, Fall, 18–23.

Crompton, J.L. and N.A. Duray (1985) 'An investigation of the relative efficacy of four alternative approaches to importance-performance analysis', *Academy of Marketing Science* 13 (4), 69–80.

Crouch, D. (2000a) 'Tourism representations and non-representative geographies: making relationships between tourism and heritage active', in M. Robinson, N. Evans, P. Long, R. Sharpley and J. Swarbrook, *Tourism and Heritage Relationships: Global, National and Local Perspectives*, Business Education Publishers, Sunderland.

—— (2000b) 'Places Around Us: embodied lay geographies in leisure and tourism', *Leisure Studies* 19, 63–76.

Crow, D. (1994) 'My friends in low places: building identity for place and community', *Environment and Planning D: Society and Space* 12, 403–19.

Cullen, I.G. (1976) 'Human Geography, Regional Science, and the Study of Individual Behaviour', *Environment and Planning A* 8, 397–410.

Culler, J. (1981) 'Semiotics of Tourism', *American Journal of Semiotics* 1, 127–40.

D'Arcus, B. (2000) 'The "eager gaze of the tourist" meets "our grandfather's guns": producing and contesting the land of enchantment in Gallup, New Mexico', *Environment and Planning D: Society and Space* 18, 693–714.

Dadgoster, B. and R.M. Isotalo (1995) 'Content of City Destination Image for Near-Home Tourists', *Journal of Hospitality and Leisure Marketing* 3 (2), 25–34.

Dalziel, F.R. (1960) *An Experimental Study of the Concept of Meaning*, unpublished PhD thesis, University of Aberdeen.

Dann, G. (1988) 'Images of Cyprus Projected by tour Operators', *Problems of Tourism* 11 (3), 43–70.

—— (1992) 'Travellogs and the Management of Unfamiliarity', *Journal of Travel Research* 30 (4), 59–63.

—— (1996a) 'The People of Tourism Brochures', in T. Selwyn (ed.) *The Tourist Image. Myths and Myth Making in Tourism*, John Wiley and Sons, Chichester.

—— (1996b) 'Tourist Images of a Destination: an alternative analysis', *Journal of Travel and Tourism Marketing* 5 (1/2), 41–55.

—— (1996c) *The Language of Tourism: A Sociolinguistic Perspective*, CAB International, Oxford.

Dann, G., D. Nash, and P. Pearce (1988) 'Methodology in Tourism Research', *Annals of Tourism Research*, 15–28.

Davis, M. (1990) *City of Quartz: Excavating the Future in Los Angeles*, Verso, London.

De Certeau, M. (1985) 'Practices of Space', in M. Blonsky, *On Signs*, Basil Blackwell, London.

—— (1988) *The Practice of Everyday Life*, trans. Steven Rendall, University of California Press, Berkeley CA.

de Saussure, F. (1966) *Course in General Linguistics*, ed. C. Bally and A. Secheehaye, trans. W. Basking, McGraw-Hill, New York.

Dear, M.J. (1981) 'Social and Spatial Reproduction of the Mentally Ill', in M. Dear and A.J. Scott (eds) *Urbanisation and Urban Planning in Capitalist Society*, Methuen, Andover, Hants.

— (1986) 'Postmodernism and Planning', *Environment and Planning D: Society and Space* 4, 367–84.

Del Casino, V. J. and S.P. Hanna (2000) 'Representations and identities in tourism map spaces', *Progress in Human Geography* 24 (1), 23–46.

Deleuze, G. (1991) *Bergonism*, Zone Books, New York.

Deleuze, G. and F. Guattari (1983) *The Anti-Oedipus: Capitalism and Schizophrenia*, University of Minnesota Press, Minneapolis MN.

Department of Employment (1984) *Census of Employment*, HMSO.

Derrida, J. (1977) 'Signature, Event, Context', *Glyph* 1, 172–97.

— (1978) *Writing and Difference*, University of Chicago Press, Chicago IL.

Deutsche, R. (1991) 'Boys Town', *Environment and Planning D: Society and Space* 9, 5–30.

Dichter, E. (1985) 'What's in an Image?', *Journal of Consumer Marketing* 2 (1), 75–81.

Dicken, P. and R.Tickall (1991) 'Competitors or Collaborators? The Structure of Inward Investment Promotion in Northern England', *Regional Studies* 26, 99–106.

Dietvorst, A.G.J., W. Poelhekte and J. Roffelson (1987) 'Hoe mer verscheiden heid aan attrcties des te aantrekk elijker de stad', *Recreatie en Tourism* 11, 441–45.

Dilley, R.S. (1986) 'Tourist Brochures and Tourist Images', *The Canadian Geographer* 30 (1), 58–65.

Domash, M. (1988) 'Boston and New York City: Two Traditions in Built Form at the Century's Turn', paper presented at the Clark Centennial Conference, *Creation of Myth, Invention of Tradition in America*.

Donald, J. (1992) 'Metropolis: The City as Text', in R.Bocock and K.Thomson (eds), *Social and Cultural Forms of Modernity*, Polity Press, Cambridge, 417–61.

— (1999) *Imagining the Modern City*, The Athlone Press, London.

Downs, R.M. (1977) *Maps in Mind: Reflections on Cognitive Mapping*, Harper and Row, London.

Dreyfus, H.L. and P. Rabinow (1982) *Michel Foucault: Beyond Structualism and Hermaneutics*, Harvester Press, Hemel Hempstead.

Driscol, A., R. Lawson and B. Niven (1994) Measuring Tourists' Destination Perceptions, *Annals of Tourism Research* 21, 499–511.

Driver, B.L., P.J. Brown, G.H. Stankey and T.G. Gregoire (1987) 'The ROS Planning System', *Leisure Sciences* 9, 29–212.

Driver, F. (1985a) 'Power, Space, and the Body: a Critical Assessment of Foucault's Discipline and Punish', *Environment and Planning D: Society and Space* 3, 425–46.

— (1985b) 'Geography and Power: The Work of Michel Foucault', unpublished typescript, Department of Geography, Royal Holloway and Bedford New College, Egham, Surrey.

— (1992) 'Geography's Empire: histories of geographical knowledge', *Environment and Planning D: Society and Space* 10, 23–40.

DRV (1995) *An Economic Impact Study of the Tourist and Associated Arts Development in Merseyside*, DRV Research, Bournemouth.

Duncan, J.S. (1980) 'The Superorganic in American Cultural Geography', *Annals of Association of American Geographers* 70, 181–98.

— (1987) 'Review of Urban Imagery: Urban Semiotics', *Urban Geography* 8, 473–83.

Duncan, J.S. and N. Duncan, (1988) '(Re)reading the landscape', *Environment and Planning D: Society and Space* 6, 117–26.

Dunford, M.F. (1977) 'Regional Policy and the Restructuring of Capital', Sussex University, urban and regional studies working paper number 4.

Eagleton, T. (1983) *Literary Theory*, University of Minnesota Press, Minneapolis MN.

— (1988) 'Resources for a Journey of Hope: the significance of Raymond Williams', *New Left Review* 168, 3–11.

Echtner, C.M. (1999) 'The Semiotic Paradigm: implications of tourism research', *Tourism Management* 20 (1) February, 47–57.

Echtner, C.M. and J.R.B. Ritchie (1991) 'The Meaning and Measurement of Tourism Destination Image', *Journal of Tourism Studies* 2 (2) December, 2–12.

Eco, U. (1986) *Travels in Hyper-Reality*, Picador, London.

Edensor, T. (2000) 'Staging Tourism: Tourists as Performers', *Annals of Tourism Research* 27 (2), 322–44.

Edwards, E. (1996) 'Postcards: Greetings from Another World', in Selwyn, T. (ed) *The Tourist Image. Myths and Myth-making in Tourism*, John Wiley and Sons, Chichester.

Embacher, J. and F. Buttle (1989) 'A Repertory Grid Analysis of Austria's Image as a Summer Vacation Destination', *Journal of Travel Research* 28 (3), 3–23.

Entrikin, J.N. (1976) 'Contemporary Humanism in Geography', *Annals of the Association of American Geographers* 66, 615–32.

— (1991) *The Betweeness of Place: Towards a Geography of Modernity*, Johns Hopkins University Press, Baltimore MD.

ETB (1980) *Tourism and the Inner City*, English Tourism Board, London.

Evans, M.R., J.B. Fox and R.B. Johnson (1995) 'Identifying Competitive Strategies for Successful Tourism Destination Development', *Journal of Hospitality and Leisure Marketing* 3 (1), 37–46.

Evans-Pritchard, D. (1989) 'How "They" See "Us": Native American Images of Tourists', *Annals of Tourism Research* 16, 89–105.

Eyles, J. and D.M. Smith (1988) *Qualitative Methods in Human Geography*, Polity Press, Cambridge.

Fairburn, K. (1991) 'West Edmonton Mall: Entrepreneurial Innovation and Consumer Response', *Canadian Geographer* 35, 261–67.

Fairweather, J.R. and S.R. Swaffield (2001) 'Visitor Experiences of Kaikoura, New Zealand: an interpretative study using photographs of landscapes and Q method', *Tourism Management* 22, 219–28.

Fakeye, P.C. and J.L. Crompton (1991) 'Image Differences Between Prospective, First-time and Repeat Visitors to the Lower Rio Grande Valley', *Journal of Travel Research* 30 (2), 10–16.

Featherstone, M. (1991) *Consumer Culture and Postmodernism*, Sage, London.

Fees, C. (1996) 'Tourism and the Politics of Authenticity in a North Cotswold Town', in T. Selwyn (ed.) *The Tourist Image: Myths and Myth Making in Tourism*, John Wiley and Sons, Chichester.

Financial Times (1995) Financial Times Survey, Cardiff, May 11.

Fish, S (1980) *Is There a Text in this Class?*, Harvard University Press, Cambridge MA.

Fisher, M.M. and P. Nijkamp (1987) 'From Static Towards Dynamic Discrete Choice Modelling: a state of the art review', *Regional Science and Urban Economics* 17 (1), 3–27.

Fjellman, S. (1992) *Vinyl Leaves: Walt Disney World and America*, Westview Press, Boulder, CO.

Fletcher, J.E. and B.H. Archer (1991) 'The Development and Application of Multiplier Analysis', in C. Cooper (ed.) *Progress in Tourism, Recreation, and Hospitality Management*, Belhaven, London vol. 3, 28–47.

Font, X. (1996) 'Managing the Tourist Destination Image', *Journal of Vacation Marketing* 3 (2), 123–31.

Foster, H. (1983) 'Postmodernism: a Preface', in H. Foster (ed.) *The Anti-aesthetic: Essays in Postmodern Culture*, Bay Press, Port Townsend WA, ix–xiv.

Fothergill, S., S. Monk and M. Perry (1988) *Property and Industrial Development*, Hutchinson, London.

Foucault, M. (1967) *Madness and Civilisation: A History of Insanity in the Age of Reason*, Tavistock, London.

— (1972) *The Archeology of Knowledge*, Tavistock, London.

— (1977) *Discipline and Punish*, Tavistock, London.

— (1979) *The History of Sexuality: Volume 1, An Introduction*, Allen Lane, London.

— (1980) *Power/Knowledge*, Harvester, Brighton.

— (1980b) *The Order of Things*, Vintage, New York.

— (1981) *The History of Sexuality: Volume 1, An Introduction*, Penguin Books, Harmondsworth, Middlesex.

— (1986) 'Of Other Spaces', *Diacritics*, Spring, 22–27.

— (1989) *Birth of the Clinic: An Archaeology of Medical Perception*, Routledge, London.

Franklin, A. and M. Crang (2001) 'The Trouble With Tourism and Travel Theory?' *Tourist Studies* 1 (1), 5–22.

Fretter, A.D. (1993) 'Place Marketing: A Local Authority Perspective' in G. Kearns and C. Philo (eds) *Selling Places: The City as Cultural Capital Past and Present*, Pergamon Press, London.

Frigden, J.D. (1984) 'Environmental Psychology and Tourism', *Annals of Tourism Research* 11 (1), 19–39.

Fullager, S. (2001) 'Encountering Otherness: embodied affect in Alphonso Lingis' travel writing', *Tourist Studies* 1 (1), 171–83.

Gale, T.J. (1996) 'Semiotics and the Reading of Cultural Texts: Possible Applications in Tourism Studies', International Conference *Higher Degrees of Pleasure*, Cardiff, July, 69–83.

Gallarza, M.G., I.G. Saura and H.C. Garcia (2001) 'Destination Image: towards a conceptual framework', *Annals of Tourism Research* 29, 56–78.

Game, A. (1991) *Undoing the Social*, Open University Press, Milton Keynes.

Gartner, W.C. (1986) 'Temporal Influences on Image Change', *Annals of Tourism Research* 13, 635–44.

Gartner, W.C. and J.D. Hunt (1987) 'An Analysis of State Image Change over a Twelve-Year Period (1971–1983)', *Journal of Travel Research* 26 (2), 15–19.

Geertz, C. (1983) *Local Knowledge: Further Essays in Interpretative Anthropology*, Basic Books, New York.

Genocchio, B. (1995) 'Discourse, Discontinuity and Difference: The Question of "Other" Spaces', in S. Watson and K. Gibson (eds) *Postmodern Cities and Spaces*, Blackwell, Oxford.

Getz, D. (1991) *Festivals, Special Events, and Tourism*, Van Nostrand Reinhold, New York.

Giddens, A. (1991) *Modernity and Self Identity*, Polity Press, Cambridge.

Gilbert, D. (2000) 'Urban Outfitting: the city and spaces of fashion culture', in S. Bruzzi and P. Church-Gibson, *Fashion Cultures: Theories, Explanations and Analyses*, Routledge, London, 7–24.

Gilbert, D. and I. Joshi (1992) 'Quality Management in the Tourism and Hospitality Industry', in C. Cooper and A. Lockwood (eds) *Progress in Tourism, Recreation and Hospitality Management*, vol. 4, Belhaven, London, 149–68.

Giletson, G. and R.J. Crompton (1983) 'The Planning Horizons and Sources of Information Used by Pleasure Vacationers', *Journal of Travel Research* 23 (3), 2–7.

Gillespie, A. (1991) *Television, Ethnicity and Cultural Change*, Routledge, London.

Glennie, P. and N. Thrift (1992) 'Modernity, Urbanism, and Modern Consumption', *Environment and Planning D: Society and Space* 10, 423–43.

Gold, J.R. (1980) *An Introduction to Behavioural Geography*, Oxford University Press, Oxford.

Gold, J.R. and S.V. Ward (1991) *Place Promotion, The Use of Publicity and Marketing to Sell Towns and Regions*, John Wiley and Sons.

Goodall, B. (1988) in B. Goodall and G.J. Ashworth, *Marketing in the Tourism Industry: The Promotion of Destination Regions*, Croom Helm, London.

— (1988) 'Market Opportunity Sets for Tourism', Geographical Papers 100: Tourism Series 1, University of Reading, Department of Geography.

— (1991) 'Understanding Holiday Choice', in C. Cooper (ed.) *Progress in Tourism, Recreation, and Hospitality Management*, vol. 3, Belhaven, London, 58–77.

Goodrich, J.N. (1977) 'Benefit Bundle Analysis: an empirical study of international travelers', *Journal of Travel Research* 16, 6–9.

Gorush, R.L. (1983) *Factor Analysis*, Lawrence Erlbaum, Hillsdale NJ.

Goss, J.D. (1993) 'Placing the Market and Marketing Place', *Environment and Planning D: Society and Space* 11, 663–88.

Gottdiener, M. (1995) *Postmodern Semiotics: Material Culture and the Forms of Postmodern Life*, Blackwell, Oxford.

Gould, P. (1976) 'Cultivating the Garden: a commentary and critique on some multidimensional speculations', in R.G. Golledge and G. Rushton (eds) *Spatial Choice and Spatial Behaviour: Geographic Essays on the Analysis of Preferences and Perceptions*, Ohio State University Press, Columbus OH.

— (1985) *The Geographer at Work*, Routledge and Kegan Paul, London.

Gould, P. and R. White (1974) *Mental Maps*, Penguin Books, Harmondsworth.

Graefe, A.R. and J.J. Vaske (1987) 'A Framework for Managing Quality in the Tourist Experience', *Annals of Tourism Research* 14, 339–404.

Graham, B. (1994) 'No Place of the Mind: contested Protestant representations of Ulster', *Ecumene* 1, 257–82.

Gray, H.P. (1970) *International Travel – International Trade*, Health Lexington, Lexington.

Gregory, D. (1989) 'Areal Differentiation and Postmodern Human Geography', in D. Gregory and R. Walford (eds) *Horizons in Human Geography*, London, Macmillan.

— (1989b) 'The Crisis of Modernity? Human Geography and Critical Social Theory', in R. Peet and N. Thrift (eds) *New Models in Geography*, vols 1 and 2, Unwin Hyman, London.

— (1994) 'Space, Time and Politics in Social Theory: an interview with Anthony Giddens', *Environment and Planning D: Society and Space* 2, 123–32.

Gregson, N. (1995) 'And Now It's All Consumption?' *Progress in Human Geography* 19 (1), 135–41.

Griffiths, R. (1993) 'The Politics of Cultural Policy in Urban Regeneration Strategies', *Policy and Politics* 21, 39–46.

Gross, J.D. (1993) 'Placing the Market and Marketing the Place', *Environment and Planning D: Society and Space*, 11, 663–68.

Grosz, E. (1995) 'Women, Chora, and Dwelling', in S. Watson and K. Gibson, *Postmodern Cities and Spaces*, Blackwell, Oxford.

Gruffudd, P., D.T. Herbert and A. Piccini (1999) '"Good to think": social constructions of Celtic heritage in Wales', *Environment and Planning D: Society and Space* 17, 705–21.

Gulliksen, H. (1958) 'How to Make Meaning More Meaningful', *Contemporary Psychology* 3 (1), 115.

Gunn, C. (1972) *Vacationscape: Designing Tourist Regions*, Taylor and Francis/University of Texas, London/Austin TX.

— (1988) *Vacationscapes: Designing Tourist Regions*, Van Nostrand, New York.

Guskind, R. (1987) 'Bringing Madison Avenue to Main Street', *Planning* February, 4–10.

Gyte, D. (1988) 'Repertory Grid Analysis of Images of Destinations: British Tourists in Mallorca', Trent working papers in geography, Trent Polytechnic, Nottingham.

Haahti, A. (1986) 'Finland's Competitive Position as a Destination', *Annals of Tourism Research* 13, 11–35.

Haahti, A. and U. Yevas (1983) 'Tourists' Perceptions of Finland and Selected European Countries as Travel Destinations', *European Journal of Marketing* 17 (2), 34–42.

Habermass, J. (1976) *Legitimation Crisis*, Heinemann, London.

Haider, D. (1992) 'Place Wars: new realities of the 1990's', *Economic Development Quarterly* 6, 127–34.

Hall, P. (1987) 'Urban Development and the Future of Tourism', *Tourism Management* 8 (2) June, 129–30.

Hall, R.H. (1968) 'Professionalization and Bureaucratization', *American Sociological Review* 33, 92–104.

Hall. S. (1973) 'Encoding and Decoding in Television Discourse', *Stencilled Occasional Paper*, Birmingham, CCCS.

Haraway, D. (1988) 'Situated Knowledges: the science question in feminism and the privilege of partial perspective', Feminist Studies 14 (3), 575–99.

Harloe, M., C. Pickvance and J. Urry (1990) *Policy, Place and Politics: Do Localities Matter?* Unwin Hyman, London.

Harrison, J. and P. Sarre (1975) 'Personal Construct Theory In the Measurement of Environmental Images', *Environment and Behaviour* 7 March, 3–58.

Hartmann, R. (1988) 'Combining Field Methods in Tourism Research', *Annals of Tourism Research* 15, 88–105.

Harvey, D. (1969) 'Conceptual and Measurement Problems in the Cognitive-Behavioural Approach to Location Theory', in K. R. Cox and R. G. Golledge (eds) *Behavioural Problems in Geography: A Synopsium*, Northwestern University Press, Evanston IL.

— (1972) 'Revolutionary and Counter-revolutionary Theory in Geography and the Problem of Ghetto Formation', *Antipode* 4 (2), 1–13.

— (1973) *Social Justice and the City*, Edward Arnold, London.

— (1989a) *The Condition of Postmodernity*, Blackwell, Oxford.

— (1989b) *Consciousness and the Urban Experience: Studies in History and the Theory of Capitalist Urbanisation* vol. 1, Basil Blackwell, Oxford.

— (1993) 'From Space to Place and Back Again: reflections on the condition of post-modernity', in J. Bird, B. Curtis, T. Putnam, G. Robertson and L. Tickner (eds) *Mapping the Future: Local Culture, Global Change*, Routledge, London.

Haywood, K.M. and T.E. Muller (1988) 'The Urban Tourist Experience: evaluating satisfaction', *Hospitality Education and Research Journal*, 453–9.

Healey and Baker (1992) *Europe's Top Cities: European Real Estate Monitor*, Healey and Baker, London.

Heidegger, M. (1967) *Being and Time*, trans. J. Macquarrie and E. Robinson, Blackwell, Oxford.

Herbert, D.T. (ed.) (1995) *Heritage, Tourism, and Society*, Mansell, London.

— (2001) 'Literary Places, Tourism and Heritage Experience', *Annals of Tourism Research* 28 (2), 312–33.

Hetherington, K. (1992) 'Stonehenge and its Festival: spaces of consumption', in R. Shields (ed.) *Lifestyle Shopping*, Routledge, London, 83–98.

Hinkle, D.N. (1965) 'The Change of Personal Constructs From the Viewpoint of a Theory of Implications', unpublished PhD thesis, University of Colorado, Boulder CO.

Hochschild, A. (1983) 'The Managed Heart', *Commercialization of Human Feeling*, University of California, Berkeley CA.

Holcomb, B. (1990) 'Purveying Places: Past and Present', Centre for Urban Policy Research, working paper number 17, New Brunswick NJ.

— (1994) 'City Make-Overs: Marketing the Post-industrial City', in J.R. Gold and S.V. Ward, *Place Promotion: The Use of Publicity and Marketing to Sell Towns and Regions*, Wiley, Chichester, 115–31.

Holcombe, B. and R.A. Beauregard (1980) 'Revitalising Cities', *Resource Publications in Geography*, Association of American Geographers, Washington DC.

Hollis, K. and J.A. Burgess (1977) 'Personal London: Students Perceive the Urban Scene', *Geographical Magazine* 50 (3), 155–61.

Home Office (2001) *Statistical Bulletin. Recorded Crime in England and Wales, 12 months to September 2000*, January 2001, HMSO, London.

Hopkins, J. (1990) 'West Edmonton Mall: landscapes of myths and elsewhereness', *Canadian Geographer* 34, 2–17.

— (1991) 'West Edmonton Mall as a Centre for Social Interaction', *Canadian Geographer* 35, 268–79.

Horne, D. (1984) 'The Great Museum', *The Representation of History*, Punto Press, London.

Hudson, R. (1976) 'Environmental Images, Spatial Choice, and Consumer Behaviour', occasional paper (new series), Department of Geography, University of Durham, Durham.

Hughes, G. (1991) 'Conceiving of Tourism', *Area* 23 (3), 263–67.

Hughes, H. (1997) 'Holidays and Homosexual Identity', *Tourism Management* 18 (1), 3–18.

— (2000) *Arts, Entertainment and Tourism*, Butterworth Heinemann, London.

Hunt, J.D. (1975) 'Image as a Factor in Tourism Development', *Journal of Travel Research* 13 (3), 1–7.

Husserl, E. (1965) *Phenomenology and the Crisis of Philosophy*, Harper and Row, New York.

— (1969) *Cartesian Meditations: An Introduction to Phenomenology*, trans. Dorion Cairns, Nijhoff, The Hague.

— (1970) *The Crisis of European Sciences and Transcendal Phenomenology: An Introduction to Phenomenological Philosophy*, trans. David Carr, Northwestern University Press, Evanston IL.

Hutt, M. (1996) 'Looking for Shrangri-la: from Hilton to Lachichhane', in T. Selwyn (ed.) *The Tourist Image: Myths and Myth Making in Tourism*, John Wiley and Sons, Chichester.

Huyssen, A. (1984) 'Mapping the Postmodern', *New German Critique* 33, 5–52.

Innes, C.L. (1994) 'Virgin Territories and Motherlands: colonial and nationalist representations of Africa and Ireland', *Feminist Review* 27, 1–14.

Iso-Ahola, S.E. (1982) 'Toward a Social Psychological Theory of Tourism Motivation: a rejoinder', *Annals of Tourism Research* 9 (2), 256–61.

Jackle, J.A. (1985) *The Tourist: Travel in Twentieth Century North America*, University of Nebraska Press, Lincoln NE.

Jackson, E. and D. Johnson (1991) 'Geographic Implications of Mega-malls, with specific reference to West Edmonton Mall', *Canadian Geographer* 35, 226–31.

Jackson, P. (1981) 'Phenomenology and Social Geography', *Area* 13, 299–305.

— (ed.) (1989) *Maps of Meaning: An Introduction to Cultural Geography*, Unwin Hyman, London.

— (1994) 'Black Male: advertising and the cultural politics of masculinity', *Gender, Place, and Culture* 1, 49–59.

Jackson, P. and J. Taylor (1996) 'Geography and the Cultural Politics of Advertising', *Progress in Human Geography* 20, 356–72.

Jacobs, J. (1993) 'The City Unbound: Qualitative Approaches to the City', *Urban Studies* 30 (4/4), 827–48.

Jakobson, R. (1960) 'Concluding Statement: linguistics and poetics', in T. Sebok (ed.) *Style in Language*, MIT Press, Cambridge MA, 350–77.

Jamal, T. and K. Hollinshead (2001) 'Tourism and the forbidden zone: the underserved power of qualitative inquiry', *Tourism Management* 22, 63–82.

James, W. (1890) *Principles of Psychology*, Dover Publications, New York.

Jameson, F. (1984) 'Postmodernism or the Cultural Logic of Late Capitalism', *New Left Review* 146, 52–92.

— (1988) 'Cognitive Mapping', in C. Nelson and L. Grossberg (eds) *Marxism and the Interpretation of Culture*, Macmillan, London.

— (1991) *Postmodernism or the Cultural Logic of Late Capitalism*, Verso, London.

Jansen, A.C.M. (1989) '"Funshopping" as a Geographical Notion, or The Attraction of the Inner City of Amsterdam as a Shopping Area', in *Tijschrift voor Economische en sociale Geografie* 80 (3), 171–83.

Jansen-Verbeke, M. (1987) 'Leisure, Recreation and Tourism: A Geographic Review on Integration', *Annals of Tourism Research* 14, 361–75.

— (1988) *Leisure, Recreation, and Tourism in Inner Cities*, CIP Geogevens Koninklijke Bibiotkeek, Den Haag.

— (1990) 'Leisure and Shopping – Tourism Product Mix', in G.J. Ashworth and B. Goodall, *Marketing Tourism Places*, Routledge, London, 128–37.

Jardine, D.W. (1998) 'Birding Lessons and the Teachings of Ciradas', *Canadian Journal of Environmental Education* 3, 92–99.

Jarvis, B. (1985) 'The Truth is Only Known by Gutter-snipes', in J. Burgess and J.R. Gold (eds) *Geography, The Media, and Popular Culture*, Croom Helm, Beckenham, 99–122.

Jeffery, D. (1990) 'Monitoring the Growth of tourism-related employment at the local level: the application of census-based non-survey methods in Yorkshire and Humberside, 1981–1987', *Planning Outlook* 33, 108–17.

Jenkins, O.H. (1999) 'Understanding and Measuring Tourist Destination Images', *International Journal of Tourism Research* 1, 1–15.

Johnson, R. (1986) 'The Story So Far and Further Transformations?' in D. Punter (ed.) *Introduction to Contemporary Cultural Studies*, Longman, London, 277–313.

Jokinen, E. and S. Veijola (1997) 'The Disorientated Tourist: The Figuration of the Tourist in Contemporary Cultural Critique', in C. Rojek and J. Urry, *Touring Cultures: Transformations of Travel Theory*, Routledge, London.

Jones, A. (1988) 'Japanese Investment – Welcome to Wales', *Welsh Economic Review* 1 (2), 60–64.

Judd, D.R. (1993) 'Promoting Tourism in US Cities', *Tourism Management* 16, 175–87.

Judd, D.R. and S.S. Fainstein (eds) (1999) *The Tourist City*, Yale University Press, New Haven CT.

Kaiser, H.F. (1974) 'An Index of Factorial Simplicity', *Psychometrica* 39, 31–36.

Kale, S.H. and K.M.Weir (1986) 'Marketing Third World Countries to the Western Traveller: the case of India', *Journal of Travel Research* 25 (2), Fall, 2–7.

Kane, J.N. and R. Alexander (1965) *Nicknames of Cities and States of the US*, Scarecrow, New York.

Kaplin, R. and S. Kaplin (1989) *The Experience of Nature: A Psychological Perspective*, Cambridge University Press, Cambridge.

Kasmar, J.V. (1970) 'The Development of a Useable Lexicon of Environmental Descriptors', *Environment and Behaviour* 2, 153–69.

Kearns, G. and C. Philo (eds) (1993) *Selling Places: The City as Cultural Capital Past and Present*, Pergamon Press, Oxford.

Kellner, D. (1992) *Critical Theory, Marxism and Modernity*, Polity Press, Cambridge.

Kelly, G.A. (1955) *The Psychology of Personal Constructs*, Norton, New York.

— (1961) 'The Abstraction of Human Processes', proceedings, 14th International Congress of Applied Psychology, Copenhagen.

— (1965) 'The Strategy of Psychological Research', *British Psychology Society Bulletin* 18 (1).

Kershaw, B. (1993) *Reminiscing History: Memory, Performance, Empowerment*, De-traditionalisation Conference, Lancaster University, July.

Kirshenblatt-Gimblett, B. (1998) *Destination Culture: Tourism, Museums, and Heritage*, University of California Press, Berkeley CA.

Knox, P.L. (1991) 'The Restless Urban Landscape: economic and socio-cultural change and the transformation of metropolitan Washington DC', *Annals of Association of American Geographers* 81, 181–209.

— (1992) review of T. Banerjee, *City Sense and City Design: Writings and Projects of Kevin Lynch*, in *Environment and Planning D: Society and Space* 10, 231–33.

Kotler, P. (1969) 'Broadening the Concept of Marketing', *Journal of Marketing* January, 10–15.

— (1972) 'A Generic Concept of Marketing', *Journal of Marketing* April, 46–54.

— (1986) *Principles of Marketing*, Third Edition, Prentice Hall, Englewood Cliffs NJ.

Kotler, P. and G. Armstrong (1991) *Principles of Marketing*, Prentice Hall, London.

Kotler, P., D.M. Haider and I. Rein (1993) *Marketing Places: Attracting Investment, Industry, and Tourism to Cities, States, and Nations*, Macmillan, New York.

Kotler, P., N. Roberto and N. Lee (2002) *Social Marketing: improving the quality of life*, 2nd Edition, Sage, London.

Krim, A. (1988) 'Inventing the Tradition of Los Angeles as Anti-tradition', paper presented at the Clark Centenial Conference, *Creation of Myth, Invention of Tradition in America*.

Krippendorf, J. (1987) *The Holiday Makers*, Heinemann, London.

L & R Leisure PLC (1995) Cardiff Strategic Tourism Plan Report (Draft), L & R Leisure Plc, Hayward's Heath, Sussex.

Labovitz, S. (1970) 'The Assignment of Numbers to Rank Order Catagories', *American Sociological Review* 35, 515–24.

Lafant, M.F. (1995) 'International Tourism, Internationalisation, and the Challenge to Identity', in M.F. Lafant, J.B. Allcock and E.M. Bruner (eds) *International Tourism: Identity and Change*, Sage, London.

Lash, S. and J. Urry (1994) *Economies of Signs and Space*, Sage, London.

— (1997) *The End of Organised Capitalism*, Oxford.

Law, C.M. (1991) 'Tourism as a Focus for Urban Regeneration', in S. Hardy, T. Hart and G. Shaw (eds) *The Role of Tourism in the Urban and Regional Economy*, Regional Studies Association, London.

— (1992) 'Urban Tourism and its Contribution to Urban Regeneration', *Urban Studies* 29, 599–618.

— (1993) *Urban Tourism, Attracting Visitors to Large Cities*, Mansell Publishing, London.

— (ed.) (1996) *Tourism in Major Cities*, Thomson International Business Press, London.

— (2002) *Urban Tourism: The Visitor Economy and the Growth of Large Cities*, Continuum, London.

Laws, E. (1999) 'Visitor Satisfaction Management at Leeds Castle, Kent', in A. Leask and I. Yeoman, *Heritage Visitor Attractions*, Cassell, London.

Laws, E. and B. Le Pelley (2000) 'Managing Complexity and Change in Tourism: the case of a Historic City', *International Journal of Tourism Research* 2, 229–46.

Lawson, F. and M. Baud-Bovey (1977) *Tourism and Recreational Development*, Architectural Press, London.

Lazarsfeld, P.F. (1958) 'Evidence and Influence in Social Research', *Daedalus* 87, 99–130.

Lees, L. (1997) 'Ageographia, Heterotopia, and Vancouver's New Public Space', *Environment and Planning D: Society and Space* 15, 321–47.

Lefebvre, H. (1966) introduction in M.G. Raymond, N. Haumont, M. Coornaert, *L'Habitat Pavillionaire*, Centre de Research d'Urbanism, Paris.

— (1967) *Position, Contre les Technocrates*, Gonthier, Paris.

— (1970) *La Revolution Urbain*, Gillinard, Du Rural a l'Urban, Anthropos.

— (1976) *The Survival of Capitalism*, trans. Allison and Busby, Blackwell, Oxford.

— (1985) 'Le projet rythmanalytique', *Communications* 41, 191–99.

— (1986) 'Hors du Centre, point de salut?' *Espaces Temps* 33, 17–19.

— (1987) 'An interview with Henri Lefebvre', *Environment and Planning D: Society and Space* 5, 27–38.

— (1996) *Writings on Cities*, trans. E. Kofman and E. Lebas, Basil Blackwell, Oxford.

Leiber, S.R. (1977) 'Attitudes and Revealed Behaviour: a case study', *Professional Geographer* 29 (1), 53–58.

Leisure Monitor, (1997) issue number 3, School of Hospitality, Tourism, and Leisure, University of Wales Institute, Cardiff.

Letendre, D. (1988) '"Explication of Texte" and the Cultural Landscape of L.A.', paper presented at the Clark Centenial Conference, *Creation of Myth, Invention of Tradition in America*.

Ley, D. (1974) 'The Black Inner City as Frontier Outpost: Images and Behaviour of a Philadelphia Neighborhood', *Association of American Geographers* 7, Washington DC.

— (1977) 'Social Geography and the Taken-for-granted World', *Transactions of the Institute of British Geographers* (NS) 2, 498–512.

— (1980a) 'Geography Without Man: a Humanistic Critique', University of Oxford School of Geography research paper 24, Oxford.

— (1980b) 'Liberal Ideology and the Post-industrial City', *Annals of Association of American Geographers* 70, 238–58.

— (1981) 'Behavioural Geography and the Philosophies of Meaning', in K.R. Cox and R.G. Golledge (eds) *Behavioural Problems in Geography Revisited*, Methuen, London.

— (1981a) 'Behavioural Geography and the Philosophies of Meaning', in R.G. Golledge (ed.) *Behavioural Problems in Geography Revisited*, Methuen, New York, 209–30.

— (1981b) 'Cultural/Humanistic Geography', *Progress in Human Geography* 5, 249–57.

— (1982) 'Rediscovering Man's Place: Commentary on Gregory's Paper', *Transactions of Institute of British Geographers* (NS) 7, 248–53.

— (1987) 'Styles of the Times: liberal and neo-conservative landscapes in inner Vancouver, 1968–86', *Journal of Historical Geography* 14, 40–56.

— (1989) 'Modernism, Postmodernism, and the Struggle for Place', in J. Agnew and J. Duncan, *The Power of Place*, Unwin Hyman, London, 44–65.

Ley, D. and K. Olds (1988) 'Landscape as Spectacle: World Fairs and the Culture of Heroic Consumption', *Environment and Planning D: Society and Space* 6, 191–212.

Li, Y. (2000) 'Geographical Consciousness and Tourism Experience', *Annals of Tourism Research* 27 (4), 863–83.

Littrell, M.A., L.F. Anderson and P.J. Brown (1993) 'What Makes a Craft Souvenir Authentic?' *Annals of Tourism Research* 20 (1), 197–215.

Lovelock, C.H. and C.B. Weinberg (1984) *Marketing for Public and Non-Profit Managers*, Wiley, New York.

Lowe, M. and L. Crews (1991) 'Lollipop Jobs for Pin Money? Retail Employment Explored', *Area* 23, 344–47.

Lowenthal, D. (1961) 'Geography, Experience and Imagination: towards a geographical epistemology', *Annals of the Association of American Geographers* 51, 241–60.

— (1967) *Environmental Perception and Behaviour*, Department of Geography, University of Chicago, Chicago IL.

— (1989) *The Past is a Foreign Country*, Cambridge University Press, Cambridge.

Luckmann, T. (1973) 'Aspekte einer Theorie der Social Kommenikation', in *Lexikon der Germanistischen Liguistik*, Niemeyer, Tubingen, 1–13.

Lynch, K. (1960) *Image of the City*, MIT, Cambridge MA.

Lyotard, J. (1984) *The Postmodern Condition: A Report of Knowledge*, Manchester University Press, Manchester.

M.T.B. (1987) *Tourism: A Flagship for Merseyside: A Consultation Draft Strategy*, Merseyside Tourist Board, Liverpool.

MacCannell, D. (1973) 'Staged Authenticity', *American Journal of Sociology* 79 (3), 589–693.

— (1976) *The Tourist: a New Theory of the Leisure Class*, Macmillan, London.

— (1989) introduction to special issue, 'Semiotics of Tourism', *Annals of Tourism Research* 16, 1–16.

— (2001) 'Tourist Agency', *Tourist Studies* 1 (1), 23–37.

Macdonald, S. (1997) 'A People's Story: Heritage, Identity, and Authenticity', in C. Rojek and J. Urry, *Touring Cultures: Transformations of Travel Theory*, Routledge, London.

MacInnis, D.J. and L.L. Price (1987) 'The Role of Imagery in Information Processing: Review and Extentions', *Journal of Consumer Research* 13, 473–91.

Madsen, H. (1992) 'Place-marketing in Liverpool: a review', *International Journal of Urban and Regional Research* 16 (4), 633–40.

Mandel, E. (1975) *Late Capitalism*, New Left Books, London.

Manning, P.K. (1997) *Semiotics and Fieldwork*, Sage, London.

Manning, R.E. (1986) *Studies in Outdoor Recreation*, Oregon State University Press, Corvallis OR.

Marin, L. (1984) *Utopics: Spatial Play*, trans. R. Vollrak, Macmillan, London.

Massey, D. (1984) *Spatial Divisions of Labour: Social Structures and the Geography of Production*, Macmillan, London.

Massey, D. and R. Meegan (1992) *The Anatomy of Job Loss*, Methuen, Andover.

Mathieson, A. and G. Wall (1982) *Tourism: Economic, Physical and Social Impacts*, Longman.

Matlass, D. (1994) 'Moral Geography in Broadland', *Ecumene* 1, 127–56.

Mayo, E. (1973) 'Regional Images and Regional Travel Behaviour', *Proceedings of the Travel Research Association, Fourth Annual Conference*, 211–18.

Mayo, E.J. and L.P. Jarvis (1981) *The Psychology of Leisure Travel: Effective Marketing and Selling of Travel Services*, CBI, Boston MA.

Mazanec, J. (ed.) (1997) *International City Tourism: Analysis and Strategy*, Pinter, London.

Mazanec, J.A. (1994) 'Image Measurement with Self-organising Maps: A Tentative Application to Austrian Tour Operators', *Revue du Tourism* 49 (3), 9–18.

McCrone, D., A. Morris and R. Kiely, (1995) *Scotland the Brand*, Edinburgh University Press, Edinburgh.

McDowell, L. (1994) 'Polyphony and Pedagogic Authority', *Area* 26, 241–48.

McGregor, A. (2000) 'Dynamic Texts and the Tourist Gaze: Death, Bones and Buffalo', *Annals of Tourism Research* 27 (1), 27–50.

McGrevey, P. (1992) 'Reading the Texts of the Niagra Falls: the metaphor of death', in T.J. Barnes and J.S. Duncan (eds) *Writing Worlds: Discourse, Text, and Metaphor in the Representation of Landscape*, Routledge, London, 256–555.

Mead, G.H. (1934) *Mind, Self, and Society*, University of Chicago, Chicago IL.

Meethen, K. (1996) 'Place Image and Power. Brighton as a Resort', in T. Selwyn (ed.) *The Tourist Image: Myths and Myth Making in Tourism*, John Wiley and Sons, Chichester.

Mellinger, W.M. (1994) 'Towards a Critical Analysis of Tourism Representations', *Annals of Tourism Research* 21 (4), 756–79.

Mellor, A. (1991) 'Enterprise and Heritage in the Dock', in J. Corner and S. Harvey (eds) *Enterprise and Heritage*, Routledge, London.

Mercer, D. and J.M. Powell. (1972) *Phenomenology and Related Non-positivistic Viewpoints in the Social Sciences*, Monash University Publications in Geography, no 1, Melbourne.

Merleau-Ponty, M. (1962) *Phenomenology and Perception*, trans. C. Smith, Routledge and Kegan Paul, London.

— (1963) *The Structure of Behaviour*, trans. A.L. Fisher, Beacon Press, Boston MA.

— (1968) *The Visible and the Invisible*, trans. A. Lingis, North Western University Press, Evanston.

— (1969) *The Primacy of Perception and Other Essays*, ed. J.M. Edie, Northwestern University Press, Evanston IL.

— (1970) *Themes from His Lectures*, trans. J. O'Neill, North Western University Press, Evanston IL.

Mersey Partnership (2000) *Destination Benchmarking 2000*, Mersey Partnership, Liverpool.

Mersey Partnership (2001) 'Make it Merseyside', *Read all about Merseyside*, Mersey Partnership, Liverpool.

Middleton, M. (1991) *Cities in Transition: The Regeneration of Britain's Inner Cites*, Michael Joseph, London.

Middleton, M.C. (forthcoming) 'Consuming the City: an evaluation of tourist behaviour within an unfamiliar urban environment', unpublished PhD thesis, University of Central Lancashire.

Middleton, V.T.C. (1994) *Marketing in Travel and Tourism*, Butterworth Heinemann, Oxford.

Mill, R.C. and A. Morrison (1985) *The Tourism System: An Introductory Text*, Prentice Hall, Englewood Cliffs NJ.

Miller, R. (1991) 'Selling Mrs Consumers: advertising and the creation of suburban socio-spatial relations, 1910–1930', *Antipode* 23, 263–301.

Mills, C.A. (1988) 'Life on the Upslope: the post-modern landscape of gentrification', *Environment and Planning, D: Society and Space* 6, 169–89.

Mills, L. and K. Young (1986) 'Local Authorities and Economic Development: a preliminary analysis', in V. Hausner (ed.) *Critical Issues in Urban Economic Development* vol. 1, Clarendon Press, Oxford, 89–144.

Mitchell, W.J.T. (1986) *Iconography, Image, Text, Ideology*, University of Chicago Press, Chicago IL.

Monicat, B. (1994) 'Autobiography and Womens' Travel Writings in Nineteenth Century France: journeys through self-representation', *Gender, Place, and Culture* 1, 67–70.

Moore, S. (1991) *Looking for Trouble: On Shopping, Gender, and The Cinema*, Serpent's Tale, London.

Mordue, T. (2001) 'Performing and Directing Resident/Tourist Cultures in Heartbeat Country', Tourist Studies 1 (3), 233–52.

Morgan, N.J. and A. Pritchard (1998) *Tourism Promotion and Power: Creating Images, Creating Identities*, John Wiley and Sons, Chichester.

Morley, D. (1974) 'Reconceptualising the Media Audience: an ethnography of audiences', *Stencilled Occasional Paper*, CCCS, Birmingham.

— (1986) *Family Television: Cultural Power and Domestic Leisure*, Comedia, London.

— (1990) 'Television and Gender', in T. Bennett (ed.) *Popular Fiction: Ideology, Production, Reading*, Routledge, London.

— (1992) *Television, Audiences, and Cultural Studies*, Routledge, London.

Morris, J. (1988) 'The Japanese are Here: For Better For Worse?' *Welsh Economic Review* 1 (1), 45–47.

Mortalieau, J.P. (1988) 'Les Macarons sur les automobiles', *Annales de la Reserche Urbaine*, Image de Memoires, Lyon.

Moutinho, L. (1987) 'Consumer Behaviour in Tourism', *European Journal of Marketing* 21 (10), 3–44.

Munt, I. (1996) 'Eco-tourism or Ego-tourism?', *Race and Class*, 36 (1), 49–60.

Murphy, P.E. (1985) *Tourism: A Community Approach*, Methuen, London.

— (1997) *Quality Management In Urban Tourism*, John Wiley and Sons, Chichester.

Myers, K. (1986) *Understains: The Sense and Seduction of Advertising*, Comedia, London.

Nash, C. (2000) 'Performativity in Practice. Some recent work in cultural geography', *Progress in Human Geography* 24 (4), 653–64.

Nash, D. (1996) *Anthropology of Tourism*, Pergamon Press, Oxford.

Natanson, M. (1970) *Phenomenology and Social Reality: Essays In Memory of Alfred Schutz*, Nijhof, The Hague.

Natter, W. and J.P. Jones (1993) 'Pets or Meat? Class, Ideology and Space', *Antipode*, 25 (2), 140–63.

Nolan, D.S. (1976) 'Tourists' Use and Evaluation of Travel Information Sources', *Journal of Travel Research* 14, Winter, 6–8.

Norusis, M.J. (1993) SPSS *for Windows, Professional Statistics, Release 6.0*, SPSS Inc., Chicago IL.

O'Barr, W.M. (1994) *Culture and the Ad: Explaining Otherness in the World of Advertising*, Westview Press, Oxford.

Olsson, G. (1980) *Birds in Egg: Eggs in Bird*, Pion, London.

Oppermann, M. (1996) 'Convention Destination Images Analysis of Association Meeting Planners' Perceptions', *Tourism Management* 17, 175–82.

Osgood, C.E. (1962) 'Studies on the Generality of Affective Meaning Systems', *Am. Psychology* 17 (1), 39–52.

Oxford English Dictionary (1979) *The Compact Edition of the Oxford English Dictionary*, Oxford University Press, Oxford.

Paddison, R. (1993) 'City Marketing, Image Reconstruction and Urban Regeneration', *Urban Studies* 20 (2), 339–50.

Page, S.J. (1995) *Urban Tourism*, Routledge, London.

— (1997) 'Urban Tourism: analysing and evaluating the tourist experience', in C. Ryan (ed.) *The Tourist Experience: A New Introduction*, Cassell, London, 112–35.

— (1999) 'Urban Recreation and Tourism', in C.M. Hall and S.J. Page, *The Geography of Tourism and Recreation*, Routledge, London, 160–77.

Page, S.J. and C.M. Hall (2003) *Managing Urban Tourism*. Prentice Hall, London.

Page, S.J. and M.T. Sinclair (1989) 'Tourism Accommodation in London: alternative policies and the Docklands experience', *Built Environment* 15 (2), 125–37.

Panel (1984) *Glasgow Tourism Development Study*, Scottish Development Agency, Glasgow.

Pannell, Kerr, Forster (1984) *Glasgow Tourism Development Study*, Scottish Development Agency, Glasgow.

Papadakis, Y. (1994) 'The National Struggle of Museums in a Divided City', *Ethnic and Racial Studies* 17, 400–19.

Parasuraman, A., V. Zeithmal and L. Berry (1985) 'A Conceptual Model of Service Quality and its Implications for Future Research', *Journal of Marketing* 49 (4), 1–50.

Parkin, F. (1971) *Class Inequality and Political Order*, MacGibbon and Kee, London.

Parlett, G., J. Fletcher and C. Cooper (1995) 'The Impact of Tourism on the Old Town of Edinburgh', *Tourism Management* 16, 355–60.

Parrinello, G.L. (1993) 'Motivation and Anticipation in Post-industrial Tourism', *Annals of Tourism Research* 20, 233–49.

Patton, P. (1995) 'Imaginary Cities: images of postmodernity', in S. Watson and K. Gibson (eds) *Postmodern Cities and Spaces*, Blackwell, Oxford and Cambridge MA, 112–21.

Pearce, D.G. (1987) *Tourism Today*, Longman, Harlow.

— (1992) *Tourist Organisations*, Longman, Harlow.

— (1998) 'Tourism Development in Paris: Public Intervention', *Annals of Tourism Research* 25, 457–76.

— (2001) 'An Integrative Framework for Urban Tourism Research', *Annals of Tourism Research* 28 (1), 926–46.

Pearce, D.G. and R.W. Butler (eds) (1993) *Tourism Research: Critiques and Challenges*, Routledge, London.

Pearce, P.L. (1977) 'Mental Souvenirs: a study of tourists and their city maps', *Australian Journal of Psychology* 29, 203–10.

— (1981) 'Route Maps: a study of travellers' perceptions of a section of the countryside', *Journal of Environmental Psychology* 1, 141–55.

— (1982) 'Perceived Changes in Holiday Destinations', *Annals of Tourism Research* 9, 145–64.

— (1988) *The Ulysses Factor*, Springer-Verlag, New York.

Pearce, P.L. and M. Fagence (1996) 'The Legacy of Kevin Lynch, Research Implications', *Annals of Tourism Research* 23 (3), 576–98.

Pearce, P.L. and G.M. Moscardo (1985) 'The Relationship Between Traveler Career Levels and the Concept of Authenticity', *Australian Journal of Psychology* 37, 157–74.

Peirce, C.S. (1931) *Collected Papers*, Vol. II, Cambridge, MA.

Peled, A. (1988) 'Explorations in Ecoanalysis' in D. Canter et al., *Environmental Perspectives*, Gower Publishing, Aldershot.

Phelps, A. (1986) 'Holiday Destination Image – The Problem of Assessment: An Example in Menorca', *Tourism Management* September, 168–80.

Phillips, R.S. (1993) 'The Language of Images in Geography', *Progress in Human Geography* 11 (2), 180–94.

Philo, C. (1984) 'Reflections on Gunnar Olson's contribution to the discourse of contemporary human geography', *Environment and Planning D: Society and Space* 2, 217–40.

— (1989) 'Enough to Drive One Mad: The Organisation of Space in Nineteenth Century Lunatic Asylums', in J. Wolch and M. Dear, *The Power of Geography: How Territory Shapes Social Life*, Hyman, London, 258–90.

— (1992) 'Foucault's Geography', *Environment and Planning D: Society and Space* 10, 137–61.

Piaget, J. (1960) *The Psychology of Intelligence*, Harcourt-Brace, New York.

Pick, D. (1994) 'Pro Patria: blocking the tunnel', *Ecumene* 1, 77–94.

Pickles, J. (1985) *Phenomenology, Science and Geography: Spatiality and the Human Sciences*, Cambridge University Press.

PIEDA (1987) *The Greater Belfast Tourism Development Study*, Northern Ireland Tourist Board, Belfast.

Pile, S. and G. Rose (1992) 'All or Nothing? Politics and Critique in the modernism-postmodernism debate', *Environment and Planning D: Society and Space* 10, 123–36.

Pine, B.J. and J.H. Gilmore (1999) *The Experience Economy*, Harvard Business School Press, Boston MA.

Pizam, A., N. Yoram and R. Arie (1978) 'Dimensions of Tourist Satisfaction with a Destination Area', *Annals of Tourism Research* 5 (3), 314–22.

Pocock, D. and R. Hudson (1978) *Images of the Urban Environment*, Macmillan Press Ltd, London and Basingstoke.

Pocock, D.C.D. (1987) 'Howarth: the experience of literary place', in W. Mallory and P. Simpson-Housley (eds) *Geography and Literature: A Meeting of the Disciplines*, Syracuse University Press, NY, 135–42.

Pool, I. (1965) 'Effects of Cross-National Contact on National and International Images', in C. Herbert and R. Kelman (eds) *International Tourist Behaviour – A Social Psychological Analysis*, Holt, Reinhart, and Winston, New York, 106–29.

Popper, K.R. (1969) *The Open Society and its Enemies. Vol.2*, 5th Edition, Routledge and Kegan Paul, London.

Porter, M.E. (1980) *Competitive Strategy: Techniques for Analysing Industries and Competitors*, Free Press, New York.

Portes, A. (1981) 'Modes of Incorporation and Theories of Labour Migration', in M. Kritz, C. Keeley and S. Tomasi (eds) *Global Trends in Migration*, Centre for Migration, New York.

Postina, A. and A.K. Jenkins (1997) 'Improving the Tourist's Experience: quality management applied to tourist destinations', in P. E. Murphy (ed.) *Quality Management in Urban Tourism*, Wiley, Chichester, 183–97.

Powell, J.M. (1978) *Mirrors of the New World: Images and Image-Makers in the Settlement Process*, Australian National University Press, Canberra.

Prentice, R.C. (1993) *Tourism and Heritage Attractions*, Routledge, London.

Prentice, R.C., S.F. Witt and C. Hamer (1998) 'Tourism as Experience, The Case of Heritage Parks', *Annals of Tourism Research* 25 (1), 1–24.

Pritchard, A. and N.J. Morgan (1995) 'Evaluating Vacation Destination Brochure Images: the case of local authorities in Wales', *Journal of Vacation Marketing* 2 (1) December, 23–38.

— (1996) 'Selling the Celtic Arc to the USA: A Comparative Analysis of Destination Brochure Images Used in the Marketing of Ireland, Scotland and Wales', *Journal of Vacation Marketing* 2 (4), 346–65.

— (2001) 'Culture, identity and tourism representation: marketing Cymru or Wales?', *Tourism Management* 22, 167–179.

Pritchard, A., N.J. Morgan, D. Sedgley and A. Jenkins (1998) 'Reaching Out to the Gay Tourist: opportunities and threats in an emerging market segment', *Tourism Management* 19, 273–82.

Probyn, E. (1999) 'Beyond Food/Sex: eating and an ethics of eating', *Theory, Culture and Society*, 16 (2), 215–28.

Queenan, L. (1992) *Conference Bureaux: An Investigation into their Structure, Marketing Strategies, and Business*, British Association of Conference Towns, Birmingham.

Raban, J. (1974) *Soft City*, Hamish Hamilton, London.

Ram, M., T. Abbas, B. Sanghera and G. Hillin (2000) '"Currying Favour with the Locals": Balti Owners and Business Enclaves', *International Journal of Entrepreneurial Behaviour and Research* 6 (1), 41–55.

Rees, P. (1988) 'Post-proprietary Philadelphia as Artefact?', paper presented at the Clark Centenial Conference, *Creation of Myth, Invention of Tradition in America*.

Reilly, M.D. (1990) 'Free Elicitation of Descriptive Adjectives for Tourism Image Assessment', *Journal of Travel Research* 28 (4), Spring, 21–26.

Relph, E. (1970) 'An Inquiry into the Relations between Phenomenology and Geography', *Canadian Geographer* 14, 193–201.

— (1976) *Place and Placelessness*, Pion, London.

— (1981) *Rational Landscapes and Humanistic Geography*, Croom Helm, London.

— (1985) 'Geographical Experiences and Being-in-the-world: Phenomenological Origins of Geography', in D. Seamon and R. Mugerauer (eds) *Dwelling, Place and Environment: Towards a Phenomenology of Person and World*, Martinus Nijhoff, Dordrecht.

— (1994) 'Classics in Human Geography Revisited. Commentary 2', *Progress in Human Geography*, 18 (3), 356–58.

Reynolds, W.H. (1965) 'The Role of the Consumer in Image Building', *California Management Review*, Spring, 69–76.

Riccoeur, P. (1971) 'The Model of Text: Meaningful Action Considered as Text', *Social Research* 38, 529–62.

Richards, G. (1996) 'Production and Consumption of European Cultural Tourism', *Annals of Tourism Research* 23 (2), 261–83.

Richards, P. (1974) 'Kant's Geography and the Mental Maps', *Transactions of the Institute of British Geographers* 61, 1–16.

Richardson, S.L. and J.L. Crompton (1988) 'Cultural Variations in Perceptions of Vacation Attributes', *Tourism Management*, 129–36.

Riley, S. and J. Palmer (1976) 'Of Attitudes and Latitudes: a repertory grid study of perceptions of seaside resorts', in P. Slater (ed.) *Explorations In Interpersonal Space* vol. 1, John Wiley and Sons, London.

Ringer, G. (ed.) (1998) *Destinations: Cultural Landscapes of Tourism*, Routledge, London.

Ritzer, G. and A. Liska (1997) '"McDisneyization" and "Post-Tourism": Complementary Perspectives on Contemporary Tourism', in C. Rojek and J. Urry, *Touring Cultures: Transformations of Travel Theory*, Routledge, London.

Robinson, F. and D. Sadler (1984) 'Consett After the Closure', occasional paper number 19, Department of Geography, University of Durham, Durham.

Robinson, M., N. Evans and P. Callaghan (eds) (1996) *Culture as the Tourist Product*, Centre for Travel and Tourism/Business Education, Sunderland.

Rojek, C. (1997) 'Indexing, Dragging and the Social Construction of Tourist Sights', in C. Rojek and J. Urry, *Touring Cultures: Transformations of Travel Theory*, Routledge, London.

Rojek, C. and J. Urry (1997) 'Transformations of Travel and Theory', in C. Rojek and J. Urry *Touring Cultures: Transformations of Travel and Theory*, Routledge, London.

Rolfe, H. (1992) *Arts Festivals in the UK*, Arts Studies Institute, London.

Rose, G. (1988) 'Locality, Politics and Culture: Poplar in the 1920s', *Environment and Planning D: Society and Space* 6, 151–68.

Rose, G. (1994) 'The Cultural Politics of Place: local representation and oppositional discourse in two films', *Transactions of Institute of British Geographers* (NS) 19, 46–60.

Rowles, G.D. (1972) 'Choice in Geographic Space: Exploring a Phenomenological Approach to Decision-making', unpublished MSc. dissertation, University of Bristol, Bristol.

Ryan, C. (1995a) *Researching Tourist Satisfaction: Issues, Concepts, Problems*, Routledge, London.

— (1995b) 'Conversations in Majorca – the over 55's on holiday', *Tourism Management* 16 (3), 207–17.

— (1997) *The Tourist Experience: A New Approach*, Cassell, London.

— (2000) 'Tourist Experience, Phenomenography, and Neural Network Analysis', *International Journal of Tourism Research* 2, 119–31.

Ryan, C. and L. Sterling (1997) 'Visitors to Litchfield Park', Proceedings of IGU Conference, 'Trails, Heritage, and Tourism', University of Otago, December.

Ryan, K.B. (1990) 'The Official Image of Australia', in L. Zonn (ed.) *Place Images in the Media: Portrayal, Meaning, and Experience*, Rowman and Littlefield, Savage MD, 35–58.

Sack, R.D. (1980) *Conceptions of Space in Social Thought, A Geographic Perspective*, Macmillan, London.

— (1988) 'The Consumers World: place as context', *Annals of Association of American Geographers* 78, 642–64.

Sadler, D. (1993) *Place Marketing: Competitive Places and the Construction of Hegemony in Britain in the 1980s*, in G. Kearns and C, Philo (eds) (1993) *Selling Places: The City as Cultural Capital Past and Present*, Pergamon Press, Oxford.

Said, E. (1991) 'Musical Elaborations', *Culture and Imperialism* 17, Columbia University Press, New York, 109.

Samuel, R. (1989) *Patriotism: The Making and Unmaking of British National Identity. Vol. 1, History and Politics*, Routledge, London.

Samuels, M. (1981) 'An Existential Geography', in M.E. Harvey and B.P. Holly, *Themes in Geographic Thought*, Croom Helm, London.

Sarre, P.V. (1973) 'Personal Construct Theory in the Measurement of the Perceived Environment', unpublished PhD dissertation, University of Bristol.

Sartre, J-P. (1948) *Existentialism and Humanism*, Methuen, London.

— (1969) *Being and Nothingness*, trans. H. Barnes, Methuen, London.

Sauer, C.O. (1925) 'The Morphology of Landscape', *University of California Publications in Geography* 2, 19–54.

Saunders, K. (1994) 'The Dark Shadow of White Australia: Racial Anxieties in Australia After World War II', *Ethnic and Racial Studies* 17, 325–41.

Savage, M. (1983) 'Walter Benjamin and Urban Meaning', working paper number 3, Department of Sociology and Social Anthropology, Keele University.

Schmidt, C.B. (1988) *The Cambridge History of Renaissance Philosophy*, Cambridge University Press, Cambridge.

Schmoll, G.A. (1977) *Tourism Promotion*, Tourism International Press, London.

Schroader, H.W. (1984) 'Environmental Rating Scales: a case for simple methods of analysis', *Environment and Behaviour* 16, 573–98.

Schutz, A. (1962) *Collected Papers, Vol. 1, The Problems of Social Reality*, ed. and trans. M. Natason, Martinus Nijhoff, The Hague.

— (1964) *Collected Papers, Vol. II*, ed. A. Broderson, Martinus Nijhoff, The Hague.

— (1970) *Reflections on the Problem of Relevance*, Yale University Press, New Haven CT.

— (1972) *The Phenomenology of the Social World*, trans. G. Walsh and F. Lehnert, Heinemann, London.

Schutz, A. and T. Luckmann (1974) *Structures of the Life-World*, trans. R.M. Zaner and H.T. Engelhardt Jr, Heinemann, London.

Scott, D.B., C.D. Schewe and D.G. Frederick (1978) 'A Multi-Attribute Model of Tourist State Choice', *Journal of Travel Research* 17 (1), 23–29.

Seamon, D. (1978) 'Goethe's Approach to the Natural World: implications for environmental theory and education', in D. Ley and M.S. Samuels (eds) *Humanistic Geography, Prospects and Problems*, Croom Helm, London.

— (1979) *A Geography of the Lifeworld*. Croom Helm, London.

Seamon, D. and R. Mugeraurer (1985) *Dwelling, Place and Environment: Towards a Phenomenology of Person and World*, Martinus Nijhoff, Dordrecht.

— (1989) *Dwelling, Place and Environment*, Columbia University Press, New York.

Selby, M. (1995) 'Tourism and Urban Regeneration: The Role of Place Image', MSc dissertation, Department of Management Studies, University of Surrey.

— (1995) 'Tourism and Urban Regeneration: The application of place image as a policy analysis instrument', *Proceedings of International Conference, The Urban Environment: Tourism*, South Bank University, London, September.

— (1996) 'Absurdity, Phenomenology, and Place: an existential place marketing project', *Proceedings of International Conference, Higher Degrees of Pleasure*, WLRA Congress, Cardiff, July.

— (2000) 'People, Place, and Consumption: conceptualising and researching urban tourist experience, with particular reference to Cardiff, Wales', unpublished PhD thesis, University of Wales.

Selby, M. and N.J. Morgan (1996) 'Reconstruing Place Image: a case study of its role in destination market research', *Tourism Management* 17 (4) June, 287–94.

Selwyn, T. (1990) 'Tourist Brochures as Post-modern Myth', *Problems of Tourism* 13 (3/4), 13–26.

— (ed.) (1996) *The Tourist Image. Myths and Myth Making in Tourism*, John Wiley and Sons, Chichester.

Shanahan, J.L. (1980) 'The Arts and Urban Development', in W. Hendon, J. Shanahan and A. McDonald (eds) *Economic Policy for the Arts*, Abt Books, Cambridge MA, 295–305.

Shapiro, M.J. (1988) 'Los Angelizing', paper presented at the Clark Centenial Conference, *Creation of Myth, Invention of Tradition in America*.

Sharpley, R. (1994) *Tourism, Tourists and Society*, ELM, Huntingdon.

Shaw, G. and A. Williams (1994) *Critical Issues in Tourism: A Geographical Perspective*, Blackwell, Oxford.

Sheenan, L.R. and J.R. Ritchie (1997) 'Financial Management in Tourism: a destination perspective', *Tourism Economics* 3 (2).

Shields, R. (1984) 'The Logic of the Mall', in S. Riggins (ed.) *Material Culture*, Mouton de Gruyer, The Hague.

— (1989) 'Social Spatialisation and the Built Environment: West Edmonton Mall', *Environment and Planning D: Society and Space* 7, 147–64.

— (1991) *Places on the Margin*, Routledge, London.

— (1992) *Lifestyle Shopping: The Study of Consumption*, Routledge, London.

— (1996) 'A Guide to Urban Representation and What to do about it: Alternative Traditions of Urban Theory', in A.D. King (ed.) *Representing the City*, Macmillan, Basingstoke.

Short, J.R. (1989) 'Yuppies, Yuffies, and the New Urban Order', *Transactions of the Institute of British Geographers* (NS) 14, 173–88.

Shurmer-Smith, P. and K. Hannam (1994) *Worlds of Desire, Realms of Power: a Cultural Geography*, Arnold, London.

Silver, I. (1993) 'Marketing Authenticity in Third World Countries', *Annals of Tourism Research* 20, 302–18.

Slater, P. (1976) 'Monitoring Changes in the Mental State of a Patient Undergoing Psychiatric Treatment', in P. Slater (ed.) *Explorations in Interpersonal Space* vol. 1, John Wiley & Sons.

Sless, D. (1986) *In Search of Semiotics*, Barnes and Noble, New York.

Smith, M. (1996) 'The Empire Filters Back: consumption, production, and the politics of Starbuck Coffee', *Urban Geography* 17, 502–25.

Smith, N. (1984) *Uneven Development: Nature, Capital and the Production of Space*, Blackwell, Oxford.

Soja, E. (1985) 'The Spatiality of Social Life: towards a transformative re-theorisation', in D. Gregory and J. Urry (eds) *Social Relations and Social Structures*, Macmillan, London.

— (1989) *Postmodern Geographies: The Reassertion of Space in Critical Social Theory*, Verso, London.

Sontag, S. (1978) *Illness as Metaphor*, Farrar Straus and Giroux, New York.

Sorkin, M (ed.) (1992) *Variations on a Theme Park: The New America City and the End of Public Space*, The Noonday Press, New York.

Spiegelburg, H. (1971) *The Phenomenological Movement*, Nijhoff, The Hague.

Spivac, G.C. (1987) *In other Words*, Routledge, New York.

— (1990) 'Explanation and Culture: Marginalia', in R. Ferguson, M. Gever, T. Minhha and C. West (eds) *Out There: Marginalisation and Contemporary Cultures*, MIT Press and the New Museum of Contemporary Art, Cambridge MA.

Sports Council for Wales (1995) cited in T. Stevens and T. Morgan, 'Capitalising on Sport – Cardiff's Future Strategy', International Conference, *Sport in the City*, Sheffield Hallam University, July.

Spurling, L (1977) *Phenomenology and the Socal World*, Routledge and Keegan Paul, London.

Squire, S.J. (1994) 'Accounting for Cultural Meanings: The Interface Between Geography and Tourism Studies Re-examined', *Progress in Human Geography* 18 (1), 1–16.

Stabler, M.J. (1988) 'The Image of Destination Regions: Theoretical and Empirical Aspects', in B. Goodall and G.J. Ashworth (eds) *Marketing in the Tourism Industry: The Promotion of Destination Regions*, Routledge, London.

Stansell, C. (1986) *City of Women: Sex and Class in New York, 1789–1860*, Alfred Knopf, New York.

Sternquist Witter, B. (1985) 'Attitudes about a Resort Area: Comparison of Tourists and Local Retailers', *Journal of Travel Research* 24 (1), 14–19.

Stevens, S.S. (1946) 'On the Theory of Scales of Measurement', *Science* 103, 677–80.

Stevens, T. and T. Morgan (1998) 'Capitalising on Sport – Cardiff's Future Strategy', paper presented at International Conference, *Sport in the City*, Sheffield Hallam University, July.

Stevenson, D. (1999) 'Reflections of a "Great Port City": the case of Newcastle, Australia', *Environment and Planning D: Society and Space* 17, 105–19.

Stock, B. (1983) *The Implications of Literacy: Written Language and Models of Interpretation in the Eleventh and Twelfth Centuries*, Princetown University, Princetown NJ.

Stringer, P. (1976) 'Repertory Grids in the Study of Environmental Perception', in P. Slater, *Explorations in Interpersonal Space* vol. 1, John Wiley and Sons, London.

Strohmayer, U. (1996) 'The Event of Space: Geographic Allusions in the Phenomenological Tradition', *Environment and Planning D: Society and Space* 16, 105–21.

Syme, G.J., B.J. Shaw, D.M. Fenton and W.S. Muller (1989) *The Planning and Evaluation of Hallmark Events*, Aldershot, Avebury.

Taylor, J. (1994) *A Dream of England: Landscape, Photography, and the Tourist's Imagination*, Manchester University Press, Manchester.

Thomson, D.A., A. Benefield, S. Bitgood, H. Shettal and R. Williams (1993) *Visitor Studies: Theory, Research, and Practice*, Visitor Studies Association, Jacksonville AL.

Thrift, N.J. (1983) 'On the Determination of Social Action in Space and Time', *Environment and Planning D: Society and Space* 1, 23–57.

— (1999) 'Entanglements of Power: Shadows?', in J. Sharp, P. Routledge, C. Philo and P. Paddison, *Geographies of Domination/Resistance*, Routledge, London, 269–77.

Thrift, N.J. and J.D. Dewsbury (2000) 'Dead Geographies – and how to make them live', *Environment and Planning D: Society and Space* 18, 411–32.

Thurot, J. and G. Thurot (1983) 'The Ideology of Class and Tourism. Confronting the discourse of advertising', *Annals of Tourism Research* 10, 173–89.

Tibbalds, Colbourne, Karski (1988) *Cardiff Tourism Study: Final Report*. Tibbalds, Colbourne, Karski, London.

Tourism Canada (1987) 'Pleasure Travel Markets to North America: United Kingdom', Market Facts of Canada, Tourism Canada, Toronto.

Tribe, J. (1997) 'The Indiscipline of Tourism', *Annals of Tourism Research* 24, 668–57.

Tuan, Y-F. (1971) 'Geography, Phenomenology, and the Study of Human Nature', *Canadian Geographer* 15, 181–92.

— (1974) *Topophilia: A Study of Environmental Perception, Attitudes and Values*, Prentice-Hall, Englewood Cliffs NJ.

— (1976) 'Humanistic Geography', *Annals of Association of American Geographers* 66, 266–76.

— (1977) *Space and Place: The Perspective of Experience*, Edward Arnold, London.

Tyler, D., Y. Guerrier and M. Robertson (eds) (1998) *Managing Tourism in Cities: Policy, Process, and Practice*, Wiley, Chichester.

Um, S. and J.L. Crompton (1990) 'Attitude Determinants in Tourism Destination Choice', *Annals of Tourism Research* 17, 432–48.

Urry, J. (1987) 'Some Social and Spatial Aspects of Services', *Society and Space* 5, 5–27.

— (1990a) *The Tourist Gaze: Leisure and Travel in Contemporary Societies*, Sage, London.

— (1990b) 'The Consumption of Tourism', *Sociology* 24, 23–35.

— (1992) 'The Tourist Gaze Revisited', *American Behavioural Scientist* 36, 172–86.

— (1995) *Consuming Places*, Routledge, London.

— (2001a) *Globalising the Tourist Gaze*, published by the Department of Sociology, Lancaster University at: http://www.comp.lancs.ac.uk/sociology/soc079.html

— (2001b) *The Tourist Gaze: The New Edition*, Sage, London.

Uzzell, D. (1984) 'An Alternative Structuralist Approach to the Psychology of Tourism Marketing', *Annals of Tourism Research* 11 (1), 79–100.

Valentine, G. (1999) 'A Corporeal Geography of Consumption', *Environment and Planning D: Society and Space* 17, 329–551.

Van de Veen, W. and H. Voogd (1987) *Gemeen tepromotie en Bedriffsacquisitie*, Geopers, Gröningen.

Van den Berg, L., J. Van der Borg and J. van der Meer (eds) (1995) *Urban Tourism: Performance and Strategies in Eight European Cities*, Avebury, Aldershot.

Veal, A.J. (1997) *Research Methods for Leisure and Tourism, A Practical Guide*, Financial Times/Pitman, London.

Veijola, S. and E. Jokinen (1994) 'The Body in Tourism', *Theory, Culture and Society* 6, 125–51.

Venturi, R., D. Scott-Brown and S. Izenour (1972) *Learning from Las Vegas*, MIT Press, Cambridge MA.

Vetter, F. (1985) *Big City Tourism*, Dietrich Verlag, Berlin.

Voase, R. (1999) 'Consuming Tourist Sites/Sights: a Note on York', *Leisure Studies* 18, 289–96.

— (2000) 'Explaining the Blandness of Popular Travel Journalism: narrative, cliche, and the structure of meaning', in M. Robinson, N. Evans, P. Long, R. Sharpley and J. Swarbrook, *Tourism and Heritage Relationships: Global, National and Local Perspectives*, Business Education Publishers, Sunderland.

Wahab, S., L.J. Crompton and L.M. Rothfield (1976) *Tourism Marketing*, Tourism International Press, New York.

Wales Tourist Board (1994) *Tourism 2000 – A Strategy for Wales*, Wales Tourist Board, Cardiff.

— (1994b) *Promotional Literature – Towards a More Rational Approach*, consultation paper, Cardiff.

— (1998) *Visitor Attractions in South Wales*, Wales Tourist Board, Cardiff.

Wallace, I. (1978) 'Towards a Humanised Conception of Economic Geography', in D. Ley and M.S. Samuels, *Humanistic Geography, Prospects and Problems*, Croom Helm, London.

Wallace, K.R. (1992) '"Roots, aren't they supposed to be buried?" The experience of place in Midwestern Womens' Autobiographies', in W. Franklin and M. Steiner (eds) *Mapping American Culture*, University of Iowa Press IA.

Walmsley, D.J. and J. Jenkins (1992) 'Tourism Cognitive Mapping of Unfamiliar Environments', *Annals of Tourism Research* 19 (3), 268–86.

Walsh, K. (1989) *Marketing Local Government*, Longman, Harlow.

Walter, C.K. and H.M. Tong (1977) 'A Local Study of Consumer Vacation Decisions', *Journal of Travel Research* 15 (4), 30–34.

Watson, S. (1991) 'Gliding the Smokestacks: the new symbolic representations of the de-industrialised regions', *Environment and Planning, D: Society and Space* 9, 59–70.

Watson, S. and K. Gibson (1995) *Postmodern Cultures and Spaces*, Blackwell, Oxford and Cambridge MA.

Wearing, B. and S. Wearing (1996) 'Refocusing the Tourist Experience: the flaneur and the choraster', *Leisure Studies* 15 (4), 229–43.

— (1998) 'All in a Day's Leisure: gender and the concept of leisure', *Leisure Studies* 7, 111–23.

Weber, M. (1949) *The Methodology of the Social Sciences*, ed. and trans. E.A. Shiels and H.A. Finck, Free Press, New York.

Welsh Office (1998) *Pathway to Prosperity, a new economic agenda for Wales*, Welsh Office, Cardiff.

Werlen, B. (1993) *Society, Action, and Space, An Alternative Human Geography*, trans. G. Walls, Routledge, London.

Whitt, J.A. (1988) 'The Role of the Arts in Urban Development', in S. Cummings (ed) *Business Elites and Urban Development: case studies and critical perspectives*, State University of New York Press, Oxford.

Whittaker, E. (2000) 'A Century of Indigenous Images: the world according to the tourist postcard', in M. Robinson, N. Evans, P. Long, R. Sharpley and J. Swarbrook, *Tourism and Heritage Relationships: Global, National and Local Perspectives*, Business Education Publishers, Sunderland.

Willems-Braun, B. (1994) 'Situating Cultural Politics: Fringe Festivals and the Production of Spaces of Intersubjectivity', *Environment and Planning D: Society and Space* 12, 75–104.

Williams, C. (1998) 'Is the SERVQUAL model an appropriate management tool for measuring delivery quality in the UK Leisure Industry?' *Managing Leisure* 3, 98–110.

Williams, C. and D. Chaplin (1999) 'Leisure and Tourism and Different: a false premise detrimental to the sustainable development of a seaside resort', paper for *International Sustainable Development Research Conference*, Leeds, March 1999.

Williams, R. (1958) *Culture and Society 1780–1950*, Chatto/Penguin, Harmondsworth.

— (1962) *Communications*, Penguin Books, Harmondsworth.

— (1977) *Marxism and Literature*, Oxford University Press, Oxford.

— (1981) *Culture*, Fontana, London.

Wilson, E. (1991) *The Sphinx in the City*, Virago, London.

— (1995) 'The Invisible Flaneur', in S. Watson and K. Gibson (1995) *Postmodern Cities and Spaces*, Blackwell, Oxford.

Wilson, K. and A. Portes (1980) 'Immigrant Enclaves: an analysis of the labour market experience of Cubans in Miami', *American Journal of Sociology* 88, 135–60.

Wittgenstein, L. (1961) *Tracatus Logico-Philosophicus*, Routledge, Chapman and Hall, Andover.

— (1968) *Philosophical Investigations*, Third Edition, Macmillan, New York.

Wolff, J. (1992) 'The Real City, the Discursive City, the Disappearing City: Postmodernism and Urban Sociology', *Theory and Society* 21, 553–60.

Wood, D. (1992) *The Power of Maps*, The Guildford Press, New York.

Wood, P.A. (1984) 'The regional significance of manufacturing service sector links', in B.M. Barr and N.M. Walters (eds) *Regional Diversification and Structural Change*, Tantalus Research, Vancouver, 108–84.

Woodside, A.G. and D. Sherrell (1977) 'Traveller Evoked Inept and Inert Sets of Vacation Destinations', *Journal of Travel Research* 6 (1), 14–18.

Woodside, A.G. and S. Lyonski (1990) 'A General Model of Traveller Destination Choice', *Annals of Tourism Research* 17, 432–48.

Wright, G.H. (1971) *Explanation and Understanding*, Routledge and Keegan Paul, London.

Wrigley, N. and M. Lowe (eds) (1995) *Retailing, Consumption, and Capital*, Longman, London.

Young, B.M. (1990) *Television Advertising and Children*, Clarendon Press, Oxford.

Zelinski, W. (1973) *The Cultural Geography of the United States*, Prentice Hall, Englewood Cliffs NJ.

Zukin, S. (1992) 'Postmodern Urban Landscapes: Mapping Culture and Power', in S. Lash and J. Friedman (eds) *Modernity and Identity*, Blackwell, Oxford, 221–47.

Index

BS
2/2/06

Understanding Urban Tourism

Tourism, Retailing and Consumption series

Edited by:
Professor Gareth Shaw, University of Exeter
Dr Dimitri Ioannides, Southwest Missouri State University

Consumption has become an important theme in geography and the social sciences and within this broad debate two key areas of concern are tourism and retailing. To date there is no series that brings together these closely related topics under a unifying perspective. Tourism, Retailing and Consumption will provide such a perspective.

The series will provide core texts for students of geography and related disciplines at first degree level. It will be wide-ranging in scope and cover both historical and contemporary debates in tourism, retailing and consumption. A number of more specialised texts suited to postgraduate study will also be included.

Also in the series:
Tourism in Transition:
Economic Change in Central Europe
Allan M. Williams and Aladimir Balaz

Tourism in the New South Africa:
Conflict, Community and Development
Garth Allen and Frank Brennan